Spider, Spin Me a Web

Also by Lawrence Block

Spider, Spin Me a Web

A Handbook for Fiction Writers

Quill
William Morrow
New York

It is the policy of William Morrow and Company, Inc., and its imprints and affiliates, recognizing the importance of preserving what has been written, to print the books we publish on acid-free paper, and we exert our best efforts to that end.

Library of Congress Cataloging-in-Publication Data

Block, Lawrence.
   Spider, spin me a web : a handbook for fiction writers / Lawrence Block.
     p.   cm.
   ISBN 0-688-14690-2 (alk. paper)
   1. Fiction—Authorship.   I. Title.
  PN3355.B558   1996
  808.3—dc20   96-14569
                                        CIP

Printed in the United States of America

First Quill Edition

      3   4   5   6   7   8   9   10

Contents

Part Two
TRAPPING THE PREY:
THE STRATEGIES OF FICTION

Part Three
SPIDER LOVE:
THE INNER GAME OF FICTION

Part Four
SPIDER DREAMS:
LIVING THE FICTIONEER'S LIFE

Preface to the Quill Edition

Those who can, write. Those who cannot, write about writing. That's what I always figured. Twenty years ago I wrote a magazine article, a whimsical piece called "Where Do You Get Your Ideas?" Next thing I knew I was writing a monthly column, and by the time the dust cleared in the fall of 1990 I'd been writing that column for fourteen years, producing four books on the subject along the way.

The first, *Writing the Novel from Plot to Print*, was undertaken at the suggestion of the publisher of *Writer's Digest*, who thought there was a need for such a volume. He seems to have been right; the book appeared in 1979 and has never been out of print. *Telling Lies for Fun & Profit*, a collection of columns, followed two years later from Arbor House and was a selection of the Book-of-the-Month Club.

My third book for writers was one I published myself. In 1983 I became convinced that it was the inner game of writing that mattered most, and that an experimental seminar might do more for writers at any stage in their development than the traditional instruction methods. I developed such a seminar and called it Write for Your Life. (A horrendous mistake, that. On more than one occasion hotels wouldn't let us book space because they wanted to steer clear of controversy. Controversy??? It turned out they figured we had some sort of position on abortion.)

The seminar was a great success. Everybody liked it but my accountant, who pointed out that Lynne and I were clearing something like fifty cents an hour for our trouble. I knew I wasn't going to run around the country giving seminars forever—financial considerations aside, after a few seasons it began to feel too much like a theatrical performance—but I wanted to make the WFYL material available to a larger audience, so that readers could take the seminar themselves at home. Like almost every writer I've known, I'd always had the fantasy of publishing something myself, and this seemed a logical candidate. I brought it out in 1985, printed five thousand copies, and sold them all. (And netted seventy-five cents an hour this time, to my accountant's considerable satisfaction.)

Finally, *Spider, Spin Me a Web* was published by Writer's Digest Books in 1988. Two years later the magazine and I came to a parting of the ways after fourteen years. I suppose it was a little like a divorce, and about as friendly as a friendly divorce.

In 1984 William Morrow brought out a new edition of *Telling Lies for Fun & Profit* as a handsome Quill trade paperback. Sue Grafton, who'd been championing the book for years at writers' conferences, furnished a glowing introduction, and the book found a heartening reception. Published without a whole lot of fanfare, it had gone through four printings the last time I checked.

And so you now hold in your hand a copy or Morrow's Quill edition of *Spider, Spin Me a Web*, and I couldn't be happier. I've always felt that it contains much of the best of my writing about writing, and I was frustrated that it never reached a wider audience. (Don Marquis, the author of *archy and mehitable*, once likened publishing a volume of poetry to dropping a rose petal into the Grand Canyon and waiting for the echo. Writer's Digest dropped the hardcover edition of *Spider* into the Grand Canyon and never brought the book out in paperback. I'm sure it was coincidental, and wholly unrelated to our friendly divorce.)

A new edition would seem to call for a new Preface. At first I thought I'd revise the book's original Preface, but I found that was trickier than it looked. In the past few years I've had a lot of my early novels brought back into print, some of them first published in the early sixties. The world has changed some in the past thirty years, and so I assure you have I; I was thus tempted to touch up those early books here and there, striking out an infelicitous phrase, smoothing a ragged transition.

I chose instead not to change so much as a comma. They were of a piece, I decided, and they were of their time, and if I started picking at them I'd wind up with nothing. Better to leave them as written.

With the *Spider* Preface, I came to a similar conclusion. Bringing it up to date was impossible. Better to chuck it out altogether and write something new.

Which is not to say that I might not profitably include some of the material from the first time around, such as this explanation of the book's title and scheme of organization:

Why a spider?
Chapter thirty-four makes the point, but I'll summarize it here. The writer of fiction is a spider. Drawing upon his inner resources and shaping them with his craft, he spins out his guts to trap his dinner.

The chapters which follow constitute a series of notes on the artful weaving of webs. But it is not a textbook, and there can be no true textbook to deal with this subject. There are no blueprints for the novel, for the short story. However well the spider may serve as a totem animal for fictioneers, there are fundamental differences between the weaving of webs and the spinning of tales.

Each writer has to find his own way to write his own story. Each writer is a stranger in his own strange land; how then can I presume to guide you through a country I myself have not visited?

Here is what I found, I said, when I traveled to such and such a place, and did thus and so. And perhaps it will be of value to you when you find yourself in some other alien land, engaged in some other monumental quest.

While my column is entitled "Fiction," and —yes, Arnold? *Oh, is that its title, sir?*

That's the overall title, yes. The individual columns have their individual titles, but the overall title is "Fiction." That's why it appears at the head of each column, and in the magazine's table of contents each month. What else did you think it was doing there?

I didn't realize it was a title, sir. I thought it might be descriptive.

Only once in a while, Arnold. Ahem. The column is called "Fiction," but the response I've received from readers over the years confirms what I've long suspected myself, which is that one need not be a fictioneer to find something of value here.

...Writers, whatever they write, are apt to find the spider an apt totem. Indeed, I've learned that writers of all sorts have far more in common than one might suppose. And, too, the distinction between fiction and nonfiction has never been that clearcut, and has grown increasingly blurry over the years.

In fiction, traditionally, the writer wants us to believe that he has made the whole thing up. In nonfiction, he wants us to believe that he hasn't.

Both weave much the same sort of web, and out of the same inner stuff.

People often ask me if I miss writing the column.

I missed it a lot at first. For all those years, knocking out my monthly riff was the only scheduled thing I did. No matter where I was, in my life or in my career, I would sit down once a month and write a letter to a few hundred thousand strangers. A lot of them wrote back.

Did I miss all that? Of course I missed it.

But at the same time I felt that I'd covered the ground and then some, that I'd said everything I had to say on the subject, and had said it all over and over again.

Still, writing this Preface has allowed me to speak again in the voice of the columns, and to talk directly once more to that enormous throng of unseen writers. And I find myself missing it all over again.

In the original Preface I wrote:

> Putting this book together has been something of a stroll down Memory Lane. The return addresses in each column's upper lefthand corner remind me how many changes I've been through during the years of this volume's composition. When the first columns were written I was living with a lady in Greenwich Village. Then I was living alone a few blocks away, and then I had moved in with someone in Washington Heights, and then I was on my own in Brooklyn, and back in the Village, and then married and in a larger Village apartment. And now Lynne and I are in Florida, and have been here for two years at this writing, and I've no idea if we'll still be here when you read this.
>
> And there have been at least as many nongeographic changes along the way.

Changes, geographic and otherwise, have continued. By the time *Spider* appeared, Lynne and I had left Florida to spend two years without a fixed address, living in motels and driving back and forth across America. We wound up back in New York and are living again in the Village, and, while we still travel whenever we get the chance, I think we're done moving. (The Village Nursing Home is diagonally across the street, visible from our windows. "We're staying *here*," we tell each other, "until it's time to go *there*.")

While I wouldn't want to try writing a column again, it seems I'm not entirely through writing about writing. Not too long ago I found myself working fifteen hours a day on a memoir of my early years as a writer; one memory led to another, and at the end of the most exhausting week of my life I had something like fifty thousand words down. I suspect I'll get back to work on it sometime in the next year or so, and while it's not instructional, it's unquestionably about writing.

And, sometime in the next year or so, I would like to update *Write for Your Life* and see it back in print. I don't ever want to present another seminar, but the material itself ought to be available.

I always enjoyed hearing from readers when I was writing the column, and that hasn't changed. While I rarely have time for a proper response, I do get out a newsletter once or twice a year as a way of keeping in touch with readers and booksellers. It's absolutely free, and, I've been assured, worth every penny. To get on the list, all you have to do is provide your mailing address. (And your name, unless you prefer being addressed as *Occupant*.) You can write to me in care of William Morrow and Company, Inc., 1350 Avenue of the Americas, New York, New York 10019, or directly by fax at 212-675-4341, or by e-mail at LawBloc@aol.com.

Building the Web
The Techniques of Fiction

*W*hat is most often associated with a spider in the minds of the majority of people? Its web! The very name spider *refers to its spinning habit, though the making of a snare is not the only use to which the spider puts its silk. The wandering spiders build no snares yet use the silk in various ways. Most spiders as they move pay out a drag-line behind them, and it is this type of line which supports the spider should it lose its footing or jump from a support. At frequent intervals the drag-line is fastened to the substratum by a large number of looped threads. This is called an attachment disc and it is from this point that the spider is supported should it drop on its drag-line.*

One of the most interesting uses to which silk is put is the parachute. The spider climbs high up on a blade of grass, on a fence, or pole, and facing the wind stands on the tips of the tarsi and tilts the abdomen upwards. From the spinnerets are emitted threads which are paid out as the air currents pull, until the buoyancy of the parachute is enough to support the spider, which releases its hold and is carried away in the breeze.

—B.J. Kaston & Elizabeth Kaston
How to Know the Spiders

1. Organic Writing

"When you sit down to write a book, how much of it do you already have fixed in your mind? Do you know how it will end? Do you know how it will get there?"

This is one of the questions that comes up most frequently when I meet my readers. (It runs a close second to "What is Bill Brohaugh really like?" and is a whole lot easier to answer.) And it's a point, certainly, that I've addressed from time to time over the years, discussing the relative merits of planning and spontaneity, the security of a detailed outline, the freedom of travelling without a formal itinerary.

I was thinking the other day that, however carefully the writer plans ahead, with or without an outline, you never *really* know exactly what's going to happen next in any truly engaging piece of fiction. Because good writing is never merely a matter of assembling a boxful of component parts according to a sheet of directions, and that holds true even when you're the one who handcrafted the parts and wrote the directions.

Writing, you might say, is an organic process. It grows as it goes. Each page is the product of everything that has gone before it, including of course the preceding page. I may know—or think I know—exactly what I'm going to write today and tomorrow. But something unplanned will happen during today's stint at the typewriter, some unimportant piece of dialogue, some bit of description—and what I write tomorrow will be changed by it.

Here's an illustration, from a letter I received from another writer a few months ago.

> In a story I'm working on now, I needed an unusual barkeep, and in creating her I gave her just three fingers on one hand. No reason, other than to make her distinctive. But by the end of the first chapter, I let her do some of the talking, and she explained how she had lost two fingers, and very shortly the loss of the fingers became important to the plot then unfolding. Including reference to the three-fingered hand was, in a sense, sowing a seed

that I harvested—by making certain fictional connec-
tions—later.

This sort of thing happens all the time. Sometimes significant plot
developments derive from minor character tags or scene dressing,
as the writer above describes it. In other instances, little bits of business which the writer drops into one chapter will create echoing elements in later chapters, in a way that seems to give the overall work
a fuller texture.

Sometimes what looks like a theme—and would very likely get
labeled one by a critic—grows out of this sort of organic accident.
An example that occurs to me cropped up in *The Triumph of Evil,* a
book I wrote some years ago under the pen name Paul Kavanagh
(and due to be reissued in a year or so under my own name). Early
on, the lead character, one Miles Dorn, watches robins nesting outside his window. Later on, his young mistress's pet cat kills a baby
robin. That scene, which led to an interesting emotional exchange
between Dorn and the girl, would never have happened had I not
had him looking out the window earlier on with no plan to make
use of what he saw there.

But that wasn't the extent of avian influence in that book. At
another point in the book, Dorn is in a city and watches a woman
feeding pigeons in the park. He muses that for all he knows the
woman is poisoning the birds, and ruminates some on pigeon eradi-
cation programs which so affect the birds that they lay eggs without
shells. And, still later, he's in New Orleans and wanders into a muse-
um where he sees row after row of glass cases containing stuffed
birds, some of them of species which have since become extinct.

If anyone were dotty enough to think *The Triumph of Evil*
merited scholarly analysis, some sort of thesis could be propounded
on the use of birds as a symbol in the book. (I wouldn't be surprised
if there were other mentions I've since forgotten.) Now we could argue that such a thesis would be pure nonsense, since the author is in
a position to attest that he had no conscious intention of using birds
as a symbol, or as a metaphor for something or other. On the other
hand, I wouldn't dream of denying that one bird reference gave rise
to another, unconsciously if not consciously, and I am perfectly willing to entertain the hypothesis that my unconscious mind may have
had some sort of grand design in mind, one way or another.

Most of us who've spent a fair amount of time writing have
come to see that the conscious analytical/intellectual part of the
mind has only a small amount to do with what winds up on the

page. It's another portion of the mind altogether that just plain *knows*, sentences after the introduction of a newly-imagined character, what that character will or won't do, say, notice, respond to, or remember. It's that obscure side of the mind, too, that keeps producing fictional ideas—not just the initial idea that sparks the creation of a piece of writing, but the endless parade of creative ideas which must follow to see the work through to completion.

"Where do you get your ideas?" That's the non-writer's perennial question, as if the initial idea is everything, as if after that one merely has the tiresome chore of filling in the blanks. But it is not like that at all. The writer's mind generates ideas without pause from the first page to the last. Whenever a character opens a door, the writer has to think of something to be on the other side of it. Some of the larger pieces of furniture in the room, if you will, are dictated by a plotline that has already been determined, but other furnishings must be dreamed up on the spot, and some of them will derive from what has gone before, and will lead to what ultimately follows.

> *The writer's mind generates ideas without pause from the first page to the last.*

My perception of my own role in this process has varied from time to time. At times I think I am the source of all my work. At other times I see myself more as channel than source, conveying stories from some unknowable well—the universal unconsciousness, the sublime music of the spheres, the mind of God, call it what you will. Perhaps everything we would write already exists in perfect form; it emerges on the page in one degree or another of imperfection, depending upon the extent to which we are open channels.

What is it, Arnold?

I was just wondering if you were going to suggest we use Ouija boards instead of typewriters, sir.

Not unless you can find one with an automatic carriage return, Arnold. No, I'm not so much recommending that we try to channel our writing as suggesting that we're *always* doing just that, that that's precisely what our imagination and intuition is always doing.

Let's return for a moment to the letter from the writer who created (or channeled, or whatever) the three-fingered bartendress, sowing a seed for later harvest.

He writes:

A lot of beginning fiction writers sow no seeds. They include no detail, or if they do include detail, it is for the sake of description or verisimilitude. It is rarely done with the intent of creating a few layers that might be mined later. The mining might be done in terms of plot, or in terms of later expanding a characterization, or in terms of creating a voice or in terms of weaving connections throughout the fiction. Because in order to weave connections, we have to have a stock of proper connecting points.

You don't know how having a three-fingered woman will affect your plot now, but it's there as fodder, to be used later. You don't know why a character's interest in collecting baseball cards affects things now, but perhaps he'll later notice that someone's alibi of going to a game that day is wrong because he mentioned a player who had been traded a year before. Or something . . .

I think the best way to sow the particular seeds my friend is talking about is simply to *allow* them to be sown, to keep the more logical side of one's mind from interfering in the process. The idea of giving the barkeep three fingers was just that, it was an idea, it came to the writer, and he allowed it to take form in his work without using logic to rule it out. He could have said, "Wait a minute here, three fingers is kind of grotesque, it seems gimmicky, why do I want to do that, what's the point of it, maybe I should think about this before I get carried away." Instead he trusted the intuitive impulse that gave him the character, and the natural organic process of writing let other things happen further on down the line, growing inevitably out of that original notion.

Here's another example of a slightly different sort. Years ago I spoke to an old friend for the first time in a long time. He informed me that his mother had died since our last contact, and related the curious circumstances of her death. A friend of hers had found an abandoned television set on the street and brought it to her apartment; the set had been booby-trapped, and when he turned it on, my friend's mother was killed by the ensuing explosion.

When I heard this, I made the appropriate sympathetic sounds, and unconsciously filed the incident away. Some seven years later I was writing a book called *Eight Million Ways to Die*, and I had my lead character, Matthew Scudder, talking to somebody, and the somebody he was talking to recounted the incident of the exploding television set, saying that it had happened to the mother of a mutual acquaintance.

Now this had nothing to do with the plot of the book. It was consistent with one of the book's themes—i.e., that the world in general and New York in particular are dangerous places—but it didn't connect specifically with anything that preceded or followed it. But it was just the right story for that fellow to tell Scudder right about then, and my mind had been holding it on a darkened shelf all these years, waiting for the time and place to trot it out.

I recounted this incident at a writer's conference, using it to illustrate that certain people tend to tell you things that prove useful in your fiction, and one person in my audience asked a question I found surprising. How, he wondered, had I known to use it where I did? What made me decide to do so? What were my reasons for the decision?

"It fit," I said. "It was perfect there."

"But how did you know that?"

I didn't know how to answer his question. How did I know it? By knowing it, I thought. I just knew it, that's all.

How did my friend decide to maim his bartender? Not through planning and calculation. Not with the thought that a three-fingered bartender just might lead to something, either. He made the decision because it just felt right. It was, thus, an intuitive decision, and he let his intuition have its head.

And, because the intuition always knows what it's doing, other things were able to grow out of the decision. Organically. Yes, Rachel?

I thought when things grow organically that means with no bug sprays or chemical fertilizers.

Well, that would describe my own writing perfectly, Rachel. I never use bug sprays, and an abundant supply of natural fertilizer is the wellspring of all my work. Is that what you were going to say, Arnold?

No, sir. I was going to ask who the writer was who had the three-fingered bartender.

That was Bill Brohaugh.

You're kidding.

Honest.

Sir, could I ask you something? What's he really like?

2. The Look of Words upon the Page

In the class I used to teach at Hofstra University, students took turns reading their assigned work aloud. Each story, upon having been read, was discussed and criticized by the author's fellow students. This workshop approach is probably the most common method of teaching writing, and one can say for it what Churchill said of democracy, i.e., that it is a terrible system, its sole virtue residing in its marked superiority to all the other systems in existence.

What is most clearly wrong with the system derives from the fact that prose fiction is not designed to be read aloud. One takes in its message with the eyes, and the ear it must please is that inner ear that hears what the eye has recorded in silence.

This is not to say that reading prose aloud is without purpose. It is of particular value, it seems to me, to the writer himself; when he has to stand up there and read his own words aloud, he is apt to be struck by those unfortunate turns of phrase, those awkward verbal constructions that seemed perfectly acceptable when they were just sitting there on the page. One student of mine last semester had a tendency to overwrite, and I noticed that his purplest passages would stick in his throat when he tried to read them to us. I understand that some writers make a point of reading each day's production aloud, either to a friend or to the unhearing walls, so that they can catch weaknesses in their writing that the eye failed to detect.

Perhaps the greatest fault of the workshop approach is that the reader's audience is in no position to judge how the story being read does or does not work upon the page. One of my students began the term by writing whole stories in single unbroken paragraphs, as endless as Faulknerian sentences and impossibly deadening to the reader's eye. I broke him of this pernicious habit, but only because I collected my students' work at the end of class and had a look (as opposed to a listen) at what they had done.

If you take a few moments to watch readers at a paperback rack, you'll see that they choose books on the basis of eye appeal. It is the visual allure of the cover that gets the book picked up in the first place, but it is the visual appeal of words upon the pages which keeps the book from being returned to the rack. Haven't you noticed how a browser will thumb through a book, barely glancing at a page here and a page there? Haven't you done that sort of thing yourself? I do it all the time, much in the manner of a prospective diner striding through a restaurant kitchen. Do things look clean? Are the smells inviting? All in all, do I want to eat here?

Or, in the bookshop, are all the paragraphs long and forbidding? Is there dialogue? Is the dialogue itself broken up now and then, or is the whole effect going to be one of reading a stage play? Does all of this look like something I might want to read?

The idea of dictating my work into a tape recorder has appealed to me from time to time. It often strikes me that I could go faster and accomplish more if I didn't have to hammer away at a typewriter. But a tape recorder won't show me how my work looks on the page. I can't see at a glance what words I used a couple of sentences back, so as to avoid repeating them. I can't tell if I've started three successive paragraphs with *I,* and thus might prefer to start the fourth with something else. Longhand bothers me for much the same reason. I can see what I've done, certainly, but I'm seeing it in a form vastly different from the printed page on which it will ultimately appear.

I want to be able to look at my work in a form as close as possible to that which will confront the reader. I can recall Noel Loomis, a writer of Westerns who was employed as a Linotype operator. He used to write his books at his Linotype machine, assembling the slugs of cast type in a chase and pulling galley proofs of his work for submission to his publisher. While I've never really considered running out and buying a Linotype machine, the idea is not without a certain appeal.

STRESS FACTORS

Just a couple of days ago, a reader wrote to ask my advice on two points. First, he wanted to know, how did you decide whether to italicize a foreign word or phrase? And did you have to go on italicizing it every time you used it thereafter? Second, how did you indicate breaks in the narrative after a flashback or some similar transition? Did you just skip two spaces or what?

I had to apologize in my reply for answering two highly specific questions in an undeniably vague fashion. But, I explained, you had to make choices of that sort yourself, and you had to base them on your own view of what did and didn't work.

Italic type is one of several tools available to the writer to indicate emphasis. When my students read aloud, they can lay the stress where they wish, interpreting their own words much as actors interpret a playwright's lines. But when a reader is making his own way through your book or story, you can't hover at his ear, letting him know how each sentence ought to strike his inner ear. Ideally, you'll write your sentences so that their stress is self-evident, but sometimes you'll <u>underline</u> something in your manuscript, and the printer in turn will render it in *italics*.

You probably won't do this too often, recognizing that less is more, and that too much is too much. *Unless,* of course, you *happen* to be writing for *Cosmopolitan,* in which case you just *might* want to lay the italics on with a *trowel.*

Italics, besides indicating emphasis, are used to indicate a foreign word. This double usage can create problems, because the reader can scarcely help stressing the foreign word each time he encounters it, and that may not be the effect you're looking for.

When a whole passage is italicized and you want to emphasize a single word within that passage, the standard method is to print that word in Roman type, like this. *I've never felt that this works terribly well. It's logical, and the reader knows how he's supposed to respond, but the eye just doesn't react to a spot of Roman in a sea of italic as it does when these proportions are reversed.*

> *I*t is the visual allure of the cover that gets the book picked up in the first place.

There are other ways besides italics to make a reader emphasize a particular word or phrase. Quotation marks are occasionally useful; by "dropping" them around a word, you give it a sort of inflection which is a little "different" from the effect you get with italics. Here again, a little goes a long way.

Capitalization is another valuable tool, useful for yet another sort of emphasis. If your object is to Make a Specific Point you might achieve it by capitalizing a series of words within the body of a sentence. Sometimes, for yet another sort of emphasis, you might want to CAPITALIZE an entire word, but I don't do that if I can help it; notice how it leaps off the page at you? All too often I find that I read the word before I come to it because of its extreme prominence. When I do want to run a word in capital letters, I usually prefer to use SMALL CAPS, like these, and I get that effect by typing the word in capitals and adding a marginal note for the printer.

My correspondent's other question concerned how to indicate transitions in a manuscript. Again, this is something for the writer to decide for himself. Most of the time I separate sections by skipping an extra space. If a section ends at the bottom of a page, I may type (leave space) at the top of the following page, then double-space before resuming with the next section.

Or I may insert a # or some similar mark between paragraphs to make it that much clearer that I want a space there. In a novel which includes long chapters, or in a lengthy short story, one might skip a few spaces at the conclusion of a subsection and place a numeral at the head of the next one. Or a date or a time, or a location—or even a name to indicate a viewpoint change.

There are innumerable ways to handle this sort of thing, and none is necessarily right or wrong. What's useful, I think, is to develop an increased awareness of how various writers indicate emphasis and transition. I rarely read anything without finding myself taking note of the choices the writer has made in matters of this sort and deciding how well his choices work. Sometimes this is a nuisance and gets in the way of my enjoyment of the story, but it usually helps make reading a learning experience for me as a writer.

It's worth noting, I think, that matters of style of the sort we've been considering are not always the writer's to decide. A magazine or newspaper editor will feel quite free to make whatever changes he deems necessary so that the work will conform to his publication's style book. If it's a matter of policy to write out street names, for instance, he's not going to let you call it 42nd Street. This seems only reasonable; stylistic variation within a single periodical would look not like artistic freedom but like sloppiness.

Book publishers, too, have their style sheets, and copy editors will frequently impose them upon one's manuscript. In this instance, however, the author has considerably more to say, especially in fiction, where the effect one is trying to achieve carries more weight than that foolish consistency which Emerson called the hobgoblin of little minds.

The point might be made that nobody ever won the National Book Award because of the way he double-spaced between sections, that nobody ever bought a story because of the surgical skill with which the writer put words in italics. If an editor objects to the way you've done this sort of thing he can always change it, or ask you to change it.

On the other hand, books and stories are unquestionably rejected because they do not work on the page, because too many overlong paragraphs tire the eye, because an overabundance of very short paragraphs impedes continuity. Editors may not know that's why they're responding unfavorably to a given work, but these factors can make a real difference.

Pay attention to the appearance of fiction—when you read, so that you can learn, and when you write, so that you can apply what you've learned.

You'll see what I mean.

3. Real People

In the ordinary course of things, the fiction writer has to demonstrate a certain degree of resourcefulness in respect to characterization. First off, he has to dream up his characters. Perhaps they spring full-blown from his psyche, like Minerva from the brow of Jupiter. Perhaps they owe their initial inspiration to a person glimpsed in passing on a crowded street, a model's expression in a magazine advertisement, or a turn of phrase that the author has managed to drape in human form. Perhaps they owe a little—or rather more than a little—to persons of the author's acquaintance. Maybe he has taken a sullen expression here, a background detail there, added another friend's brave smile and an old enemy's withered arm to create someone new.

Having done all this, our writer has to create a history for each character and cap the performance by devising a name which is at once memorable and believable, and which manages to fit the character without being too obvious about it.

A tricky business, when you look at it that way. Is it any wonder then that some writers cut the Gordian Knot of characterization by filling up their books with real people? Why knock yourself out by working up a whole body of character traits and mannerisms for a fictional wife of an American president, say, when you can just call the good woman Eleanor Roosevelt and be done with it? We would certainly be hard put to create a fictional character as vivid and memorable as the genuine article, and consider the edge we have by casting Mrs. Roosevelt in our fiction. No sooner have we brought her on stage and mentioned her by name than has every reader (every reader of a certain age, anyway) given an immediate nod of recognition and formed an immediate image of her. Many of our readers will hear the woman's voice every time we furnish her with a line of imaginary dialogue.

Mrs. Roosevelt comes to mind because she has made several appearances in recent fiction, including the leading role in a detective story written by her son Elliot. Another writer who has employed her as a guest star is Stuart Kaminsky, whom I met at a gathering of mystery fans and writers in Chicago. Mr. Kaminsky's writings include a series of period detective stories set in the '40s and feature one Toby Peters, whose investigations bring him into contact with such persons as Judy Garland, Howard Hughes, Mae West . . . and Eleanor Roosevelt.

In the course of a talk on how he writes his books, Mr. Kaminsky explained that he was not trying to depict real people accurately in his fiction as much as he was using his impressions of these real people to create fictional characters. His Eleanor Roosevelt, he said, derived in large measure from that woman's portrayal in a book by Joseph Lash, who was himself a friend and admirer of Mrs. Roosevelt and by no means an impartial observer. Mr. Kaminsky did not suppose that his Eleanor Roosevelt had much to do with the Eleanor Roosevelt of objective reality, and he didn't care. His object, after all, was fiction, and his character was as much a work of fiction as the plot he devised for her.

Donald E. Westlake makes similar use of real characters in *A Likely Story,* although his real people have writing rather than speaking parts. The book is the diary of a writer named Tom Diskant, whose task it is to solicit contributions from prominent authors for a coffee-table volume with a Christmas theme. Consequently, the list of offstage characters includes Isaac Asimov, Norman Mailer, Truman Capote, Henry Kissinger, Mickey Spillane, Roddy McDowall, Arthur C. Clarke, Isaac Bashevis Singer, and many many more.

Here is Mr. Westlake's introductory note:

This is a work of fiction. All of the characters in this book are fictional, and my creation. Some of these characters wear the names of famous real persons. I have not attempted to describe the true personal characteristics of these famous real persons, whom in most instances I do not know. In each case, I have put that famous name with what I take to be the public perception of that individual (the equivalent, for instance, of suggesting that Jack Benny the person was really a tightwad, though in fact his public persona was that of a tightwad while he was very generous in private life).

I have deliberately chosen not to follow the accepted pattern of changing the name and keeping the public personality, to have a baseball pitcher named Jim Beaver, for instance, who led the Mets to the World Series in 1969. I think that method is arch, crass and deplorable.

The famous names herein are just that: famous names. In looking behind them, the reader will not find the actual human beings who hold those names, nor satires on those human beings. The reader will find only what I believe is the generally held view of that famous name's public self. . . .

A likely story. I quote Mr. Westlake at length not merely out of a base desire to be paid for what he has written, but because he expresses so well what many writers do when they tuck real people into works of the imagination. I don't know that I would label the alternative arch, crass and deplorable. (I seem to recall Arch, Crass & Deplorable as an advertising agency that had its heyday in the early '70s, but I could be mistaken.)

There is a whole school of pop fiction, some examples of which might merit the designation of arch, crass and deplorable, purporting to tell the real story of celebrities in the guise of fiction. Sometimes the writers merely use the character's public perception, as Mr. Westlake calls it, as a jumping-off point. In other instances, the writer

Some writers cut the Gordian Knot of characterization by filling up their books with real people.

collects all available unprintable anecdotes about the celebrity, fills in the gaps with his own imagination, and winds up with a book that owes its marketability to the reader's inference that he's getting the lowdown on a prominent person. I could name names of some writers who make a specialty of this sort of thing, or I could change the names, but I don't think I'll bother. Books of this sort almost always bear a disclaimer notice, in which the author gives us his solemn assurance that none of the characters is based on any real person, living or dead. Readers who like these books read the disclaimer notices with a knowing smile, although the notices are often more accurate than one would suppose; many of the authors' creations bear precious little resemblance to anyone, living or dead, real or imaginary.

It's also possible to write a good book, even a great book, based to a greater or lesser extent upon a real person, and perhaps a prominent one. One often bases one's fictional characters upon persons of one's acquaintance. If one is acquainted with the famous, why should that preclude one's so employing them?

The Disenchanted, Budd Schulberg's powerful portrayal of

the alcoholic dissolution of a famous novelist, quite clearly grew out of Mr. Schulberg's acquaintance with F. Scott Fitzgerald, nor was this a very closely held secret at the time of the book's publication. Mr. Schulberg did elect to call his lead character by another name and change elements of his background and circumstances; he was not trying to transfer Fitzgerald to the printed page but to create a character of his own deriving from his perception of Fitzgerald. As a way of distancing his lead character from the real F. Scott Fitzgerald, he mentions Fitzgerald in a list of writers with whom his fictional lead character is himself acquainted.

Somerset Maugham's fiction occasionally drew inspiration from real people, and sometimes prominent ones. In *Cakes and Ale,* Edward Driffield owes a lot to Thomas Hardy, while another character puts one in mind of Horace Walpole. The painter Charles Strickland in *The Moon and Sixpence,* while hardly a clone of Gauguin, leads a life based upon Gauguin's. It is hard to deny that these two books owed some of their commercial success to the recognition factor; on the other hand, the books work perfectly well as fiction for those of us who know nothing of their real-life counterparts, or are unaware of their factual bases.

It is in period pieces that real people most frequently make cameo appearances. E. L. Doctorow's *Ragtime* is an example that comes quickly to mind, but any number of books set a few decades or more in the past have real people on hand to lend a note of verisimilitude. In John Jakes's historical novels, which have as one of their aims the recounting of history, such characters play an important role. In others, where they are less essentially a part of the story, they help recreate the past for the modern reader. Why invent a fictional mayor of New York when you can usher Jimmy Walker or Fiorello LaGuardia on stage? Why invent a headline for your character to read with his morning coffee when you can have Lindbergh cross the Atlantic, or Roosevelt elected by a landslide?

Once in a while these time machine glimpses seem jarring to me. Recently I read in manuscript the forthcoming novel by Harold Adams, *The Naked Liar.* It's the fourth book in a series set in a small town in South Dakota during the Depression, and it contains in passing a reference to the Lindbergh kidnapping. In that instance, I felt the author's fictional universe was so wholly realized that anything outside, like a real-life newscast, perversely disturbed the book's essential reality.

Sometimes the choice between using a real name and fictionalizing is a tricky one. In *The Day of the Jackal,* Frederick Forsythe's titular antihero spends the book attempting to assassinate Charles de Gaulle, who bears that name in the novel.

Now this would seem to gut the book of some of its suspense. We who are its readers know that General de Gaulle survived any number of assassination attempts, dying at last of natural causes. If Mr. Forsythe had made the Jackal's target some de Gaulle type named, say, General Pousse-Café, we'd have no way of knowing how the book would turn out.

The counter-argument, I suppose, is that calling the man de Gaulle made the book seem somehow more important. Just as we suspend our disbelief in order to get involved in the fiction we read, so did we in that instance suspend our knowledge of the book's inevitable outcome. We knew full well that de Gaulle would be alive at the book's end, but while we read it we told ourselves that we couldn't be absolutely certain.

A note on the legality of all of this, prefaced by the admonition that I am not a lawyer, nor am I much interested in this sort of legal question. Generally speaking, one may make relatively free use of real persons once they are dead. If they are alive, it gets trickier. Public personages may usually be given off-stage mention and cameo roles with no trouble. Any character may be more safely portrayed in a good light than a bad one; it's hard to sue for libel and claim massive damages of someone who has said only good things about you.

In the main, I would say that this is not something a writer has to worry much about while writing a book; afterward, he can always consult with his own or the publisher's lawyer before bringing the book out.

4. Jyl's Story

Last August I spent a few days on Fire Island, where two of my daughters were spending the summer in gainless employment. One of them, Jyl, had written a short story. Would I care to read it?

Of course I would. Jyl (whose name used to be spelled J-I-L-L until she fell down and broke her crown) has been writing the occasional story for a couple of years now. Her ear for dialogue is excellent, she has a fine sense of the proper shape of a sentence, and her ability to sustain an extended narrative bodes well. She has, as they say, all the moves. This doesn't mean she'll make it as a writer, but it suggests that she probably *can*—if she wants to badly enough.

Jyl's stories run heavily to dialogue, and some of them amount to virtual prose plays composed almost entirely of free-standing dialogue. In this respect, the story I read was atypical. It was in the first person, and in it the narrator discussed her friendship with another young woman named Marni and the changes that friendship had undergone over a period of several years. The two had met during a summer at Fire Island while both were in high school. Although their backgrounds and off-season lives were dissimilar in several respects, they'd become quite close and maintained their friendship back in the city as well. A second island summer further deepened their relationship, which was characterized by a feeling of closeness and the ability to share thoughts and experiences conversationally.

Then, after each had spent a year at college, the two of them met for a third time on Fire Island and found that something had changed between them. Marni, the narrator complained, was different. She'd become a sort of artsy hippie in contrast to the preppy narrator, and she no longer fit in with her old crowd on the island. The sharing and intimacy that had existed between the two girls wasn't there anymore.

Finally the narrator went on to explain that now, in 1993, she's just seen Marni again, having gone to an art gallery where her former friend had a show opening. As the story ended, one saw how the two lives had taken very different paths.

After I'd finished the story, I walked Jyl over to Mike the Greek's. (Perhaps he'll change that to Myk the Grique's.) We took a window table, and the waiter brought coffee for Jyl and tea for me. We stirred our respective beverages reflectively, as people are wont to do on such occasions, and cleared our respective throats.

"Nice job," I said. To Jyl, not the waiter.

"Thank you," she said.

"Of course it's not really a story. It's more of a recollection. Nothing actually happens in it."

"I know."

"It's unusual for you. The style, I mean."

She nodded. A friend of hers had written a story and showed it to Jyl, and it had inspired her to try writing in a narrative voice rather than her usual scenes-with-dialogue approach.

"Well, that's good," I said. "I think it's very useful to try different things in your work. The opportunity to fool around with a new technique can be reason enough to write a particular story in the first place. I, uh, gather this story is based on experience."

"My stories always are," she said, with one exception of which she reminded me. "People say it's not really fiction because I just put down what happens."

I shook my head. "They don't know what they're talking about. You fictionalize. You create dialogue—it's never like a transcribed tape recording. It's shaped and constructed. And you change things. The narrator here is preppier than you are, for instance. As I recall, you and your sister Amy both spent the past winter in men's overcoats from the Salvation Army."

"You don't like my coat."

"I said it made you look like a bag lady. But I never said I didn't like it." I sipped some tea. "The point is that your stories definitely qualify as fiction. But I gather the friend you're writing about here is one you've told me about before." And I named the other girl, but let's call her Marni.

"Right," Jyl said. "She was out here two weeks ago and things were different between us, and I thought about it, and I, like, wanted to write about it."

"That's good, too," I said. "Fiction can be a useful way of finding out how you feel about something. I've found out a lot about myself by looking at my own work." I tapped the manuscript. "There's one thing here that's very jarring," I said, "and that's your jump-cut eleven years into the future. All along the reader's assumed he's reading something narrated in present time by someone who is describing the changes in a relationship in the recent past. He visualizes the narrator as a nineteen-year-old woman in today's world, and all of a sudden you tell him it's 1993 and the narrative voice he's been listening to is that of a thirty-year-old. You can surprise a reader in this fashion, but only if you have a good reason, only if it makes a strong dramatic point. Here it's just wrong."

"I didn't know it was going to turn out that way," she admitted. "I was like looking for a way to end it."

"That's what I figured." I made a little tent of my fingertips, a sign that I was about to turn ruminative and philosophical. "You know," I said, "you make the point that Marni and the narrator both go in straight lines from this point of divergence. Each goes on in the direction she's headed at that last meeting, and they're never friends again, and ten years later one's an artist and the other's a hausfrau."

"Right."

"That's interesting, the idea of two roads diverging and carrying them on their separate paths forever. Of course, straight line projection is almost always wrong. People who try to forecast social changes always tend to predicate them on the indefinite continuation of present trends, and present trends never continue indefinitely. The same thing's true for human lives. Maybe the direction Marni's taking is permanent, but then again maybe it's a way station en route to the suburbs."

I t's very useful to try different things in your work.

"Maybe."

"Do you remember *Same Time Next Year*? A man and a woman met once a year for twenty-five or thirty years and each time spent a night together. And they were both going through profound changes from one scene to the next, swinging like metronomes never quite in synch one with the other. Remember?"

We kicked this around for a while. Then I ordered us another round. "One reason this isn't a story," I said, "is that we don't see anything. We have to take the narrator's word for it. You do a nice job of showing how this rift between the two girls impacts upon the narrator, how she feels and what she thinks about it, but you don't make us see it. I don't get a sense of any change in Marni's behavior. How was she different?"

"She was so out of place here," she said, remembering. "At

school she lives in this organic commune where they buy whole grains in bulk and don't eat anything with additives, and everybody out here is into pizza and Haagen-Dazs. Same as *she* was a year ago."

"Uh-huh."

"And she just, oh, everything's different about her. She doesn't shave her legs anymore."

"I'm surprised they let her on the ferry."

"I know it's a small thing, but it just seemed to sum up the whole thing. Like a bunch of us were sitting around Windswept and Marni had these hairy legs, and she kept pulling at the hem of her skirt. She couldn't leave her skirt alone. Like she was embarrassed and uncomfortable about it but she wasn't going to run to the bathroom and shave. It's a little thing, but—"

"It's terrific."

"Huh?"

"It's perfect. You couldn't pick a better way to illustrate her discomfort. Here she is with her legs unshaven, and she's self-conscious about it, but she can't go shave her legs to conform to standards here because that would be phony, and even if she wanted to she can't because she'd feel phony going back to her Back-to-Nature friends with shaven legs. She's changed in the past year, maybe, but it's still a tentative change. She's got a foot in both camps, even if they're both at the end of hairy legs, and she's uncomfortable that way." I looked at her. "That belongs in your story."

"I can see that."

"There's nothing wrong with a story that's composed entirely of the narrator's reflection, without scenes or dialogue. You could write the story that way and still use an example like the hairy legs incident to highlight the whole thing. And that's such an ideal example. It's the kind of thing writers make up—when they're lucky enough to think of it."

We talked some more about the story, and about other things. The next day, while we waited for the ferry that would take me and my youngest daughter, Alison, back to the mainland, I thought of the story again. "You know," I told Jyl, "what you really ought to do is rewrite that story about you and Marni."

"And put in the bit about shaving her legs?"

"Not just that," I said. "Rewrite it—but make Marni the narrator."

"Oh, wow," she said. Or words to that effect.

"You'd still be using your experience, but you'd have to give your imagination a little more of a workout. Because you'd be seeing the same material through somebody else's eyes."

She gave me a look through her own.

"Listen," I told her, "you've got it easy. Think about what I've got to do with the same material. I've got to sit down at the typewriter and turn it into a *Writer's Digest* column. I've got to make up dialogue for both of us, and I've got to put in little bits of business like the waiter coming over with the coffee. Here's the ferry now. Why does it swing wide like that instead of pulling straight in?"

"Nobody knows."

"Well, I'll put it in the column that way. Give the thing a sense of immediacy. Of course it'll be harder writing the story from Marni's viewpoint. When did I ever tell you it was going to be easy?" I hoisted my backpack, took Alison by the hand. "I'll send you a copy of the column," I said.

"Just spell my name right," said Jyl.

5. Following in Jane Austen's Footsteps

> It is a truth universally acknowledged, that a single man in possession of a good fortune must be in want of a wife.
>
> However little known the feelings or views of such a man may be on his first entering a neighbourhood, this truth is so well fixed in the minds of the surrounding families, that he is considered as the rightful property of someone or other of their daughters.
>
> "My dear Mr. Bennet," said his lady to him one day, "have you heard that Netherfield Park is let at last?"
>
> Mr. Bennet replied that he had not.
>
> "But it is," returned she; "for Mrs. Long has just been here, and she told me all about it."
>
> Mr. Bennet made no answer
>
> "Do not you want to know who has taken it?" cried his wife impatiently.
>
> "You want to tell me, and I have no objection to hearing it."
>
> This was invitation enough.

It's enough, all right—if you want more you'll have to read it yourself. *Pride and Prejudice,* by Jane Austen, and you could find a worse use for a couple of hours than to spend them in that lady's company. The book's opening sentence is one of the more well-known beginnings of English prose, and a quick perusal of the portion I've copied out shows that its author knew how to get a story started. But for a few turns of phrase that sound awkward to a modern ear, this passage would still do to start a story 170 years after its original publication.

All of which has next to nothing to do with the subject that concerns us. I selected *Pride and Prejudice* neither for its excellence nor for its occasional archaism but simply because it was there, and because it's old enough to be planted firmly in the public domain. Thus I could copy it without a second thought, and that's what I wanted to do. I wanted to copy it.

I suppose you'll tell us why, sir.

Why, certainly, Arnold. I'll be glad to, and I'll do so by copying something else, in this case a portion of a letter from Craig Broude, of Northridge, California. Mr. Broude noted that I'd drawn an analogy between painting and writing in a recent column, and went on to raise this point:

> *Are you aware that many painters, when they're first studying their craft, try to duplicate the works of the masters? Not just the techniques, but the actual works themselves. This is supposed to allow them to see first-hand the various techniques necessary to create certain effects.*
>
> *Here's the question: Are you aware of any writers who have tried to improve their craft by copying the works of others they admire? (As an exercise, I mean, not as a plagiarism intended for publication.)*
>
> *Do you see any value in doing this? I myself am undecided. The idea of simply typing out—copying—page after page of another writer's work, doesn't seem so beneficial at first glance. But then I've never done it . . . Does it seem like a good idea to you, or a ridiculous one?*

I'll tell you one thing. It seems like a soft touch if there ever was one to get paid for sitting here copying Ms. Austen and Mr. Broude. But let me earn a little of this month's stipend by giving the question some serious thought.

My first reaction is that the analogy with painting doesn't hold water. (Or oil, or acrylic, or whatever.) A novice artist who copies a sketch or painting is attempting to create an effect identical to what some master has created before him. Depending on his skill, he will produce a good or bad copy of the original, but in any case he will produce a copy, and one which can be readily distinguished from the master's work. Through his efforts to make his copy as good as he can, he will learn how to achieve certain artistic effects through the application of certain techniques. It is not difficult to imagine how he could learn a considerable amount in this fashion.

In contrast, anyone who copied any writer's work would be quite capable of copying it perfectly. I need no literary skill whatsoever to copy Ms. Austen's novel. I can get it perfectly right, word for word and comma for comma, even to the "u" in neighbourhood and the curious semicolon after "she," and so could anyone with two fingers and a typewriter. When one writer copies another's work, whether with a typewriter or a quill pen, it is not at all like copying the Mona Lisa in oil paint but far more like taking a photograph of it.

The point's too obvious to belabor. The painter's technique is a matter of mind and hand and eye; the writer's is more exclusively mental.

Having dismissed the analogy, can we as easily dismiss the whole idea of copying another's work as a useful learning device? I should think not. The theory underlying this business of copying is that it brings one a little closer to the writer's process of creation. By taking the author's words one at a time and laying them on paper one experiences a piece of created prose in a deeper fashion than if one merely reads it. You go through the words at a writer's pace, not a reader's pace.

I don't know how many teachers make their students do this sort of thing. I know I've read occasionally of this sort of copying technique's being recommended to young writers, but the more I think about it the less I can imagine anyone's willingly participating in it. It would seem to me to be an unutterably boring task.

The object, after all, is to develop one's own writing style.

Does this mean I think the process would be utterly valueless?

Well, not exactly. I don't for a moment think it's worth doing, and if I had had to do it in order to become a writer I think I'd probably have found another line of work, but I don't know that it's completely pointless. I'm willing to believe, for instance, that this sort of copy-typing can help a person tell good writing from bad writing. Manuscript typists with no particular interest in writing report that it's easier to type something well written. The words flow better, and it's less of a strain to be a part of the process. I knew a Linotype operator who found some reporters' stories infinitely easier to set than others; his fingers grew more agile when the prose he was setting had the right sort of rhythm to it.

In a few days Mr. Bingley returned Mr. Bennet's visit, and sat about ten minutes with him in his library. He had entertained hopes of being admitted to a sight of the young ladies, of whose beauty he had heard much; but he saw only the father. The ladies were somewhat more for-

> *tunate, for they had the advantage of ascertaining from
> an upper window that he wore a blue coat, and rode a
> black horse.*

You tell 'em, Jane. There are other ways to copy which might or
might not prove useful to a student of writing, and which instructors occasionally promote as exercises. One consists not of verbatim copying but of imitation. I might ask you, say, to write a particular scene in the manner of Jane Austen, or J. D. Salinger, or Ernest
Hemingway, or anyone at all.

This is usually a popular exercise because it generally turns out
to be fun, especially in a classroom situation where students can
amuse one another with parody. Occasionally it leads to confusion,
when a student proudly reads a scene he wrote in the manner of Ms.
Austen, say, and his classmates praise him for his excellent imitation of Salinger.

I don't know, though, that it has much to do with writing, or
that the ability to do this sort of thing well correlates in any way
with the ability to produce viable fiction. The object, after all, is to
develop one's own writing style, not to refine the ability to imitate
other writers.

Now it's possible that imitation might be a useful path toward
developing one's own style. And it's certainly true that the facility
for writing in a style suitable to a particular genre is essentially an
imitative one.

If I were to decide tomorrow to write a romance, for example,
I would promptly go out and buy copies of a dozen typical specimens, and I would read them all thoroughly. I would immerse myself in these books until I had acquired a sense of what did and did
not constitute a successful romance novel. I would know what sort
of characters with what sort of backgrounds would interact in what
sort of ways in order to add up to an acceptable story. And then my
imagination would obligingly come up with an appropriate plot
and some suitable characters, and I would get to work.

And the style of my writing, the tone and rhythm of my prose
and dialogue, would amount to a sort of unconscious synthesis of
what I'd read, all of it overlaid on the basic style that comes naturally to me. I wouldn't set out to imitate any particular romance writer,
or even to imitate the overall style of the genre; it would happen almost automatically. And I don't think it would happen any more effectively for my sitting down and typing up verbatim extracts from
the latest Harlequin romance.

> *Elizabeth made no answer, and, without attempting to persuade her ladyship to return to the house, walked quietly into it herself. She heard the carriage drive away as she proceeded upstairs. Her mother impatiently met her at the drawer of the dressing-room, to ask why Lady Catherine would not come in again and rest herself.*

Whatever you say, Ms. Austen. If I were sentenced to copy any writer, I think my fingers would wind up fighting back. Before long I'd almost certainly find myself rewriting what I was typing, rephrasing something that struck me as clumsy, repunctuating, changing a word here and a word there. Now that might be something of a creative exercise, though it doesn't sound like a whole lot of fun, either.

Because ultimately what makes writing work or not work is the life that we do or don't breathe into it, and that life is rather more than a matter of prose rhythms and word choice. The damning thing about most unsuccessful amateur writing is not that the clauses are too long or the vocabulary too small but that the sentences lie lifeless upon the page and the pages lack all conviction. The reader doesn't believe what he's reading because he somehow senses that the writer didn't believe it, either.

And the breath of life that animates fiction can't be copied. So I'm afraid I would not advise anyone to try schooling himself by performing a task at which (to paraphrase John Randolph of Roanoke) the carbon paper is one's equal and the Xerox machine one's superior. When all is said and done, you're all alone with a blank sheet of paper, and you have to think up the words with which to fill it.

6. The Shadow Knows

> *Officer: Awright, soldier. Suppose an enemy sub surfaced and ran aground on that beach over there, and suppose she offloaded fifty enemy troops. What would you do?*
>
> *Soldier: Sir, I'd blow 'em off the sand with concentrated mortar fire, sir.*
>
> *Officer: Where would you get the mortars?*
>
> *Soldier: Same place you got the sub, sir.*

Our subject this bright summer afternoon is foreshadowing, and we could do worse than define it as the technique of making both the submarine and the mortars acceptable to the reader. Through skillful foreshadowing, the writer prepares the reader for a sharp turn in the plot without tipping his hand altogether. The reader knows the turn is coming but doesn't know what sort of beast is lurking around the bend.

Let me give you an example from something I read just a couple of nights ago. *The Danger Within* is an early effort of Michael Gilbert, a British suspense novelist of considerable ability. The book is set in a POW camp in Italy during the Second World War, and concerns the unmasking of an enemy agent during preparations for a mass escape.

One of the prisoners is moved to a jail. He is to be hanged unjustly, but gets a last-minute reprieve when the camp command changes upon Mussolini's overthrow. Released, he's debriefed by the head of the escape committee, at the conclusion of which we have this exchange.

> *"Was there anything else you picked up that might be useful?"*
>
> *"Well—no. Nothing in particular." For a moment Byfold looked almost embarrassed.*
>
> *"Certain?"*
>
> *"Yes, quite certain. If I do think of anything I'll let you know."*

What he's let *us* know, of course, is that there is indeed something else he picked up but he just doesn't think it's worth mentioning. And we know at once that it is worth mentioning, and we're impatient for him to get off the pot and mention it.

Immediately thereafter Byfold is further debriefed by the Senior British Officer, and this conversation concludes as follows:

> "Did you pick up anything else that might be useful while you were over the other side?"
> "No, sir. Nothing startling."
> If there was, once again, a certain hesitancy in Byfold's manner, Colonel Lavery apparently did not notice it.

Again Mr. Gilbert has teased us a little, letting us know that Byfold heard something significant. But he's not ready to let us know what it is yet, nor is he ready to hand that information over to the two men who have interrogated Byfold. A few scenes later, it's time for us to have the information, and he spoons it to us by having Byfold confide haltingly to his bunkmates:

> "I—look here, you've got to keep quiet about this, because I may be quite wrong—although they both asked me—but something did happen while I was in the carabinieri hut . . . It wasn't at all easy, and you couldn't hear anything very distinctly, but I suddenly realized that something rather odd was going on. At least one of the voices was English . . ."
> "Was it distinct enough," said Goyles, "for you to pick up any sort of intonation?"
> "Yes," said Byfold, "that's just it. There was. I'm prepared to swear it was either an American or a Colonial speaking."

We have now been given a clue, and the foreshadowing helps us to recognize it as such. At the same time, it keeps us from wondering why Byfold said nothing of this to either of the officers who debriefed him. He *almost* said something, we realize, and we recognized as much at the time, and that keeps us from feeling cheated when we learn what he's been holding back.

Toward the end of *The Dead Zone*, Stephen King's novel which pits a clairvoyant against a potential despot, the plot is literally advanced by a bolt out of the blue. Johnny Smith, the prescient hero, is given the foreknowledge that a roadhouse where a graduation party is to be held will be struck by lightning. He tries to get the party canceled, whereupon . . . well, read it yourself.

Lightning strikes, of course, as we know it will. Now this business of moving things along with a stroke of lightning might ordinarily strike us as relying rather heavily on coincidence. How convenient, we'd say, that the lightning just happened to come around at the right time. How handy for Mr. Smith, not to mention Mr. King.

But we don't react this way at all. Because a couple of hundred pages earlier the author has foreshadowed precisely this development. He planted a scene in which an itinerant lightning rod salesman stops for a beer at a New England roadhouse and tries mightily to peddle his wares to the proprietor, pointing out that the place is a natural target for lightning and that the rods would pay for themselves in reduced insurance premiums.

The owner, of course, isn't interested. The salesman drinks his beer and goes his way. (Maybe it wasn't beer. I don't have the book handy, and it doesn't matter.) If we stop to think about it, we realize that sooner or later this place is going to get in the way of a bolt of lightning, but since none of the characters figure in the rest of the story

Through skillful foreshadowing, the writer prepares the reader for a sharp turn in the plot.

and we have no idea how the roadhouse is going to fit into future plot development, we don't dwell on it much. We turn the page and keep reading, engrossed in the story.

But we're prepared. When Johnny Smith envisions that lightning striking, we know damned well it's going to happen. That place is going to burn, and he knows it and we know it, and it makes perfect sense to us. After all, we were there when the dumbbell missed his chance to protect himself, weren't we? We'd forgotten all about that roadhouse and those lightning rods, but *now* we remember, and we're pleased with ourselves for remembering.

Sure, we think. Sure, *that's* what King was setting up. Knew he was getting at something or other. How clever of him to manage it that way. How clever of us to be ready for it. And how stupid of the roadhouse proprietor to have sent that salesman on his way.

Is it any less of a coincidence that the roadhouse is struck by lightning during the graduation party? It's still the same bolt from the blue, isn't it?

Sure it is.

But we're ready for it, and it seems perfectly plausible to us. Because of the foreshadowing.

How admirable of Stephen King to have laid the groundwork so carefully. How meticulously he must have plotted his book in advance in order to have set up that business with the lightning rods. Why, he had to be almost as clairvoyant as Johnny Smith himself, knowing so early on that he was going to be burning down a roadhouse hundreds of pages down the road.

Right?

Maybe. And maybe not.

Because for all you or I know, Mr. King never even thought of a roadhouse fire until it came time to write about it. Whereupon he wrote the scene and realized that his readers would not be prepared for it. Whereupon he backed up and wrote the foreshadowing scene and dropped it into a suitable place in the book.

Now I don't know which way *The Dead Zone* was written, and it doesn't matter very much. The point is that you don't have to foresee plot developments in order to foreshadow them. When something happens in your story that demands foreshadowing, you can drop back a few yards and slip in a sentence or a paragraph or a scene that will properly set things up. Writers, unlike construction experts, build their castles in the air; thus we have the luxury of being able to lay the groundwork after the fact if we don't think to do it before.

Mystery writers do this all the time, planting the appropriate clues after the fact. Well, not *all* the time; some of us know who the killer is from the beginning, have the plot outlined in more or less detailed fashion, and plant our clues as we go along. But a book is an organic entity. It grows as it goes, and often a plot will take turns unanticipated in an outline. Afterward the writer can go over the manuscript at leisure, get his clues and red herrings pointed in the appropriate directions, and generally tidy things up.

Similarly, when I'm writing a book and am not sure who will turn out to have done the dirty deed, I'll often toss in the odd clue without knowing just what it's a clue to, or who will be ultimately tripped up by it. This sort of scattergun foreshadowing sometimes pays off in that it aids in plot development. I wind up getting ideas by trying to figure out my own puzzle.

This is rather along the lines of the advice given by a mystery writer—I think it was George Harmon Coxe—who advised beginners that whenever the action seemed to be lagging, they should "bring in a man with a gun." It didn't matter, he explained, that you didn't know who the man was or what he wanted. His presence would serve to heighten tension, and sooner or later his role in the proceedings would clarify itself.

You may find it useful to pay attention to foreshadowing in its various forms in the reading you do. If you have a taste for daytime television, check out the soap operas. They make frequent, albeit heavyhanded, use of foreshadowing, to the point where virtually every extraneous element may be presumed to be a harbinger of developments to come. On the soaps, when a character reacts to stress by fixing himself a drink, we know he's going to turn out to have a problem with the sauce. If a woman mentions an upset stomach, it's either a terminal illness or a baby on the way. It's never just an upset stomach. (On the commercials, it's always an upset stomach, and she gets to trade a headache for it.)

Soap opera foreshadowing is rarely allowed to go unnoticed. When one character does or says something that's supposed to let us know of impending whatever, another character picks up the cue and we're treated to a reaction shot. And the organ music serves as the underline key on a typewriter, putting everything noteworthy in italics.

Now they do this on daytime TV because it works. The plots twist around like a snake with a motor dysfunction, and the focus hops from one group of characters to another, and some viewers miss some episodes because the nine-year-old has to be taken to the orthodontist, and others can't concentrate fully because some attention has to be devoted to doing the ironing. So the viewer has to have a good idea what's coming next without knowing for sure what's coming next, and that's one of the things foreshadowing provides.

If it can do that while making the implausible plausible and setting up the plot's punchlines, it would seem to be a technique worth mastering.

7. A Stitch in Time

As I write this, I'm at my desk in Brooklyn. It's the last week in January and I've got a column due. That's okay, because I know what I'm going to write about and I have a pretty good idea how I'm going to approach the topic.

A week ago I was somewhere in Pennsylvania or West Virginia, driving an aunt's car from Buffalo to Pompano Beach. The weather was medium-rotten, and the wheels of other cars kept splattering my windshield, and the windshield washer was frozen solid. I'd hoped to think about my column while I drove, but I wound up thinking of other things. Homicide, for example.

Listen, forget all that. It doesn't matter what I went through coming up with a topic for this column. It doesn't even matter much to *me*, and there's no reason why it should matter to you. This column's first two paragraphs are there to introduce the topic, which is flashbacks. And the second paragraph *is* a flashback, albeit a brief one. It takes me back seven days in time, and moves me from Brooklyn to Pennsylvania or West Virginia or wherever I was. (Once I got into Virginia the road surface cleared up, and somewhere in the Carolinas the fluid in the windshield washer melted. Just in case you were wondering.)

I've discussed flashbacks a couple times before. In *Telling Lies for Fun and Profit*, two consecutive chapters ("First Things Second" and "Spring Forward, Fall Back") deal with ways of departing from a strictly chronological narrative flow. In the first, I explained the trick of beginning a book with the action already in progress, then dropping back in the second chapter to fill the reader in. In "Spring Forward, Fall Back" I talked about ways of jumping ahead in a story, then backing and filling.

But there are innumerable other ways in which flashbacks can enhance prose writing, and perhaps we can profit from a look at some of them. The flashbacks which make themselves most obvious are the lengthy ones, ranging from a chapter to the greater portion of a book, but they're only one of many methods of backing up, of taking a stitch in time.

In multiple-viewpoint novels, the flashback is a particularly handy way to give a reader information about a character. It's awkward, every time a character is introduced, to feed the reader as much information about the new character as you might want him to have. Nor is there necessarily any great need to give the reader all this data immediately. At an appropriate time, however, you can tell as much or as little as you wish of that new character's story in a flashback.

Let's say your lead character goes into a nightclub and chats with the piano player. That piano player is going to play a lot more than "Stardust" in the chapters to come, and you want the reader to know something about his lousy first marriage and how he lost part of his left foot in Vietnam. Now you could cram this in on the spot by having your lead discuss these points with him, but maybe that would be an artificial conversation, the sort in which the principals are speaking only so that they may be overheard by the reader.

Instead, you can write your scene naturally, with perhaps some kind of teaser; you might have your lead unable to keep from staring at the pianist's tapping foot, for instance, without explaining any more about it.

Later on, perhaps when the pianist has a viewpoint scene of his own, you say what you want to about him. The material won't get in the way of a scene in progress, and you can let scenes in your flashback come fully to life; the reader's there for them instead of eavesdropping on them.

A flashback's like a swimming pool. You can ease into the water or take a running jump.

For example:

> *Clavenger segued smoothly into the opening bars of "More Than You Know," his foot tapping, keeping the insistent tempo. He winced at a stab of pain in the foot, then smiled sardonically at the sensation and his response to it. He hardly ever felt it anymore, ghost pain in a foot that had been amputated years ago. Now, tapping its wooden replacement, he let himself remember that morning in Vietnam.*
>
> *It had been a murderously hot day, with the sun blazing relentlessly in a cloudless sky. PFC Barton Clavenger, nineteen years old, lay on a cot in his hootch, smoking a Lucky and blowing smoke rings at the ceiling. On the cot beside him . . .*

I leave you to decide for yourselves who or what was on the cot beside him. That, in any case, is one way to do it. Here's another, in which we begin the scene or chapter by going directly into the flashback:

> *When Bart Clavenger was nineteen years old, the Army dressed him in khaki and sent him to Vietnam. One murderously hot day, with the sun blazing relentlessly in a cloudless sky, he lay on a cot in a hootch outside Da Nang, a cigarette smoldering between his fingers . . .*

There are advantages in either transitional method. If you ease away from present to past time, perhaps by letting your character remember, you don't take the reader quite so far away from the present time story. The story still has one foot in the here and now, since Clavenger's tickling the old ivories and remembering what happened. After he's remembered as much as you want him to, he can sigh, shake off the reverie, and play something else.

Flashbacks needn't be lengthy or elaborate.

On the other hand, the fast cut is clean and sharp and simple, and avoids much the same sort of artificiality that made us put this material in a flashback instead of an overheard conversation. In our first example, we might wonder why Clavenger happened to remember this incident just now. Oh, it's been explained that a phantom pain triggered the memory, but why did the author trigger the phantom pain? So that Clavenger could conveniently remember what the writer would like the reader to know.

Flashbacks needn't be lengthy or elaborate, nor are they only useful as ways to convey essential material. Consider the following backward glance, from my own novel *Eight Million Ways to Die*. The narrator, an ex-cop named Scudder, is paying a visit to a murdered woman's apartment:

> *The police had been through the place earlier. I didn't know what they were looking for and couldn't say what they found. The sheets in the file Durkin showed me hadn't said much, but nobody writes down everything that comes to his attention.*
> *I couldn't know what the officers on the scene might have noticed. For that matter, I couldn't be sure what*

might have stuck to their fingers. There are cops who'll rob the dead, doing so as a matter of course, and they are not necessarily men who are especially dishonest in other matters.

Cops see too much of death and squalor, and in order to go on dealing with it they often have the need to dehumanize the dead. I remember the first time I helped remove a corpse from a room in an SRO hotel. The deceased had died vomiting blood and had lain there for several days before his death was discovered. A veteran patrolman and I wrestled the corpse into a body bag and on the way downstairs my companion made sure the bag hit every single step. He'd have been more careful with a sack of potatoes.

I can still recall the way the hotel's other residents looked at us. And I can remember how my partner went through the dead man's belongings, scooping up the little cash he had to his name, counting it deliberately and dividing it with me.

I hadn't wanted to take it. "Put it in your pocket," he told me. "What do you think happens to it otherwise? Somebody else takes it. Or it goes to the state. What's the State of New York gonna do with forty-four dollars?"

. . . . I put it in my pocket. Later on, I was the one who bounced bagged corpses down the stairs, the one who counted and divided their leavings.

Someday, I suppose, it'll come full circle, and I'll be the one in the bag.

None of the material in this passage is essential to the story. There's no information presented that the reader will need later on, nor is the story's action advanced in any way by Scudder's recollection.

So why did I include it?

Well, for one thing, I thought it was terrific material. I knew a fellow who lived in flophouses for many years, and he'd told me the way cops treated derelicts who died in such circumstances. And I knew a cop who'd robbed the dead for years, and whose conscience troubled him on that score. I'd filed the information, knowing it would find its way into a book sooner or later.

It stayed in my mental files for several years. I saved it until I had just the right spot for it, and I'm glad I did. It was a very natural thing for Scudder to remember in the context of where he is, what he's doing, and what frame of mind he's in. The recollection sets the mood for the scene that follows, gives us an illuminating view of Scudder at a couple different stages in his life and career, and ends with a nice little stinger.

I am, I must admit, immoderately proud of this passage. Let me hasten to point out that I could have run it longer or shorter. The first two paragraphs quoted above, for instance, could have been followed by this:

> *I remember the first time I helped remove a corpse from an SRO hotel. My partner divided the dead man's cash and insisted I take my share. I hadn't wanted to, but later on I was the one who bounced bagged corpses down the stairs, the one who counted and divided their leavings.*
>
> *Someday, I suppose, etc.*

That's a quicker way to convey the same information. It doesn't interrupt the action as much. In contrast, I could have chosen to stretch the same scene over several pages, using it as a vehicle to show more of Scudder's past, introduce other characters from his early years, and reveal other aspects of his character.

Flashbacks, like any other aspect of writing technique, are best learned by observation of their use in one's own writing and the writing of others. By seeing what works and what doesn't, by considering alternatives, you can develop your ability at weaving portions of the fictional past into the fictional present.

Remember, though, to keep it as natural as possible. In *Point Blank*, a suspense film, the director used a staccato stop-frame technique to show the lead character's remembrance of past action.

A friend took exception to it. "I could accept it when Lee Marvin shot a guy and remembered other times he shot people," he said, "but I couldn't buy the idea that looking out a window would make him remember every other time he looked out a window."

Most readers (and viewers) aren't that critical. Even so, the more your flashbacks grow naturally and organically out of your story, the less risk you run of calling attention to the strings from which your characters dance, and thus chucking believability out the window.

8. The Art of Omission

Okay, trivia buffs. Some seasons ago there was a relatively witless afternoon game show called "You Don't Say." Who was the host, and what was the tag line?

The host was Tom Kennedy, and the thing he said at the end of each program was, "Remember, it's not what you say that counts, it's what You Don't Say." (I may have the wording slightly wrong, or you may remember it differently. Please don't write and tell me as much. Let me persist, blissful in my ignorance.)

Did you want to say something, Arnold?

I just wondered why you were telling us all this, sir.

Because I was reminded of it just the other day, Arnold. I was at the American Booksellers Association convention in San Francisco, a few days ago as I write this, some months ago as you read it. Elmore Leonard was on hand to sign hardcover copies of his bestseller, *Glitz*, for whatever booksellers cared to stand in a long line in order to secure one. And what came to mind then—and comes to mind now, for that matter—is something Leonard was quoted as saying in explanation of his writing style.

"I try," Dutch said, "to leave out the parts people skip."

I liked that when I first read it, and I decided I liked it even more when I saw that double line of autograph seekers. When professional booksellers queue up to meet an author and get an autograph, one senses that the author in question must be doing something right. After all, Dutch wasn't an actress peddling a confessional autobiography or a defrocked politician flogging a diet book. He was a solid professional novelist who's been writing his own books for thirty years, and a whole host of bookstore people were there to show they approved.

"I try to leave out the parts people skip."

With that in mind, I remembered sitting in a jazz club years ago listening to Ellis Larkins playing piano. "I really like the notes he plays," someone at our table said. "That's funny," said a jazz pianist sitting across from him. " 'Cause I like the notes he *doesn't* play."

Sometimes, see, it's not what you say. It's what you don't say.

All art is selective. In any medium, the artist is constantly making decisions, consciously or unconsciously, putting this in, leaving that out. The painter decides what to reproduce on canvas, what to suggest, what to omit. The photographer decides where to point the camera and how to focus and where to crop the negatives and which negatives to print. We all play some notes and leave other notes unplayed.

We could hardly do otherwise. Put down this book for a moment and look around the room. Suppose you were to set a fictional scene in that room. Why, if you were to describe the room completely, if you were to tell everything you knew or could find out about every object in the room, its precise description and history and every association it called up for you, you'd require more words than it would take to write your whole novel. Every piece of writing, even the richest and most lushly detailed, is selective in that something which might have been included has been left out.

How do you decide what to leave out?

One could do worse, it would seem, than attempt to emulate Elmore Leonard and leave out the parts people skip. If you must omit something, make it the part the reader wouldn't read anyway. That way nothing's lost. But isn't that pretty obvious? Don't all writers try to leave out the dull parts?

Some, to be sure, are better at it than others. And some of us, at least some of the time, do a lot of conscious padding.

Some years ago, during Grover Cleveland's second administration, I wrote a slew of softcore paperback sex novels under a variety of pen names, low ceilings, and threats of exposure. The books, while affording a good deal of leeway in terms of plot, setting and characters, were quite formulaic in certain respects. They had to be a certain number of pages long, and they had to have a fully developed erotic scene in each chapter. I wrote one of these a month, and after I'd written six or eight of them and the novelty had long since worn off for me, the chief challenge lay in making the story stretch over two hundred typescript pages.

There were various tricks to that trade.

One lay in writing a lot of one-sentence paragraphs.

Like this.

Short ones.

Fragments, really.

Punchy.

Pithy.

Filling up space effortlessly.

And all in the name of style.

Another trick lay in letting dialogue sequences, and scenes in general, run longer than they had to. The longer a scene played, the fewer scenes one had to invent. During those days, I assuredly wrote parts I knew people would skip. I would have skipped them myself, given the opportunity.

I had to learn, in succeeding years, to break that habit, to avoid including anything simply because it would fill space in an inoffensive fashion. And I've had to do this not by trying to guess what parts my reader might or might not be inclined to skip, but by writing for myself as reader, and leaving out the parts *I* would skip while including those that I myself would want to read. I'm sure that's the yardstick Elmore Leonard uses, and I think it's the only sound one.

> *I try to leave out the parts people skip.*

Omission means more than leaving out the dull parts, the parts readers would skip. It can also mean surgically excising anything that would blunt the point or dilute the impact of one's writing. To recall the pianist's observation, it is the unplayed notes that enhance the performance.

I recently read *"B" Is for Burglar*, Sue Grafton's second novel about private investigator Kinsey Millhone. (The first is *"A" Is for Alibi*, and I hope there are twenty-six before she's through, and I hope I get to read them all.) At one point Kinsey realizes her apartment has been burgled. She takes a careful inventory, and then:

> *I called a locksmith and made an appointment to have her come out later in the day and change all the locks. I could replace the window glass myself. I did some quick measurements and then headed out to the street . . .*

We have not been previously introduced to the locksmith, so it is news to us that she is a woman. What I especially like here is that Kinsey just slips this in without calling attention to it. There's no comment to deaden the point, no intrusive presence of either the author or the narrator. The locksmith Kinsey calls happens to be a woman, and Kinsey finds this sufficiently unremarkable to fail to remark upon it, and that *is* remarkable. It is an unplayed note that gives us more to listen to than a whole progression of chords.

Avoiding unnecessary explanations and rhetorical overkill is one aspect of the art of omission. Self-restraint is another. I sometimes have trouble resisting the temptation to show off.

Research creates problems in this respect. If I've done a lot of research as background to a novel, and if some of that research has yielded up interesting material, I'm naturally inclined to shovel it all at you, for your education and entertainment and to prove what a busy little boy I've been. Sometimes the material *is* fascinating, and the trick lies in including only that which may be kept in without getting in the way of the story.

And just how much is that? It depends, certainly, on the type of story one is telling. In some types of fiction, the background is one of the attractions for the reader, who comes to the book wishing to gain information or to be submerged in a sense of time and place. In other sorts of fiction, any attention paid to the background detracts from the story itself.

One could write, say, a fact-filled novel about a city visited by a plague, stuffed full of information about the role of plague in human history. Or one could do as Albert Camus did, writing *The Plague* as a very spare philosophical novel, with background data kept to a bare minimum. Either approach is right or wrong depending upon what type of book you've set out to write.

In either case, though, one has to read over one's work with an eye on those sentences and paragraphs that have the smell of the library upon them. If the reader stops to admire what a great research job you've done, he's being drawn away from the story.

Humor's another danger spot. Even in a book specifically designed to be funny, it can be a mistake to stick something in simply because you think it'll get a chuckle. If a particular exchange is out of character, or if it throws off the tempo of a scene, it's not worth the laugh it might get. One useful test, I suspect, is whether the reader will find a given bit of business acceptable even if he or she doesn't happen to find it amusing.

In *After the First Death*, the narrator disguises himself by renting a military costume from a theatrical supply house. The following paragraph appears in the sixteenth chapter:

> *I lit a cigarette. My fingers shook, and after I shook out the match I watched the trembling fingers with clinical interest. I wondered what was shaking me up. It wasn't the uniform. I had been walking around in it for enough hours to make me quite accustomed to it, if not*

entirely comfortable in it. My performance as Major Breakthrough (whose comrades in arms include Private Bath, Corporal Punishment, and General Nuisance) had improved somewhat.

Oh, dear. I wrote that book twenty years ago, and I wish I could reach back through time and remove the twelve words within the parentheses. It isn't that it is or isn't funny. It's the author talking, sticking his head in and trying to be clever, and it has no business there.

Ah, well. The moving finger writes, and all that. The book was reprinted last year, and since the reprinter simply photo-offset the original edition, all that cuteness survives to haunt me anew. Perhaps I'll learn a lesson from it, and be a better person for it.

Whatever lesson I learn, I hope it's not absolute. Because all the rules have exceptions to them. If something comes to me that's really funny enough, I mean really riotously funny, I don't care if I have to stretch to a point to include it. If you make the reader fall on the floor laughing, he's not going to hold it against you. (Hold what against you? The floor? Never mind.) But it had better really be funny, and it had better not be something you heard elsewhere and decided to tuck into your own book. There's something very disquieting about encountering in fiction, as if for the first time, a joke you already heard in a saloon. It takes you right out of the story and makes you want to give the author a smack.

Yes, Rachel?
You said there were exceptions to everything, sir.
I did. Was that unwise of me, Rachel?
Would there even be exceptions to Elmore Leonard's rule, sir? About leaving out the parts people skip?
There might. John O'Hara claimed he wrote long fact-filled paragraphs with the intent of slowing down the reader. I don't know that he quite anticipated readers might skip those paragraphs, but they clearly would read them with less excitement and enthusiasm. And some writers structure the climax of a suspense novel so that you're in a rush to find out what happens, and skip over some paragraphs en route.
How many paragraphs like that did you have in this chapter, sir? The kind you figured people would skip?
I don't know, Arnold. Why don't you read it again and see for yourself?

9. Details, Details

I once taught a twelve-session writing workshop under the auspices
of Mystery Writers of America. One of my students became increasingly apprehensive as her novel began to grow. As soon as the murder in her book took place, the police would begin their investigation. And she didn't know a great deal about police investigatory
procedures, and didn't know how to secure the information she
lacked. Her novel, after all, was set in Honolulu, so even if she managed to determine how the New York police would handle a case,
how could she be sure the Honolulu cops would follow a similar
procedure?

I told her not to worry about it. No one was likely to turn to
her book for a crash course in police procedure, island or mainland
variety. Hers was not that sort of book. She was writing a novel
about a singer working as a waitress in a nightclub. The club's manager is murdered, and subsequently the heroine survives attempts
on her own life and ultimately solves the murder. The official police
investigation is not an important element of the story she has to tell.
It has to take place or the story would lack credibility, but it needn't
spend much time in the spotlight. The author doesn't have to know
whether cops from a specific precinct or from Police Headquarters
would turn up at a murder investigation, or whether the Honolulu
police have a separate Homicide Bureau. Would the officer in
charge be a sergeant or a lieutenant or a detective or what?

It doesn't matter. It never hurts to get this sort of thing right,
but it can hurt to spend too much time and effort on details like this.
Ninety-eight percent of your readers won't know whether the information is accurate or not and the rest won't care. Furthermore,
there's even a danger in over-researching certain areas. There's a
strong temptation to use the fruits of research whether they fit or
not, and, if our author were to immerse herself sufficiently in Honolulu police procedure, she might include a disproportionate amount
of detail, until her real story got lost in a welter of lab reports and in-
terdepartmental memoranda.

Does this mean details are unimportant?

No, absolutely not. It doesn't even mean that details of police procedure are unimportant. Consider the 87th Precinct novels of Ed McBain, in which the mechanics of the police investigation constitute the skeleton of the story. Consider the novels by ex-cops like Joseph Wambaugh and William Caunitz, in which the authentic cop's-eye view of urban crime is what draws the reader in the first place. If these authors were to gloss over details they'd be cheating their readers and diluting the impact of their books.

I was thinking about this recently when I read Tom Wicker's excellent novel of the Civil War, *Unto This Hour*. Wicker's whole 640-page book takes place during what you may call either the Second Battle of Bull Run or Second Manassas, depending on which side of the Mason-Dixon Line is home to you. A great cast of characters play out their parts on this stage, and the battle is rendered in extraordinary detail.

And the detail, we are assured, is authentic. An author's note explains this authenticity. Mr. Wicker takes pains to assure us he has not written "faction," or a "nonfiction novel," or some sort of reportage in the guise of fiction. He lets us know which characters and military divisions are the creation of his own imagination and which are historical personages. And he explains that the remarks and attitudes he attributes to historical personages can be substantiated, if not in the scene he has created:

> *"Sometimes I have taken slight liberties with the context of actual events. In Chapter Two, for example, Generals Lee and Longstreet have dinner with a Virginia farm family on the night of August 26, 1862. The fact that, with some of their staff officers, they did dine that night at a country house is amply recorded; but the family that invited them is not identified in any source I could find. So I invented the family, invented the other officers, and placed Lee and Longstreet, with historical accuracy, in a scene that is imaginary in all other respects.*
>
> *"In this scene, General Lee speaks twice—once about Pope, once about his nephew, Louis Marshall, who had scandalized Virginia by serving on Pope's staff. Both quotations are historically recorded; but of course Lee made these remarks on other occasions. I consider it plausible, however, that he might have said these same things at that wartime dinner table at which he actually sat."*

Wicker goes on to explain that most of the incidents which happen to his fictional characters, in and out of the battle, did actually happen to various real people. The actual military events of the battle are reproduced as accurately as human effort can manage, and the ground upon which it was fought, as it was then and as it is now, is vividly familiar to the author.

Not a week after I finished Wicker's novel, I picked up a used paperback collection of short fiction of the Civil War, a batch of short stories and excerpts of novels by William Faulkner, Scott Fitzgerald, Ambrose Bierce, MacKinlay Kantor, and others. In his introduction, the editor wrote about one of the selections, a chapter from Stephen Crane's classic, *The Red Badge of Courage*. He mentioned in passing that Crane's novel was set at the battle of Chancellorsville, but that Crane never says so; he was not sufficiently interested in the larger context of the war to mention the battle by name.

I don't think I'd have paid much attention to that observation if I hadn't so recently read *Unto This Hour*. As it was, I was struck by the vastly different approaches undertaken in two

The best research is generally easy to do.

worthy novels. Wicker had taken a battle and labored hard to get it all down, to make it as accurate a rendition as possible, to use real characters wherever possible and to put into their mouths only words that historically belonged there. Crane, too, had placed his story within a single battle, but had limited the novel's focus to a single fictional character, and one with no more overview of the battle of which he was a part than an ant might obtain of an oil painting by walking across it. Crane's hero doesn't see the whole battle, and neither do we, and it is ultimately not even important for us to know the battle's name.

The lesson here, it seems to me, is that both authors found the right way to do it. Each provided just the right amount of detail for the particular book he was writing. A wealth of detail enriches Wicker's book, and palpable historical inaccuracies would weaken it. Crane's book, centering itself utterly upon the fear and courage of a single soldier, can take liberties with history where they serve the story, while an excess of detail and a glimpse of the bigger picture would dilute the book's impact.

How much background information should you provide in your fiction? What details shall you offer up to the reader? How important is the accuracy of the background you supply?

Well, it depends. It depends whether you're at Bull Run or at Chancellorsville. It depends, that is, on just what kind of a book or story you're trying to write.

Sometimes the background is what we're there for. An Englishman named (pen-named, actually) Jonathan Gash writes a series of mystery novels about a half-shady antique dealer Lovejoy. Lovejoy knows a great deal about antiques, as I assume does his creator. A large portion of the appeal of the Lovejoy books lies in the information with which we are abundantly supplied. Lovejoy tells us how to spot a fake, how crooked dealers operate, what classes of antiques are over- and underpriced, and generally furnishes the equivalent of an adult education course on the subject in the space of a brief novel. The books would be immeasurably impoverished without this material. Another mystery-writing student of mine shares with her husband the duties of superintendent of an apartment house on the edge of Greenwich Village. She chose as the lead character for her first novel a man not unlike her own husband, a graduate student working his way through college as a building super. While discussing one of her early chapters, she questioned whether she ought to include material on what such a life is like. Would readers be at all interested in the details of the life of an apartment superintendent in the Village?

Indeed they would, I assured her. In fact, they'd probably be more likely to buy her book for its local color than for anything else. Oh, she would have to have a good story and a cast of interesting characters, but the fascination inherent in the background of her novel would lead potential readers to pick it up and leave another mystery on the shelf. On the other hand, it is always possible to tell readers more than they want to know about a subject rather dearer to its author's heart than to anyone else's. The book which comes quickest to mind in this context is one which a good number of mystery fans regard as a timeless classic—*The Nine Tailors,* by Dorothy Sayers. The book is a lengthy one, and it centers upon bell ringing at a village church in England, and both the murder and its solution are largely lost in a glut of detail on the curious pastime of bell ringing. It's been years since I read *The Nine Tailors,* and rare is the incentive that would move me to read it again, but I recall that the ringers were greatly excited about ringing something called a Treble Bob Major, whatever that is, and that I emerged from the book with no clearer idea of what they were doing than I'd had going in. Let alone why they were doing it.

Now Sayers's book is considered a classic, and there are people who relish all of that bell stuff, just as I understand there are those who read *Moby Dick* for a lesson in whale anatomy. But I would point out that Dorothy Sayers was at the height of her reputation when she wrote the book, with her novels of Lord Peter Wimsey already enjoying a large following, and I submit that, had *The Nine Tailors* been a first novel, someone would have made her cut two-thirds of that bell ringing business before publication.

But if I had the job of defending *The Nine Tailors* from the charge I've just leveled at it, I'd say that the strongest argument for the retention of the bell ringing lore is that the book's author wanted to include it. I don't think every author is necessarily the best judge of what belongs in his or her book, but I think the writer's sense of what does or doesn't *feel* appropriate should weigh heavy in the balance. Somewhere along the line, you as writer must decide just what book or story you're writing, and what does or doesn't belong in it.

Some of us are inclined to skimp on details and research—perhaps out of laziness, perhaps out of impatience to be done with the task, perhaps because we are insufficiently confident that what interests us will interest others. (And what interests us will almost *always* interest others, above and beyond the innate interestingness of the material; our own enthusiasm, or lack thereof, tends to be contagious). Others of us do too much research, generally out of fear— fear that we don't know enough to write the book on our own, fear that what we have to say isn't enough, and simple fear of writing; research provides us with a respectable excuse for procrastination. Years ago, when I was first getting started in this dodge, I decided to write a novel about three people who live and die in the Irish Civil War of the 1920s, and I ultimately assembled a vast research library including a six-volume history of Britain before the Norman Conquest. I set out to read all of this before beginning my novel, and of course I still haven't written it a quarter of a century later, and surely never will.

The best research is generally easy to do; it involves learning interesting things which will still be interesting when you share them with your readers. Not every last bit of essential research is interesting; there are things you have to know, matters of fact that will trip you up if you get them demonstrably wrong. But how much research you undertake and how much detail you ultimately furnish are a function of the particular piece of fiction you're writing and the particular individual who is writing it.

10. The Story Behind the Story

What were your characters doing before you put them into a book? What sort of lives did they lead? Where did they come from, and how did they get to the point where your story begins?

How much do you have to know about this? And what use can you make of that knowledge?

In one type of novel, the entire life of the protagonist constitutes the fictional narrative. Such books—J. P. Marquand's *The Late George Apley* is an example, as are John O'Hara's *Ten North Frederick* and *From the Terrace*, and Colleen McCullough's *The Thorn Birds*—follow a principal character more or less from the cradle to the grave, and amount to the biographies of their fictional heroes.

Other novels examine a portion of a character's life. While the segment observed may be as long as several decades or as brief as an hour, there is in any case a story behind the story, a span of time in the lives of the characters which precedes the novel's focus.

There are a variety of ways in which we can treat this background material.

One choice is to leave the past unexplored and unreported. Films frequently operate in this fashion; we see characters in action, and the filmmaker makes no effort to inform us of what the characters did or were before the onset of the film. Watching, we may draw inferences, and indeed every viewer may cloak a character with a slightly different prior history, but the film itself remains resolutely in present time.

Some books are like this, telling us little about the characters before we meet them. (Two that come readily to mind are Dashiell Hammett's *The Maltese Falcon* and Albert Camus' *The Stranger*.)

In other novels, elements of the characters' history are introduced from time to time. There are innumerable ways to manage this. A character may remember something, or may muse on the past in an internal monologue. He may recount some past history in dialogue, telling a friend that this particular bowl of chili tastes just like what his aunt used to cook back home in Elyria, Ohio, say, and then imparting as much or as little information as seems fitting about his days as a chili-eating Elyrian.

To focus more directly upon a portion of the past, the writer may employ a flashback, dropping back in time to the remembered event or the illustrative incident and presenting it in narrative just as one has been presenting the primary storyline. Flashbacks may be long or short, sketchy or detailed, as one prefers.

Occasionally, the prior history of the character or characters is given sufficient prominence that it becomes one of the novel's narrative threads. When this is the case, the story behind the story is commonly called a "back story."

I had occasion to create a back story recently when I wrote a novelization of a film script. (The author of the original screenplay elected to bar publication of the book version, so it will remain forever unavailable.)

In the film, one of the characters has made a career of marrying wealthy men and murdering them. There's no particular indication in the screenplay as to what she might have done before turning her hand to this unquestionably profitable occupation, or what sort of childhood she might have had. I doubt that a viewer would feel at all deprived for lack of this information.

I decided, though, that the inclusion of this information would enrich the novel for the reader. Accordingly, some seventy pages into the book, I dropped back in time for a chapter that reported on the character's childhood and adolescence. I made her father a sexually abusive drunk, and had her ultimately stab the man dead and leave home, never to return. I went on to describe how she had managed to educate herself, how she had created and discarded identities, and how she had transformed the slum brat she had been into the polished sophisticate capable of being all things to all men.

What did I accomplish by adding this chapter of back story? Well, for one thing, I made the book a little longer. My publishers had determined that they wanted a more substantial novel than the typical novelization of a screenplay, and had requested a manuscript in the neighborhood of a hundred thousand words. (Novelizations more commonly run 50-60,000 words.) A back story chapter would fill some space.

More to the point, it would fill space without feeling like padding. The easiest way to write a book long rather than short is to fatten scenes up by writing them longer and fuller. One can describe in more detail, one can let conversations ramble, one can allow characters to muse interminably in internal monologue, and in no time at all one can thus increase a book's length enormously without adding to it anything of substance. That's easy, all right, but the result is a puffy padded piece of work that feels as though it would deflate to a third its size if someone pierced it with a pin.

To enlarge a book without merely inflating it, one has to include additional elements. You can write more scenes, add more characters, insinuate a subordinate plot line. Or you can incorporate some of the back story, in one or more extended flashbacks.

Sometimes the back story gets as much or more space than the book's present-time story. *The Fools in Town Are on Our Side*, by Ross Thomas, is an excellent example of the successful employment of an extensive and detailed back story. The book's primary concern is the effort of a group of people to clean up a politically corrupt southern city, but close to half the book's text is devoted to the prior history of one of the men, one Lucifer Dye. His whole life is told in the back story, from his upbringing in a lush bordello in China through his career as an intelligence agent. Some of the scenes in the back story are as fully realized as any in the book.

> *The story behind the story is commonly called a "back story."*

Without the back story, *The Fools in Town* would be a taut and satisfying story of crime and action and political chicanery. With it, it is all that and more; it has dimension and scope it would otherwise lack. It is still the same story, but reading it is a richer experience.

Could any story be similarly augmented with a back story? Yes, but the result would not necessarily be similarly successful. The back story works here largely because it is as interesting as it is. If Lucifer's life were less fascinating, we might find ourselves impatient to return to the "real" story, and might regard the back story as padding and a waste of our time.

What function does the back story have besides pure entertainment? Well, it can make the reader care more about the character. To know all is to forgive all, one is told, and the more one knows about a character, the greater the likelihood one will sympathize and identify with that character. In the novelization, the back story I developed seemed likely to make the character's murderous acts somewhat more comprehensible, if not necessarily more palatable, to the reader. Her motivation inferentially became something subtler and more interesting than simple greed.

Another use of back story is for the writer's own enlightenment. While the text of the novel may be limited to a single contemporary storyline, the writer may write out a considerable amount of back story in order to learn more about his characters. He may ultimately keep almost all of what he discovers to himself, sharing rather little of his characters' past histories with his readers. All the same, this preparation may make it easier for him to write convincingly and consistently about the characters.

I don't generally do this myself, but then I rarely work up written character sketches of any sort before beginning the actual writing of a manuscript. I do, however, often know a fair amount about my characters before I start writing, and this knowledge may include historical information about them that I will not wind up spelling out in the text.

Do you have to know the back story before you start writing? Is it something that belongs in your outline?

Not necessarily. It seems to me that how much one knows or has to know about any aspect of a book varies considerably from writer to writer and from book to book. In the novelization I've been discussing, I hadn't given a conscious thought to the character's past history while I wrote the book's first seventy pages. Then I felt it was time to find out who she was and where she'd come from, and I invented a back story that seemed to me to be consistent with her personality as it had defined itself for me in those seventy pages. I'm comfortable working this way, and tend to find out things about my characters as they create themselves on the page. It's no less natural to find out things about their past than about their present.

Much of my writing over the years has involved series characters. Some, like Matthew Scudder, were originally conceived of as characters to be employed in a continuing series of books; others, like Bernie Rhodenbarr, were created to appear in a single book and wound up booking themselves for return engagements. Over the years, back stories tend to accumulate for series characters, not through extended flashbacks but as anecdotes and reminiscences and bits of data build up. Sometimes it's difficult to keep all of this straight, and series writers are apt to let some inconsistencies slip through in the ongoing back story.

Back story can be great fun to write. Some years ago I wrote a big multiple-viewpoint novel set in a small town; there were eight or ten major characters and a number of supporting players. From time to time I would supply an extensive back story for a character, sometimes at the character's first appearance, sometimes later on after the character had already been on-stage several times. In one instance, I remember, I recapped a character's life-until-now in three or four dramatic pages, then had virtually nothing for the character to do in the actual story; she owned a restaurant, and never did much more than show a couple of characters to their table, but I liked the back story and it seemed to fit.

Ultimately, your sense of fitness will best enable you to decide when and to what extent to employ back story. There are times when it would seem to be indicated—the reader simply has to know more about the characters in order to be involved in their fate—and there are times when it ought to be kept to a minimum lest it wind up being the tail that wags the dog. But much of the time you can legitimately go either way, opting for either substance or streamlining. Make the choice that feels right.

PART TWO

Trapping the Prey
The Strategies of Fiction

*S*piders are exclusively carnivorous, and in fact generally seize only live animals, as the spider's attention is attracted by the movement of the prey. Very occasionally one learns of a snake or mouse accidentally caught in the snare of a spider, but ordinarily the spiders of our region feed on insects. Dolomedes, however, sometimes captures small fish, such as minnows. Most species are not particular as to the insects eaten but will take whatever happens to come their way. However, it is true that some species will not accept everything. Only a few eat ants, many refuse wasps and hornets, and many cast bugs and beetles out of their webs.

The spider's appetite may often appear insatiable, the abdomen swelling to accommodate the added food. Most species can survive long periods of fasting, and although many can do without water for weeks some species will die if deprived of moisture for only a few days.

Spiders may feed on other spiders, and because of this tendency to cannibalism a social or communal life is hardly to be expected.

—B.J. Kaston & Elizabeth Kaston
How to Know the Spiders

11. What Do Editors Want?

What do editors want?

What are publishers looking for?

These two questions come up again and again whenever writers are gathered together. They crop up in informal shop-talk sessions at writers' conferences. They are often the first questions asked of a speaker.

Implicit in them is another question, generally unspoken—

What should I write?

I would like to suggest that, when you ask what editors and publishers are seeking, and by extension what you should be writing, you're asking the wrong question. What do editors want? Why, they want world peace, and recognition from their peers, and more money for less work, and a more exciting love life, and a five-pound weight loss without dieting. What do you think they want? What does *everyone* want, for heaven's sake?

Oh.

You mean what do they want to buy from you?

That's their business.

Quite literally. Deciding what one wants to buy, and then buying it, is quite properly the business of an editor. And because it's the editor's business, it's not yours.

Your business, on the other hand, consists of dropping the word "should" from your internal vocabulary and focusing instead on the problem of writing what you *want* to write.

What *should* I write? The only piece I *should* write is one for which I have some sort of contractual obligation. Aside from such considerations, it is at once my duty as a writer and the best means of advancing my career for me to find the book or story I most want to write—and then write it.

An inspiring thought, wouldn't you say? All a-sparkle with high-flown artistic purpose. What is it you call it when I talk like this, Arnold?

You mean "the old to-thine-own-self-be-true bit," sir?

That's it, all right. The Polonius peroration. Follow your own star. Cleave to the truth. And, like a valiant old buffalo hunter, let the chips fall where they may. It certainly has a nice ring to it, but aren't there a couple of things wrong with it?

For one thing, it loses sight of the fact that, for most of us, simply writing something isn't enough. We want to publish what we write, and we want to be paid for it. Isn't that desire incompatible with this business of going one's own way? It might work for geniuses and the literary creme de la creme, but isn't it bad advice for the ordinary workaday fictioneer?

After all, publishers have guidelines. They want books and stories of a certain length, avoiding certain themes, with or without a certain background. In some categories of popular fiction the guidelines are wide open, in others they're harder to pass through than the eye of a camel, but in any instance are we simply to ignore them altogether?

Not quite.

But close to it.

A few months ago I was one of several speakers at a monthly writers' group centering largely upon romantic fiction. Another speaker, an editor, spoke about what sort of books she was buying and looking to buy. One recent acquisition she spoke highly of was in the sub-genre of Time-Travel Romances.

Time-Travel Romances?

What, I promptly asked someone, was a Time-Travel Romance? I was informed that it was very much what the name implied, a romance novel in which the heroine travels backward or forward in time, where she not too surprisingly falls in love and acts upon it to a greater or lesser degree, the fervor of her participation depending, no doubt, on whether this particular volume is destined to be a Sensuous Time-Travel Romance or a Chaste Time-Travel Romance, and perhaps skirting danger if the book turns out to be a Time-Travel Romantic Suspense, sensuous or otherwise.

I found this to be astonishing information. What great editorial genius had dreamed up the Time-Travel Romance? What farseeing publisher had decided the world was ready for such a category of fiction?

But of course that's not how it happened at all. Instead, a writer sat down and wrote the first Time-Travel Romance, and did so without any way of knowing that this breach of guidelines and departure from tradition would even prove to be publishable, let alone the start of a sub-genre.

That, it seems to me, is how all manner of genres come into existence.

In a recent interview in the revived *Black Mask Magazine*, Robert B. Parker makes the point that categories of fiction are useful to everyone but the author. It's handy for people in the book trade to know how to refer to a particular book, and it's useful for readers to know where to look in a bookstore or library for the sort of reading matter they like, but none of this really applies to the writer. He is not writing a book because it fits the precise dimensions of a particular pigeonhole, but because it is the book he most wants to write. Categorization, then, is what people other than the author do with a book after it has already been written.

Hemingway said somewhere that we all have two choices, we can break new ground or we can try to beat dead men at their game. There's an element of art-as-competition in that statement to which I'm disinclined to subscribe, so I might say the same thing differently. The choice, as I see it, is this: I can write my own book, or I can try to write someone else's. I have every reason, it seems to me, to do the former; I am the single person in the whole world best qualified to write my book, and have no special qualifications beyond a measure of professional facility when it comes to writing someone else's.

> *The only piece I should write is one for which I have a contractual obligation.*

This seems clear enough, and may even make sense. But does it make dollars as well? Is it a commercially sound decision to write what one wants to write?

In my own experience, it has always proved to be the right thing to do from a commercial standpoint—and I have learned this both by doing it and by not doing it. Whenever I have tried to write someone else's book, the results have been disappointing in every respect. Whenever I have written the book I wanted to write, often with cavalier disregard of market considerations, the results have been favorable—usually in the short run, and always in the long run.

Let me furnish an example. In the mid-seventies (the century's, not my own) I wrote three novels about an alcoholic ex-cop named Matthew Scudder. The books were published by Dell as paperback originals. They did not sell well, in large part because they were not very well distributed. While they did receive some favorable critical attention, including a gracious quote from James M. Cain, they were a long way from setting the world on fire.

A couple of years later, I realized that what I really wanted to do was write a fourth book about Scudder. While this was not quite equivalent to the Ford Motor Company's bringing out a new edition of the Edsel, it was certainly in the same ball park. Dell wouldn't want to proceed further with Scudder, nor would other publishers fight for the privilege of taking over a series someone had already failed with. The more sensible course would seem to be to consign Scudder to limbo and dream up another character to carry whatever story I wanted to tell.

But I wanted to write about Scudder.

I talked to my agent. He told me to write the book I wanted to write. (And, he pointed out, if it didn't work out we could always change the guy's name.)

So I wrote the book, and Arbor House published it, and Berkley reprinted it, and it was a Literary Guild selection and did better commercially than any of my previous books. And the book that followed it was also about Scudder. It was called *Eight Million Ways To Die*, and it ran 444 pages in manuscript, which is about twice as long as a first-person detective story is generally supposed to be. I worried about that, but I wrote it that way anyway because the story I was trying to tell seemed to need that length, and the book got an Edgar nomination and won the Shamus award and became the basis of a film, and its success helped bring back into print from Berkley all those earlier Scudder novels.

Should I applaud myself for my moral fiber? I don't know that I can take a whole lot of credit for writing my own book, at least not in recent years. It's been easy for me to do just that because I haven't had any choice. I'm spoiled. Having written what I've wanted to write, I can no longer grit my teeth and write what I *don't* want to write. It's no more a matter of pride than it is one of ethics. My books just plain don't get written unless they're what I want to do. The well goes dry. The words don't get on the page.

Don't let me give the impression that good work has to fly in the face of market trends, that every successful book is wildly experimental. This is by no means the case. My own books, to be sure, fit very comfortably within the boundaries of a long-established and popular genre. The book you want to write may fit neatly into a precise category, and there's certainly nothing wrong with that. What's essential is merely to keep one's priorities in order, and give first priority to the old to-thine-own-self-be-true bit.

Editors know this. For all that their guidelines attempt to codify their requirements, I have heard no end of editors say that the manuscript they most hope to find on their desks is the one that breaks all their own unbreakable rules—but that grabs them so hard and moves them so much that they have to buy it anyway. That's the kind of fiction that expands the bounds of a genre, or creates a whole new one. And it's that kind of ingenuity and integrity on the part of writers that's responsible for the endurance of fictional categories; like anything else living, they must either grow and change or wither and die.

Does this mean studying the market is a waste of time? Does this mean *Writer's Market* is a pointless addition to one's library, taking up shelf space that could be better devoted to *The Wit and Wisdom of Polonius?*

Absolutely not. There's a way to study the market, a way to study other books as preparation for writng one's own.

Turn the page and I'll tell you all about it.

12. Be Prepared

Good morning, boys and girls.

Good morning, sir.

Today we're going to be talking about some of the ways to prepare yourself to produce the kind of fiction editors will buy and readers will read with pleasure. After all, for many of us the desire to publish is part and parcel of the desire to write, so naturally we want to turn out books and stories that will see print, not waste their fragrance on the desert air, as Mr. Gray would put it. Furthermore, many of us would just as soon grow rich and famous as a result of our literary efforts, and toward that end—did you say something, Arnold?

No, sir.

Funny, I could have sworn . . .

He said, "Would you look at the old boy contradicting himself all over the place again."

Thank you, Mimi. Contradicting myself, Arnold? How?

Sir, didn't you just say . . .

Oh, of course. Last chapter I told you to forget about what editors want and focus on telling your own story, on writing the story you most want to write.

You said to follow our own star, sir. To hunt the buffalo and let the chips fall where they may.

My very words.

But that was then and this is now, eh, sir?

Not at all, Arnold. What we'll be talking about today is how you can best prepare yourself so that your story, the one you most want to write, is one that will be published with pleasure and read with satisfaction.

In a new book called *Higher Creativity*, Willis Harman, head of the Institute of Noetic Sciences, writes at length about the creative process and the manner in which creative breakthroughs occur. He makes the point that such transcendental illuminations rarely come about as the direct result of conscious thought. The true quantum leaps in creativity, be they artistic or scientific in nature, seem rather to bubble up from the unconscious, a gift from that shaded corner of our minds to our consciousness.

This bubbling up may take the form of dreams, of spontaneous illuminating thoughts or images or metaphors. A composer may suddenly hear new music in his head. An inventor may be abruptly struck by the notion of trying a tungsten filament in his light bulb. A writer may just as suddenly be gifted with the plot of the next book, or the personality of a character, or the way out of a plotting dilemma, or, indeed, the solution to any variety of writing problem.

How does this happen? What ethereal transportation system delivers the goods to the right place, so that, for example, my own subconscious mind slips me the notion of my burglar Bernie Rhodenbarr's stealing a teddy bear instead of, say, giving me the idea for a salad dressing made with raspberry vinegar (which, now that I think of it, doesn't sound half bad)?

According to Mr. Harman, creative breakthroughs come about through a four-step process. The four steps are Preparation, Incubation, Illumination and Verification.

What does this amount to? Well, in the first stage you prepare yourself so that the unconscious mind knows precisely what problem it is supposed to solve. You furnish it with all the necessary data, give it the materials to work with.

Then, in the second stage, you take James Thurber's advice and Leave Your Mind Alone. You go to the movies or pitch horseshoes or take a walk in the woods or lift weights or lie down for a nap.

In the third stage, you Get an Idea. And, finally, you verify it by sitting down at the typewriter (or at the word processor, or with a quill pen, whatever level of technology you're most comfortable with) and getting down to the serious business of putting words on paper (or on the screen, or parchment).

Let's look at the first stage, preparation. Suppose you've decided that you want to write a romance novel. Perhaps you've read a few over the years and think that it might be easy and enjoyable to write one yourself. Perhaps you haven't ever read one but have heard that the field is a good place to break in. Perhaps you just intuitively sense that a romance novel would be the right thing for you to try your hand at.

How do you prepare yourself to do just that?

For openers, you *read* romance novels—one after another,

book after book after book. You fill up a tub with romance novels and you soak yourself in it. You gobble up the things until they're coming out of your ears.

I can't stress this too strongly. A while ago I led a mystery workshop at a writers' conference on Cape Cod and toward the end one student stood up and complained that I hadn't fulfilled his expectations.

"I was hoping you'd tell us *how* to write a mystery," he said, "how to bring in characters, how to plant clues, what a mystery really is, what you can and can't do in a mystery."

"Oh, you want to learn all that?" I replied. "That's easy. You don't need me standing up here and lecturing to you. Just go home and read five hundred mysteries." Because, I added, that was what I had done, and what most people I knew had done.

During this stage, any of several things may happen. You might find the reading impossible, might discover that you just plain don't like romance novels and have no respect for the genre. If this is the case, you probably ought to find something else to write.

Take James Thurber's advice and Leave Your Mind Alone.

I would not go so far as to state this as an absolute. Every once in a while publishable books are written by a writer who has done relatively little reading in a genre, and who in some cases has nothing but contempt for the genre. Every once in a while such a writer is not only published but hugely successful. Such instances, however, are very much the exception. In the vast majority of cases, successful fiction is written by people who enjoy reading the very sort of fiction they write, and who regard it as worth writing.

I had a letter a while ago from a woman who was sure she could write a romance, because she had just read a couple and thought they were garbage. I told her perhaps she was right, but that her contempt for the field would almost certainly work against her, communicating itself subtly to her readers. Some of us think we have to regard other writers in our chosen field with contempt, as if the alternative to that would be awe that would keep us from taking chances—but I think we have more choices than that.

All right. You've read a ton of romances, and you've liked them. You like some more than others, as you increasingly learn to tell a good romance from a bad one, and develop a sense of what does and doesn't work within the bounds of the genre.

You may find that you have an affinity for a particular type of romance novel. Perhaps a Regency romance by Megan Daniel particularly strikes you. You read some other Regencies by other writers to see whether it was the pure novelty of the book, or the admitted excellence of Ms. Daniel's writing style, that won you. If you determine that you genuinely like Regencies, you may want to concentrate your further reading upon them. And you may also want to start reading historical texts dealing with that period—memoirs, social histories, biographies, etc.

This isn't research. Research may come later, when you know what you are going to write and need to discover certain specific data. Right now you'll be reading historical material with no goal in mind beyond that of supplying your unconscious mind with a load of information. You read, and soak up general knowledge of the period, and that computer within your unconscious sets about programming itself.

At this point you may discover that you don't like this sort of reading. If you try a variety of kinds of historical reading and don't enjoy any of it, it may be that, for all that you like reading Regencies, you won't enjoy writing them. If so, time for a change in direction. If not, press onward.

About now you'll probably want to start studying the markets. In a sense you've been doing that by reading the books—you've been seeing exactly what's turning up in the market as opposed to reading someone else's survey thereof. But now you'll want to go over market lists in *Writer's Digest* and pertinent sections in *Fiction Writer's Market* to find out what editors have to say about their own particular requirements. (*FWM* is currently titled *Novel & Short Story Writer's Market.*) You may even want to send to various publishers for guidelines to their specific dos and don'ts.

I would suggest that you scan this material without paying too much conscious attention to it at this stage. You don't want to try to frame your story with a conscious regard to specific market requirements. Rather, you want your subconscious mind to synthesize those requirements, so that the ideas it sends up lend themselves to the realities of the marketplace.

That's much of what you've been doing by reading book after book. Your subconscious mind has been synthesizing what you've read so that it *knows* what a romance is and what does and does not belong in one. It's one thing to know intellectually, say, that a romance ought to run 60-70,000 words, and another to have so incorporated the structure of these books into your subconscious mind that you automatically know what sort of plot will combine with what sort of writing style to extend the desired length. In the first case one knows how long a book ought to be; in the latter instance, one knows what such a book *is*.

In *Writing the Novel from Plot to Print* I explain a method of outlining a book—not the one you intend to write, but one you've already read. By breaking the book into scenes and writing down what happens in each scene, you are able to see a book much as an anatomist can see a body by examining a skeleton. This is a useful method, especially for those of us who approach our first novels with some uncertainty, but in a sense we are doing this informally every time we read a book and consign its essence to the growing program taking shape in our internal computer.

What else? You may want to start calling yourself a romance writer, and join an organization of romance writers, and make plans to attend a conference. You may think that amounts to whistling in the dark, but it's more than that. It's a way of telling your subconscious that you're serious about all of this and that you expect it to tell you a story.

And, having so instructed your subconscious, you can turn everything over to that part of yourself. Just let the idea for your book come to you in your own good time.

And it will. And, when it does, it will be your own idea for your own book, the book you yourself want to write. Your subconscious will have sifted through all of the material with which you have supplied it and will incorporate elements of you—your own areas of knowledge, your own personal experience, your own thoughts and feelings and perceptions, everything that is uniquely yours. The result will be an idea for a book that you were meant to write and that an editor will be eager to purchase for publication.

Is that clear, class? Any questions? Arnold, did you say something?

Not a thing, sir.

Mimi?

He said, "The old boy got out of that one pretty neatly, didn't he?"

I'm sure he said it respectfully. But I won't let it go to my head, because one of these days I want to talk to you about humility.

13. Let's Hear It for Sex and Violence!

Through the rifle's telescopic sight, Dattner watched the man and woman making love. They were young and beautiful, and as their lovemaking progressed a thin sheen of perspiration bloomed on the assassin's upper lip. His hand, too, dampened with perspiration, and he wiped it from time to time on his trouser leg. As the culmination of their efforts approached, Dattner studied the woman's face through the gunsight, centering the crosshairs upon her temple. He caressed the trigger. Gently, gently, he squeezed it . . .

Did I get your attention? I'm not surprised. The traditional method of getting a mule's attention consists of hauling off and clouting him between the eyes with a two-by-four, and graphic scenes of sex and/or violence offer a similar means of causing a reader to sit up and take notice. The material to follow, you will be relieved and disappointed to learn, has nothing to do with Mr. Dattner and the cavorting couple. They don't exist, not even as fictional characters; the scene you just read was written specifically for this occasion, to get your attention while introducing a discussion of the functions of sex and violence in the writing of fiction.

When Bill Brohaugh proposed this piece, I couldn't deny that I was an obvious choice to write it. A look back at my checkered career suggests that, but for sex and violence, I'd have spent the past quarter of a century standing in a breadline or, God help me, doing some sort of honest work. I started out writing crime stories for pulp magazines and soft-core paperback sex novels, and in the years since then either sex or violence has been a major component in virtually everything I've written.

I don't recommend this road to others. I see no particular virtue in writing about sex and violence, and I believe a writing career could be every bit as fulfilling if one wrote, say, instructive moral fables about lovable bunny rabbits. (On the other hand, one of my favorite books in recent years was Richard Adams's moral fable about lovable bunny rabbits, *Watership Down,* and it absolutely overflowed with sex and violence.)

What roles do sex and violence play in fiction? How can a writer best use these elements, and best avoid abusing them? What works and what doesn't? What's appropriate and what isn't?

First, a word about what we're not going to discuss. We're not going to talk about legal aspects of censorship, or the social effects of pornography. We're not going to investigate these topics because I feel neither qualified nor inclined to lead such an investigation. I'm here today as a writer, seeking to share with other writers some thoughts on some of the technical aspects of the writer's craft.

You may believe that excessive sex and violence in books and films is eating great holes in the homespun fabric of American society, and you may be right. You may believe that candid writing about sex and violence is leading us out of centuries of denial and repression and hastening the dawning of the Age of Aquarius. And you may be right.

I tend to believe both of these notions at various times, and a few other notions at other times, but right now what I believe is beside the point. For the time being you and I are writers talking about writing. We can be philosophers and social critics on our own time.

Some people think sex and violence are what makes a book sell. Ladle in sufficient quantities of both and the result is a bestseller.

Often implicit in this line of thought is the idea that the writer goes against his own inclinations when he lards his manuscripts with sex and violence. Perhaps he's grudgingly acceding to his crass publisher's demands, perhaps he is cynically providing the tasteless public with what it craves. If he were true to himself and true to his Art, he wouldn't be staining his pure paragraphs with all of this heavy breathing and bloodletting.

I don't think it works that way. With surprisingly few exceptions, writers who become successful do so by doing the very best they can and by expressing their own selves to the fullest possible extent. Those writers who do well with books laced with sex and violence are generally doing so in obedience to an inner calling, not in response to public demand.

It's hard to prove this, but I've come to believe it on the basis of my own experience. The books that I have written in an attempt to give readers "what they want" have done relatively poorly. The books I've done with little or no regard for market considerations and popular appetites have had the greatest critical and commercial success. I do best when I write my book, not someone else's.

Every eighteen minutes, a Hollywood starlet tells an interviewer, "I would do a nude scene if it was essential to the integrity of a film. But I have strong objections to nudity for its own sake."

In much the same way, readers and writers will tell you that they don't object to sex and violence. What they object to is *gratuitous* sex and violence.

When does the nasty stuff become gratuitous?

Hmmmm.

It seems to me that certain categories of books have as a cardinal element a dose of sex and/or violence that would have to be labeled gratuitous. Certainly the soft-core sex novels I wrote in my misspent youth come under this heading. Every fifteen or twenty pages, two or more of the characters got into some sort of erotic tangle, which was then described in a manner designed to arouse the reader as much as possible without violating the censorship restrictions of the day. That may not have been gratuitous, come to think of it, in that the sexual content was the whole purpose of the work, but it was certainly sex for sex's sake.

Some people think sex and violence are what makes a book sell.

In today's market, with censorship no more than a historical curiosity, pornography is hard-core and of little use as a writer's training-ground. Other genres, however, use sex as the soft-core books did twenty years ago.

Adult westerns come quickly to mind. There are a good many of these on the stands now, most of them in the form of series following a single character and authored by a single pen name—although most series have multiple authorship. I've read a few volumes each in the *Longarm* and *Slocum* series, and have glanced through the odd volume from several others.

The formula is simple enough. The typical book consists of a more or less standard novel, a variation of a traditional Western plot. The quality of the book will vary with the skill of its writer and the degree of enthusiasm and inspiration he brings to the task. Four or six or eight times in the book's course, however, a graphically described full-blown sex scene will blossom right there in front of God and everybody.

An English lady is supposed to have said she didn't care what people did among themselves, so long as they didn't do it in the road and frighten the horses. In adult westerns, people are doing it in front of the horses.

Now that's gratuitous sex. It's also the right way to write an adult western, which pretty much dooms the category to mediocrity. It's possible, of course, to write a solid western novel in which sex is treated with unblushing candor. Such a book would not be an adult western but a genuine novel of the West, which is something rather different.

Ages ago I worked at a literary agency. Our card files included a description in several sentences of the plot of each manuscript being marketed. Westerns were always tagged either KG or KH, standing for Kisses Girl or Kisses Horse.

I wonder what initials they use nowadays?

In sex and violence, less is often more.

I'm talking now in terms of impact, not of taste. An abundance of detail in the depiction of sex or violence might well be of dubious taste, but that's not what I'm getting at just now. Let's postulate that the point of erotic writing and of violent writing is to engender a response in the reader, to make him feel something. (That's the point of all fiction, and arguably the point of all writing, so why shouldn't it be the point of the sex/violence scenes?)

And, toward that end, less can be more. Understatement can jolt the reader far more effectively than excess.

This is not to say that excess never works. Some writers describe scenes of mayhem with a wealth of photographic detail, producing the verbal equivalent of a Kung Fu movie. Others are similarly devoted to sexual representation.

I've certainly read enough examples of this sort of thing to stock a fair-sized library, yet what stays with me most is the underplayed scene. I remember a line of Dashiell Hammett's Continental Op: "I hit him with the door repeatedly." There is a level of matter-of-fact violence in that line that does more for me than any page-long description of a barroom brawl.

Similarly, I can recall a scene in a novel of John O'Hara's, probably *A Rage To Live*. One character tells another about a sexual episode that took place years ago, and the result is more genuinely erotic than all the sense-numbing footage of *Deep Throat*.

A violent scene very early on, perhaps involving the sacrifice of a minor character, is an excellent way to get the reader's attention. It lets him know right off the bat that he's reading a book in which violent death can strike at any time. It prepares him so he can accept violence later on, and in the process it whets his appetite.

In *The Maltese Falcon*, Hammett's detective Sam Spade tells an apparently pointless story about a missing husband he'd searched for once. The man had been narrowly missed by a beam falling from a construction site, whereupon he left his job and family, moved to another state, and, when Spade found him, was living a life similar to the one he had abandoned. As Spade sees it, the man discovered he lived in a world where beams fell, and he adjusted his life accordingly. Then, when no more beams fell, he adjusted to a world in which they didn't fall.

An early act of violence lets the reader know he has stepped into a world where beams fall, where guns go off, where blood flows. And he adjusts his reading self accordingly.

I said earlier that a discussion of the social effects of writing about sex and violence upon the reader would lie outside the scope of this article. But what about the effects thereof on the writer?

They can be considerable. For a couple of years, virtually every book I wrote—and I wrote more than one a month—was full of sex. I don't know that this had any particular effect on my sex life, although I suppose it must have. I do know that it did affect my ability to write sex scenes in fiction.

When I moved on to better books, I had trouble writing candidly about sex. Like the starlet who told her husband on her honeymoon that she wouldn't do certain things anymore now that she was respectable, I found myself almost prudish when the context of a suspense novel demanded a realistic sex scene. *You're respectable now*, an inner voice tells me. *You don't have to do those things anymore.*

A similar experience with violence had a considerably more marked effect upon a good friend of mine. For years he wrote westerns and suspense novels in which the realistic treatment of violence played a role. Then he wrote a book, rather more violent than usual, in which the protagonist, goaded beyond endurance, takes the law into his own hands. The book was a modest success, but it was made into a film which was an enormous success, critically if not commercially. The film was infinitely more violent than the book, and its violence was overblown where the book's was understated, even as its underlying philosophy was mindlessly simplistic where the book's was thoughtful and reasoned.

My friend wound up trying to live the film down, publicly deploring its violence and going on to write several books in a row which were determinedly nonviolent. To my mind, these books suffered for their lack of violence, but I can well understand why their author was impelled to write them as he did. They were his way of making amends for the film.

A couple of years ago I was reading a first novel by a man who has since gone on to some success in the suspense field. His first book was rather good, but scattered here and there in it were several starkly pornographic sex scenes.

All I could think of was a line that has been bandied about by several people over the years. Most recently Gore Vidal said it to Norman Mailer: "You behave, sir, as if you had no talent."

I thought of it because it struck me that the writer did not need to stuff scenes of excessive sexual detail into his narrative. It succeeded admirably without them, and their addition was distinctly counterproductive. It was as if he did not trust his ability to sustain his novel without them; i.e., he behaved as if he had no talent.

I don't believe I've done this sort of thing, cramming scenes of sex and violence into books where they don't belong, but I can relate to the writer's insecurity. For quite a while after I ceased writing sex novels, I was anxious that I wouldn't be able to hold the reader's attention. My apprenticeship had left me believing that, if somebody didn't have sex or get shot every twenty pages, the reader's mind would wander.

This anxiety may well have had good long-term effects. It led me to seek out other ways of holding the reader's attention and keep the narrative interesting. Some writers seem to operate on the principle that it's the reader's job to keep interested. I think it's my job to keep him interested, and I can do so either by developing my talent to the fullest or by behaving as though I had none.

When I met Elmore Leonard recently, he talked about how characters come to life and wind up dictating changes in a novel's plot. In *Cat Chaser*, he'd originally planned on the lead character's ultimately confronting the Cuban secret-police villain. "But that wouldn't work," Leonard said, "because the Cuban would just torture Moran, and Moran would cave in and tell him what he wanted to know, and what kind of an ending is that for a book? So this other character got more important than I thought he would, and he wound up in the showdown with Moran."

I found myself remembering a problem I'd had years ago with a book called *Here Comes a Hero*. It was the sixth of seven novels I wrote featuring a character named Evan Tanner, a sort of adventurer and secret agent given to living by his wit and his whimsy. In this particular book, Tanner goes off to rescue a former girlfriend who has been sold into white slavery in Afghanistan. Her trail leads him to the man in London who led her down the primrose path, and Tanner has to extract information from the villain.

But Tanner's is not an intimidating presence. The bad guy simply refuses to talk, calling Tanner's bluff, whereupon my hero muses that his problem is one of image, that he simply lacks credibility as a torturer. He threatens to lop off one of the villain's fingers, the villain assures him that he's bluffing, and Tanner does what he threatened to do, to everyone's considerable astonishment.

It was a tricky scene to write and I'm still not sure how convincingly it came off, and whether it cost Tanner the sympathy of some of the readers. It seemed to me to be consistent with his nature and the exigencies of the situation, and if there was a better way to handle it I couldn't figure out what it was.

You can avoid having the reader manifest skepticism like that of Tanner's English adversary by foreshadowing a character's capacity for violence or brutality. Earlier we talked about killing a minor character to let the reader know we're playing for keepsies. Similarly, by showing a violent character in action—especially a villain—the reader is prepared to take him seriously at a later date.

Ages ago a guitarist friend of mine was waiting to audition at a folk music club. Another performer, a blues singer, preceded him. The guy commenced singing risque material, and each verse got dirtier than the one before it. Twelve-bar blues consist of a line sung twice and followed by a rhyming line, like this:

Oh, I got the blues and it made me awful mean
Yes, I got the blues and it made me awful mean
I'm gonna drown the dog in a bucket of kerosene.

And so on.

Anyway, my friend would hear the first line, think *Oh, no, he's not really gonna sing that one*, and then the guy would do it. Repeatedly.

The singer eventually walked off stage and came up to my friend with a woebegone look on his face. "You want to know the worst thing in the world?" he demanded. "The worst thing in the world's when you're singing dirty blues and not going over, and you don't know if it's 'cause you're too clean or too dirty."

Same thing in fiction. Are your sex scenes too sexy or not sexy enough? How about the violence? Too much? Not enough?

Raising such a question might seem a betrayal of the to-thine-own-self-be-true argument advanced earlier. But I don't think one compromises one's artistic integrity by seeking to avoid being too clean or too dirty, too rough or too tame. A sex scene that is too graphic for the particular work that contains it will sabotage that work, appearing to the reader as pornographic. A scene that's underwritten will lack useful impact.

In category fiction, an analysis of the usual treatment of sex and violence should be part of your study of the market. If you're trying to write a particular sort of book, an adult western or a romance, a male action-adventure or a gothic, you'll certainly read a minimum of half a dozen representative specimens before attempting your own. Pay attention to the manner in which sex and violence are portrayed. Mark the scenes that strike you as particularly effective, and pay attention to their length, the extent of their detail, and the tone in which they are presented.

More important than consistency with the standards of the genre is consistency with the rest of the work itself. Here your own intuition has to substitute for market analysis.

In recent years I've written two series of mystery novels, one featuring a burglar named Bernie Rhodenbarr, the other an ex-cop named Matthew Scudder. Both are written in the first person and set in New York, but the two vary considerably in style and tone. The burglar books are light and airy, all good clean fun, while the Scudder books are serious and uncompromisingly downbeat.

Not surprisingly, sex and violence demand different treatments in these books. In the Rhodenbarr books, people do get killed, but we rarely see violence or its aftermath straight on. Bernie rarely hears a shot fired in anger, and certainly never fires one. In *The Burglar Who Studied Spinoza*, he brings down the killer with a dart from a tranquilizer gun; in *The Burglar Who Liked to Quote Kipling*, the killer is pointing a gun at Bernie in his own bookstore when his sidekick Carolyn Kaiser comes to his rescue:

> *Killing women's bad policy. Ignoring them can be worse. He'd forgotten all about Carolyn, and he was still running his mouth when she brained him with a bronze bust of Immanuel Kant. I'd been using it as a bookend, in the Philosophy and Religion section.*

Bernie leads a reasonably active sex life, but I've tended to keep details to a minimum. This is not because well-developed sex scenes don't belong in light airy mysteries. Richard S. Prather's Shell Scott novels are light and airy as flawless souffles, and their sexual content is considerable. My own Chip Harrison mysteries, recently reissued in a dual volume as *a/k/a Chip Harrison*, combine light and presumably amusing detective stories with a generous dollop of sex. It just seems to me that such scenes would be out of place in Bernie's casebooks.

Here, from *Spinoza*, is a typical Rhodenbarr passage at arms:

> The piano player was a young black kid who kept reminding me of a Lennie Tristano record I hadn't listened to in years. We got out of there when the set ended and cabbed to my place, where I dug out the record in question and put it on. We had a nightcap and threw our clothes on the floor and dived into bed.
>
> I did not find her to be gawky and bony. I found her to be warm and soft and quick and eager, and the music's eccentric harmonies and offbeat rhythms didn't interfere with the pleasure we took with one another. If anything, it gave a nice brittly atonal edge to our lovemaking.

Sex is handled at least as obliquely in the Scudder books. Here's an example from *A Stab in the Dark*:

> I joined her on the couch and ran a hand over her fine hair. The sprinkling of gray hair enhanced its attractiveness. She looked at me for a moment out of those bottomless gray eyes, then let the lids drop. I kissed her and she clung to me.
>
> We necked some. I touched her breasts, kissed her throat. Her strong hands worked the muscles in my back and shoulders like modeling clay.
>
> "You'll stay over," she said.
>
> "I'd like that."
>
> "So would I."
>
> I freshened both our drinks.

There's sometimes a fair amount of sexual content in the Scudder novels, with plots involving pimps and prostitutes, transvestites and homosexuals. But rather little sexual activity happens onscreen, and when it does it's not rendered in detail.

Violence, on the other hand, gets a fuller treatment. Scudder's

New York is very much a city of violent death, a fact particularly stressed in *Eight Million Ways To Die*, in which the brooding detective reads the tabloids every morning and obsessively recounts the most appalling homicides. (While writing the book, I read the *Daily News* every afternoon once the day's work was done. Each day's atrocities were typed out the following morning for Scudder to ponder.)

Scudder's confrontation with the murderer is not always violent, and on several occasions he's taken the killer gently in tow, leading him peaceably off to the police station. But several of the books have included a scene of what might well be called gratuitous violence. In *The Sins of the Fathers*, Scudder goes bar-hopping, pretends to be drunker than he is, makes himself a target for a mugger, and deliberately vents his pent-up rage by beating his assailant. In *A Stab in the Dark*, Scudder braces and frisks a youth who may or may not have planned to rob him. And, in *Eight Million Ways to Die*, Scudder jumps a man who's about to shoot him in a Harlem alleyway. After he's kicked the gun out of the man's hand:

> *He came off the wall, his eyes full of murder. I feinted with a left and hit him with my right in the pit of the stomach. He made a retching sound and doubled up, and I grabbed that son of a bitch, one hand gripping the nylon flight jacket, the other tangled up in his mop of hair, and I ran him right into the wall, three quick steps that ended with his face smacking into the bricks. Three, four times I drew him back by the hair and smashed his face into the wall. When I let go of him he dropped like a marionette with the strings cut, sprawling on the floor of the alley.*

A page later, after wrestling with the question of what to do with the attacker-turned-victim, Scudder does this:

> *I stretched him out across the alley on his back with his feet up on the ledge and his head wedged against the opposite wall. I stamped full force on one of his knees, but that didn't do it. I had to jump into the air and come down with both feet. His left leg snapped like a matchstick on my first attempt, but it took me four tries to break the right one. He remained unconscious throughout, moaning a bit, then crying out when the right leg broke.*

None of these scenes are completely beside the point. While they are not intrinsically a part of the plot of their respective books, they make a point about the lead character and the world he operates in. They seem to me to fit the tone of the books, and to give the reader enough without giving him too much.

That, of course, is a matter of judgment. The last quoted paragraph could have been rendered in a sentence: *Before I left him in the alley, I smashed both his legs by jumping up and down on them.* Or it could have been presented in greater and more violent detail; the victim could have regained consciousness, could have begged for mercy.

Dick Francis has a chapter in every book he writes in which the narrator is seized by bad guys and mistreated in astonishing detail. I find those chapters a little much, but the reading public doesn't seem to mind. Ross Thomas has scenes of violence that sprout up as spontaneously as mushrooms; all of a sudden mild-mannered characters are squeezing triggers and popping off at one another.

The options are infinite. Read the writers whose work you enjoy and see how they do it, and how it works.

No matter what you do in the area of sex and violence, you will alienate some of your readers. The ones you hear from will likely be those complaining of too much sex, too much violence. I had an altogether reasonable letter a while back taking me to task for four-letter words; the writer found such words upsetting, liked my work otherwise, and argued that I didn't have to pepper my work with words she found obscene and distasteful. I could only reply that my first obligation was to artistic truth, and that if anything my characters were rather milder in their choice of language than their real-world prototypes.

Another woman expressed her considerable dismay at my writing sympathetically about Bernie's buddy, Carolyn Kaiser, who is after all a lesbian and thus a disgusting and unworthy person. I found this astonishing, but I recalled how Mort Sahl used to close his act, saying that he wanted to apologize if there was anyone present whom he'd failed to offend.

I know there are people who find my books disappointing because they're not sexy or violent enough. Readers rarely write a letter to uphold that position, but they'll cast their ballots at the newsstand. And I'm sure the reader mentioned in the last paragraph is balanced by another somewhere who thinks I'm exploiting lesbians, and that Carolyn is a nasty caricature of female homosexuality.

Ah, well. You can't please everybody and you're crazy if you try. I try to shrug off the negative reactions and enjoy the positive ones. Just yesterday a friend came up to me to report his reaction to *Eight Million Ways*, and he singled out the scene I quoted above.

"I stopped halfway through the scene," he said, "and I closed the book, and I tried to figure out what Scudder could do. Because he couldn't take the guy in, and it would be too much to kill him, and what could he do, just leave him there to rob and murder somebody else? And then he broke that bastard's legs, and I'll tell you, I felt so *good* about it."

Every once in a while someone reacts to a scene exactly as you intended. You know what? That's more fun than sex and violence.

14. Where's the Story?

In *Only In America*, the late Harry Golden wrote of a sign he'd seen in the offices of a company which traded in flour. A milling firm, I suppose they were. *"Does It Sell Flour?"* the sign demanded. If it didn't, one was given to understand, then the hell with it.

I probably ought to hang a sign like that over my desk. I'd have to change the wording, since I'm not in the flour-selling business. I am, on the contrary, in the story-telling business. That's my primary purpose as a fictioneer, and when my doodling on the typewriter keys fails to advance the story I'm telling, I'm not keeping my eye on the ball, my shoulder to the wheel, and my nose to the grindstone. I'm not selling flour, and it's gonna cost me.

"Where's the Story?" That, I submit, would be a useful sign to hang over almost any writer's desk. And such a sign would need regular dusting and cleaning, because it seems to me that the longer one practices this trade, the easier it is to lose sight of one's chief objective. It is often the veteran writer with considerable technical facility who is most likely to wander off on a tangent—and leave his story somewhere in the lurch. (The lurch is situated right between left field and the boondocks.)

Here are some of the tangential byways off on which you might find yourself wandering:

1. *Anecdotage.* Ever since *The Friends of Eddie Coyle*, I've greatly admired the writing of George V. Higgins. His prose is lean and crisp, his dialogue crackles with authenticity, and his stories are tough-minded and affecting. Lately, though, I've found his books harder to get through, although any individual page of writing is as appealing as ever. The problem I have with the books is that the storyline gets completely lost in a web of anecdotal material.

   Kennedy for the Defense, the most recent Higgins I've read, is a good example. Every time any two characters are talking, one of them is reminded of a story and tells it at length. The titular narrator is similarly anecdotal. Now the anecdotes are all good material and Higgins's characters tell them well, but a third of the way through the book I found myself gasping for breath. I wanted to grab the author by the throat and insist that he get on with it.

2. *Small talk.* The 87th Precinct police procedurals which Evan Hunter writes as Ed McBain have maintained a consistently high level of quality for over a quarter of a century. The plots are involving and the cop characters well drawn and appealing. At least once in almost every book, however, two homicide cops named Monaghan and Monroe make their appearance, and they banter. They toss the old repartee back and forth, and then they go away and leave the case to the boys of the old 87th, and I'm always relieved when they get off the stage.

Monaghan and Monroe have a mercifully brief turn at bat, but their particular sin is one that some authors commit in every chapter. Cute exchanges between the characters, flip remarks tossed back and forth, are hard to resist. If you have the knack for that sort of thing, they're easy to write; one line feeds right into the next and the pages pile up like crazy. And they're easy to read, but reading whole books full of this stuff is like making a meal of popcorn. Your dinner is mostly air, and you wind up tired of chewing and still oddly hungry.

3. *Character tags.* "I have a great idea for a mystery novel," people write me. "The detective is an Albanian dwarf who hybridizes gladioli, and he lives in a packing case in an abandoned subway station, and his girl friend is a Korean giantess with three breasts, and he always wears one blue sock and one black sock, and he drinks stingers before dinner and Orange Crush after dinner, and he insists on being paid exclusively in silver bullion, and . . ."

Now there's nothing inevitably wrong with all of this, although I don't think I could possibly enjoy reading about anyone who would drink stingers before dinner, but my point is that it's all too easy to let the external trappings of character get in the way of your story. It's especially apt to happen in series novels, in which you've created a whole trunkful of props for your lead character in the course of several books. Every time you open the trunk, you're tempted to trot out everything it holds.

In my first Bernie Rhodenbarr novel, my hero hadn't yet defined himself. By the third book, he had a bookstore and a best friend. In the fourth book a character introduced in book two emerged as his girlfriend. And by the fifth book I was in a little trouble. I had too much stuff in Bernie's trunk, and I had to remember not to dump it all out on the floor whenever I reached in for a wig or a pair of gloves.

I wound up starting that book over after writing 175 pages of it. One problem was that it needed replotting, but that wasn't all that was wrong with what I wrote. It was pumped airily full of repartee—Bernie and Carolyn and Ray Kirschmann and friends all found too many witty things to say to each other—and it was topheavy with bookstore bits and poodle salon bits and, oh, assorted junk from Bernie's trunk.

There may be too much of that kind of stuff in the final version, and only those of you who go out and read *The Burglar Who Painted Like Mondrian* can say for sure. But it was a lot easier to avoid excesses in that direction in the final draft because by then I knew where I was going with the plot, and I didn't have to mark time.

In a sense, every novel is a balancing act.

4. *Marking time.* I just gave that a separate heading, and not only because it's about time for another numbered entry. I wanted to stress it because I think it explains why some of us find it easy to wander away from the story on one or more of the above-described tangents. In the first draft of *Mondrian*, such tangents were a welcome alternative to the horrible chore of figuring out what would happen next. When I didn't know what turn the plot ought to take, I could kill time by having one character tell a story to another, or by having Bernie exchange mal mots with Ray or Carolyn, or by letting something cute happen in the bookstore, or whatever.

This provided me with the illusion that I was working, that the pages were piling up beside the typewriter, and that the book was getting written. It wasn't. I was getting farther from the beginning without getting closer to the end because I was not getting the story told. I was running in place. I was shuffling my feet. I was marking time.

5. *Library paste.* I do a fair amount of research, and spend plenty of time and money on it. But when people tell me they can see that I did a whole lot of research for a piece of writing, I know I've done something wrong.

Research is best when it doesn't show. It underscores the work, supplying an authentic grace note here and there, a detail that reinforces the impression of reality. If you write a book set in Florence in the fifteenth century, you're going to have to do considerable research and some of it's going to have to show. But if the reader's constantly dazzled by how much you know about the time and place, if he's getting a lesson in art history even as he's reading your story of love and betrayal, your research may very well be getting in the way of your story. It's like watching a dancer and being constantly aware of the performer's virtuosity. If the performance were truly first-rate, you wouldn't be aware of the skill involved; it would seem altogether natural, and you'd be caught up entirely in your response to its artistry.

Local color's much the same. Whether you're publishing your research or showing off your own firsthand familiarity with a locale, you can put so much work into the background that the story pales against it.

Some years ago I wrote a series of novels about an adventurer named Evan Tanner. The books danced all over the globe, which was more than could be said for their author. I found to my surprise that I was most at ease writing scenes in settings where I hadn't been, and which I had researched minimally. Otherwise my research, on the spot or from books, tended to get in my way. I could get bogged down trying to provide a realistic description of rural Ireland, say, or the Montreal Expo, both of which I'd visited. But I could make up areas of Eastern Europe out of the whole cloth and cut them to fit the plot at hand.

THE STORY ISN'T EVERYTHING

Early on, I mentioned that the problems we're examining here are apt to be the faults of experienced and accomplished writers. One reason, of course, is that they can get away with it; a best-selling novelist can throw the cat and the kitchen sink into a book, and who's to tell him to take them out?

Another reason is that these faults are often skillful faults, faults to a purpose. Because, paradoxically, the story isn't everything.

We read fiction for more than its story line. We read some writers—James Michener comes quickly to mind, and Leon Uris and Irving Wallace—at least as much for the factual material they provide as for the fictional framework into which their data is arranged. We read others for the glimpse they give us into areas of our world that we are unable to experience firsthand. We read books for the dialogue, and because we enjoy spending time with the characters. We read them, too, to appreciate an author's masterful use of language, yet this too can be tangential in that it leads us away from the story.

In a sense, every novel is a balancing act, and every writer is forever faced with the task of keeping its various elements in proportion. Every component which enriches the reading experience must be allowed full expression—as long as it doesn't get in the story's way.

Sometimes you get to feel like a juggler. I had that feeling writing *Eight Million Ways To Die*, a book which was very specifically concerned with two major elements beside its story. One was the decay of New York City and the perils of life therein; the other was the lead character's alcoholism and his struggle to get sober and stay sober. These were central themes and they deserved a lot of ink, but I had to keep them from eclipsing the primary story, which dealt with the detective's efforts to solve a murder. If other concerns slowed down that story, the whole book would suffer.

It's hard, in that sort of situation, to know to what extent you're successful. A few readers thought there was too much emphasis placed upon alcoholism. Others felt the booze theme was the book's greatest strength, and that it was realized without cost to the story.

I hope they're right, because the story has to come first. It's not everything, but without it nothing else really has a chance to work. If it doesn't sell flour, they'll have to shut down the mill.

15. Mirror Mirror on the Page

On my most recent trip to California, I was talking with a bookstore proprietor about the just-published first novel of a local writer. The store owner said that it wasn't really his kind of book, nor was he overly fond of the way it was written. "But it's set here in Santa Barbara," he said, "and of course I really enjoyed the local scenes."

With that for an introduction, I picked up the book expecting it to be positively overflowing with local color, a veritable insider's guide to the region. I found instead an agreeable novel that might as easily have been set in Wichita or Watervliet or, I suppose, Walla Walla. The novel did not disclose any Santa Barbara secrets, nor did it abound in descriptive or historical material. Streets and parks were named, and the various characters were identified as living in particular neighborhoods, about which a line or two of sociological description occasionally appeared. A character might be said to have gone to a particular school, to shop at a particular store.

Why should these little details make the book at all special to another Santa Barbaran? The answer seems simple enough. By setting his book in Santa Barbara, by providing even a handful of local allusions, the author facilitated the phenomenon of *reader identification* for those of his readers who inhabited or were otherwise familiar with the book's setting.

Hmmmm. Reader identification.

What's that mean?

Well, I'll tell you what I always thought it meant. When I was first getting a glimmering of the elements of fiction, I was given to understand that one thing a story needed was a strong and sympathetic lead character with whom the reader could identify. In other words, the reader would see himself in the lead character, would share the lead's thoughts and emotions, and would care what happened to the lead because of this process of self-identification.

This sort of identification certainly has a great deal to do with whether or not we find a piece of fiction involving enough to stay with it, and it helps determine how much emotional impact the plot developments will have on us. The more I can feel that the lead character is a person like me, that he thinks and reacts as I do, that he wants what I want, the more caught up I am in his actions and the greater my concern for his fate.

This is a fairly obvious point, and it helps to explain certain phenomena which scarcely need explaining, such as the tendency of young readers to prefer stories with young protagonists. We want to read about people like ourselves because it is then easier for us to put ourselves into the story. When the skill of a writer and the urgency of a story are great enough, we can stretch the perimeters of our identification, somehow seeing ourselves in the ancient fisherman in *The Old Man and the Sea*, the rabbits in *Watership Down*, or the extraterrestrials in assorted science fiction. In Michener's *Centennial*, we can find ourselves caught up in the prehistoric life-and-death struggles of a dinosaur. But it is generally easier for most of us to identify with members of our own species, and the greater their similarity to us, the more specific is our identification.

WINDOWS AND MIRRORS
What does all this have to do with Santa Barbara?

Well, I would submit that this capacity to see oneself in a fictional character is only one aspect of reader identification. The reader seeks in fiction not merely a window opening onto another world but a mirror in which he may see his own world reflected.

Does this seem curious? It did to me for the longest time. I sort of assumed that readers wanted fiction to map new lands for them, not to present fresh charts of familiar territory. Much of my own work is set in New York City, and I thought that those settings would be of the greatest interest to readers who lacked firsthand familiarity with New York and could pick some up painlessly in the course of reading a suspense novel.

What I came to discover—and perhaps this will strike you as obvious, and something I should have guessed all along—is that my New York settings were of the greatest interest to people who were already familiar with them.

Some of them were former New Yorkers. The proprietor of a mystery bookshop in San Francisco said that many of his customers were transplanted New Yorkers with a hunger to read about their hometown. Well, I could understand that. Nostalgia is not without appeal. But I have learned that my fictional New York settings are at least as popular with readers who have not moved away from them, and who in fact get to see their real-life counterparts every day of their lives.

Consider this. A friend, a Brooklyn native, reported that he had been an hour early for an appointment in the Wall Street area. He went into a coffee shop, ordered a cup of coffee, and took out a paperback novel of mine. "And in the part of the book I was reading," he said, "Scudder [my detective] goes into a coffee shop on the same block. And I thought, this is the same coffee shop, and I'm sitting here reading about it. And I really liked that."

"I was walking west on Twelfth Street," another friend said, "and I must have walked that block hundreds of times, and this time it hit me that I was following the same route that Bernie and Carolyn took pushing the wheelchair in *The Burglar Who Painted Like Mondrian*. And I really got a kick out of that."

Why? What is there about the phenomenon of encountering the familiar in fiction that makes it such an enjoyable experience? Why do we get a good feeling about both the real world and the fictional world when the two overlap like that?

Familiar settings have the further virtue of bringing scenes more fully to life.

I'm not sure, but I can think of a couple of possible explanations. For one, the presence of real parts of our own real world helps convince us that the writer knows what he's talking about. If I read a scene set in a neighborhood I know intimately, or reflecting an occupation or background with which I am closely familiar, and if the author gets the material right, I can allow myself to trust him in respect to other matters. "This guy knows New York," I can say. Or he knows stamp collecting, or bricklaying, or country music, or what you will. The more I can accept the idea that the author knows whereof he writes, the easier it is for me to believe further that the fictional story he's relating is true—and it is upon this voluntary suspension of disbelief that fiction depends for much of its power to move us.

To a reader who does not know New York, or stamp collecting or bricklaying or country music, the same piece of fiction may have substantially less appeal. The background may *look* authentic, but if I personally have no way of proving its authenticity, I can only take it on faith.

SEEING AND BELIEVING
Familiar settings have the further virtue of bringing scenes more fully to life. I can much more easily visualize a scene if it takes place in an area with which I am at least glancingly familiar, and the greater my familiarity, the easier the process of seeing what the writer

would have me see. It's an easier matter for me to picture a scene set in Bryant Park, even if the park is only sketchily limned, than one placed on the Serengeti Plains, however many pages of description of the Serengeti may preface the scene. All I have to do is read the words "Bryant Park" on the page and a photographic image comes to mind, an image clearer than any number of words about an unseen location can form in my mind.

And it's more than a matter of seeing. A scene set in Bryant Park (which, for non-New Yorkers, is the little park around the main public library at 42nd Street and Fifth Avenue, haunted almost exclusively in recent years by unregistered pharmacists hawking their wares) immediately calls up for me every association I have with that park, every flash of memory that is a part of my mental response to that piece of real estate. Even if I have only walked past the park once, it and I have at least that much common history, which endows any scene situated there with a personal dimension for me beyond what the writer himself actually put on the page.

It is one of fiction's functions, certainly, to teach us things, to illuminate for us portions of the world and areas of human experience of which we have previously known little or nothing. Many readers were drawn to Colleen McCullough's *The Thorn Birds*, not only because it was widely heralded as a good read, but because it promised to make the broad sweep of Australian history and culture painlessly accessible. And James Michener's novels are surely read not just for their stories but because of the knowledge the author imparts about Poland, about Israel, about the Chesapeake region.

But it seems to me that we are even more eager to seek to have the familiar explained and illuminated for us. Michener's next book will be about Texas, and I don't doubt that it will be avidly read by non-Texans curious about the Lone Star State—but what state do you suppose will contain the highest proportion of the book's customers? Texas, of course.

We go to fiction for a mirror that will give us a view of ourselves we can get nowhere else. For all that it serves us as an escape *from* our own lives, so too does it function to show us our own lives and allow us, if you will, to escape *into* them.

I remember when I saw the film *Diner* a couple of years ago. I went because I heard it was a good movie, but I loved it as much as I did, and chose to see it again, because it so utterly recaptured a piece of my own past. While it was set in Baltimore, the world it depicted and the lives it showed were completely interchangeable with my own late teens in Buffalo. I don't know that I especially saw myself in the film, but I knew all those guys in the film, and I had never seen that part of my life so accurately recreated.

Why should that have led me to sit through it twice and tout it to innumerable friends? I hadn't enjoyed those days all that much while they were happening; why should I want to see them brought back to life on the screen?

And what lesson is the writer to draw from all this musing upon mirrors? I don't know that there's any logical way to write with the aim of increasing this sort of reader identification. I suppose the lesson, if there is one, is the very one to which I find myself forever returning, like Cato ending every speech with a call for the destruction of Carthage. To wit: write for oneself, write what you yourself would most identify with, write honestly and unsparingly and fearlessly. It's nothing new, but it keeps proving out in new ways.

16. Purely Coincidental

A letter from a reader in Syracuse, New York, raised some interesting questions. We've examined the writer's reponsibility to mirror reality. To what extent is it his job to distort it?

"I realize the phrase *All characters in this book are fictional and any resemblance to persons living or dead is purely coincidental* is a catchall to protect the writer," Leonard J. Milbyer writes, "but does it? If in the course of a story you mention a specific telephone number, is it the writer's responsibility to research that number to make sure it doesn't belong to anyone? Or do you just make up a number and hope it's attached to a pay phone in a deserted warehouse?

"Additionally, what about character names? I recently wrote a short story in which I mentioned a Mrs. Perry of Lynn, Massachusetts. Although I had been to Lynn on one occasion I had no idea if there was a Perry family living there. Is it my duty as a writer to research character names in association with places?

"Lastly, what about the names of businesses? In your book, *The Burglar in the Closet*, Bernie seeks information about Crystal at a bar called the Recovery Room. You mention specifically where it is, first floor of a brickfront building on Irving Place, a few blocks below Gramercy Park. Is there a Recovery Room, an Irving Place, a Gramercy Park?

"And what if the owner of the Recovery Room objects to having the name used, especially if the writer doesn't treat the place too kindly—i.e., 'Den of thieves, pimps, and drug addicts, I had misgivings about entering the Recovery Room.' "

There is indeed an Irving Place, named for Washington Irving, as it happens. There is also a Gramercy Park. And I have just learned, through consultation with the telephone directory, that there is a bar and restaurant in the East Seventies called the Recovery Room. I didn't know this last fact when I wrote the book, although the information doesn't surprise me. I had to invent a batch of names of bars for Bernie to visit, and the Recovery Room sounded right for the sort of place I had in mind. I might not have used the name if I had happened to know that an establishment with the same name existed uptown, but I didn't feel it was important enough to check. On the other hand, if a Recovery Room had in fact existed at the location I picked for it, and had I been familiar with it, I might well have used it with its name unchanged; after all, nothing I said reflected adversely upon it, nor were any of its employees implicated in the plot of my fictional story.

Before I take this further, let me note that I don't know much about the legal aspects of all of this. The question of the extent to which one may base characters upon real people is by no means clear-cut, especially after the well-publicized case in which the decision went against writer Gwen Davis, and I'm not equipped or inclined to comment. I'm more interested in the point Mr. Milbyer raises about purely coincidental use of real names and addresses and phone numbers and the writer's responsibility to guard against such coincidence.

The question of phone numbers is interesting. The telephone company, presumably convinced that a fair number of lunatics tends to call whatever numbers they hear on television or read in books, has made certain numbers universally available to writers of fiction. As I understand it, any number beginning with 555 or ending with 9970 is, in Ma Bell's unmistakable cadence, not a working number. While I somehow doubt that, as a direct result of this policy, lunatics all across the country have found themselves muttering their obscenities to recordings, I think it's nice the phone company takes an interest.

I, on the other hand, don't. Because too many readers are aware of this dodge, and when they hit a 555 number in print it's a red flag shouting at them that they're reading fiction, just one more hook to yank them out of the fictive world the writer's been working so hard to create. Even when the reader doesn't know about the phone company's scam, or is willing to overlook it, suppose you've got a whole list of numbers in your story? Are they all going to start with 555? Or end with 9970?

The easiest way around this, of course, is simply to avoid being specific. More often than not, you can refer to a phone number without reeling out its seven digits. But if there's a reason why the whole number must appear, I can't let myself get terribly concerned about the person to whom that number may belong in the real world. I've known any number of people who have had to have their telephone numbers changed because of the activities of telephone pests, and not a one of them owed his plight to having had his number appear in print or on television.

When I have to make up a number, I more often than not will select one I myself have had in the past. This doesn't mean it hasn't by now been reassigned to some other lucky subscriber. I do this chiefly to avoid having to look up the number later on. Similarly, whenever I need a license plate number, I tend to use LJK-914, a plate I had for several years in New Jersey.

Publishers are unpredictable in this area. In *The Burglar Who Liked to Quote Kipling*, I set several scenes in a building on Riverside Drive and described it quite precisely. Jackie Farber, then my editor at Random House, seemed disappointed to learn that I had essentially invented the building, although it was certainly appropriate to its location. On the other hand, when *A Stab in the Dark* was being readied for publication, Jared Kieling, then my editor at Arbor House, wanted my assurance that none of the addresses I cited were the addresses of existing buildings, whether they were as I described them or not. He was evidently concerned about the possibility of a nuisance suit resulting from the coincidental use of a real address.

I would strongly advise you against using the names of real people of your acquaintance.

I know that some writers take pains to avoid using real addresses, and sometimes it's evident in what they write; I occasionally spot addresses in books set in New York which I know do not exist. 1200 West 53rd Street, for example, would be located somewhere in the middle of the Hudson River.

I don't like to do this. It bothers me as a reader and it would bother me as a writer. It interferes with believability, and I like to believe in fiction, whether I'm reading it or writing it. In the books I've written about Matthew Scudder, the city of New York is almost a character in the stories, and I make a special effort not only to get neighborhoods right but to use real establishments and real addresses. I know readers respond to this approach, and I know that it helps me as a writer by anchoring the books in reality.

It seems to me, though, that I would feel considerably less free to mix in doses of reality in a book that was not set in New York or some comparable metropolis. In a pseudonymous novel set in New Hope, Pennsylvania, for example, I changed the names and identities of all commercial establishments, and considered changing the names of streets and even of the town itself while I was at it. In a book currently in the works, the town I'm using is imaginary.

When it comes to character names, there's no way the writer

can preclude the possibility of coincidence. If you call your character George Miller, say, one of the thousands of George Millers out there may share certain of your character's idiosyncrasies. If you call him Byron Onderdonk, somewhere out there in Readerland a real Byron Onderdonk will wonder why you've singled him out.

I certainly wouldn't worry, if I were Mr. Milbyer, about the possible existence of a Perry family in Lynn, Massachusetts, or about the existence of a Lynn family in Perry, Georgia, come to think of it. These are common names, and even with uncommon names I don't see that it is the writer's job to establish their non-existence, or to do anything about it if they do exist. The standard disclaimer notice, after all, means what it says—that the characters are fictional, and that coincidence is coincidental.

I would, however, strongly advise you against using the names of real people of your acquaintance—unless, as sometimes happens, you have their permission. When *Breakfast at Tiffany's* appeared, the writer Bonnie Golightly brought suit against author Truman Capote, who had named the book's protagonist Holly Golightly. Her case was considerably strengthened by the fact that she and Capote were acquainted with one another—and, of course, by the fact that her surname was by no means a common one.

In the '40s, the late James T. Farrell published a novel entitled *Bernard Clare*. A man with that name brought suit, and in subsequent novels about the same character, his surname was changed to Carr as part of the lawsuit's settlement. I don't recall whether Farrell and Clare were acquainted, nor do I know that it matters much.

In *A Stab in the Dark*, I changed the name of one character when it was pointed out that a man with that very name was prominent in the publishing world. I did not know the man and was not familiar with his name, although I may have registered it subliminally somewhere along the way. I changed the character's first name and am glad I was able to do so, although if the name had been left unchanged it would have attracted no attention outside of the narrow world of New York publishing. For all I know, the name I changed it to might be as well or better known in some other area—aerospace, or banking, or whatever—than the original name is known in publishing. So be it. There are coincidences for which I can be held responsible, others for which I cannot.

Ah, well. It's important, I submit, to remember that what we are all writing is fiction, that however we struggle to make them real our creations are nothing but a pack of lies. Must we rush to apologize when one of them is endowed by coincidence with an unintended grain of truth?

17. How Long, O Lord?

When she was in the second grade, my daughter Jyl (nee Jill) brought me to class for show-and-tell. It was her teacher's idea. She thought it would be a prime educational experience for the kids to meet a real live writer. I went, talked a little, answered some questions, passed around some page proofs and galleys, and, all in all, had a terrible time.

One kid had a good question. "How long," he wanted to know, "does it take you to write a book?" I hemmed. I also hawed. It depended, I told him, on the nature of the book, on the length of the book, on the air temperature and barometric pressure, on . . . "Well," he said, "how long does it take you to write the Bible?"

My stammered response is mercifully lost to memory. But the child's question echoes in my mind whenever someone asks me how long my books take me.

My usual answer, as equivocal as ever, is It Depends. Some books have taken a matter of days. Most take months. Some take forever. It Depends.

But let us for once be specific rather than general, precise rather that vague. My most recent book, *Eight Million Ways To Die*—how long did it take to write the thing?

That's an easy question to answer. I put the first sheet of paper into the typewriter a day or two into January of 1982. I took the last sheet out a day or two before the end of February. As a round figure, say the book took two months, start to finish. Two intense months, two work-filled months, but two months nevertheless, and one of them a short one in the bargain.

Not bad, huh? Now if I could just be that productive all the time and turn out half a dozen books a year, why . . .

Wait a minute.

Plotting a book is part of the work therein, isn't it? Well, I did some outlining in December. It would be fair to say that I spent the week between Christmas and New Year's getting the plot in shape and writing a rudimentary outline. So that stretches the writing time to what? Nine, ten weeks?

Still pretty quick.

Wait another minute.

Sometime in the fall of '81, I guess it must have been October, I got a call from Arnold Ehrlich, my editor at Arbor House. Could I supply a title and a hint of the plot for the novel I planned to deliver next? That way the book could be included in the catalog currently being prepared. I was at the time hard at work on a mystery about Bernie Rhodenbarr, for a series published by Random House, and I told Arnold my next Arbor House book would be about private detective Matthew Scudder, but that was all I knew about it.

A day or two later I called him back. My title, I advised him, was *Eight Million Ways to Die*. He assured me that it was a terrific title. And could I tell him what it was about?

"A call girl gets killed," I said, "and her pimp's the leading suspect, and he hires Scudder to find out who really killed her."

"Sounds fine," Arnold said. "Do you suppose I could say 'Spellbinding tension'?"

"You could," I said. "You could even throw in 'Edge-of-the-chair suspense' if you think it'll help."

"It couldn't hurt," said Arnold.

I went on working on the Burglar book and it ran right into a stone wall. Sometime in late November or early December I stopped working on it, and sometime in late December I officially turned my mind to *Eight Million Ways To Die*. But one might argue that I had unofficially turned my mind to the new Scudder book the day Arnold first asked what its title would be, and that my mind had been engaged in sifting plot and character components for the book ever since.

Which would lengthen the time devoted to its composition from two months to—what? October, November, December, January, February. Five months. Well, that's still a pretty short time to spend on a long book.

Of course there's another way to look at it. In December of 1980, I finished up a book called *A Stab in the Dark*, which was the fourth book in the Scudder series. Aside from my monthly column for *Writer's Digest* and one or two short stories, I didn't do any writing after that until I started the Burglar book in the fall. I ran several marathons, traveled across the country and back, put in a couple of weeks on a screenwriting project in Hollywood, but didn't get my teeth into a book until the fall. So it's not unrealistic to argue that all the time after the completion of *Stab* could legitimately be charged to the account of *Eight Million Ways*.

What's that come to? Fourteen months?

Hmmmm.

Back in the fall of '76, I sat down with Bill Grose, who was at Dell at the time. I had an idea for a big book about a pimp. Bill was encouraging and I was encouraged, and I went right to work on it. I did about a hundred pages of the opening of the novel, and I did about eighty-five pages of flashback, covering the guy's life before he became a pimp, and in the course of doing all this writing I also did a fair amount of research on African art, which the pimp collected. I even bought a couple of pieces, a Dan mask and an ancestor statue from Cameroon, because purchase and ownership help me get the feel for that sort of thing. I bought a lot of books, too, and spent a lot of time reading them, and going to museums, and talking to people.

*S*ome books have taken a matter of days. Most take months. Some take forever. It Depends.

The book didn't work out. I don't know why, exactly, but it didn't. Five years later, though, that pimp came back to life and became Scudder's client. He'd changed some in the intervening years, naturally enough. I'd originally conceived of him as a white pimp, an anomalous Caucasian in a predominantly black trade, but he became a black pimp in *Eight Million Ways To Die*. His name changed from Davy Starr to Chance, but he still collected African art, still maintained a secret residence, and indeed was still the highly original character I'd dreamed up all those years ago.

I didn't go back for a look at what I'd written originally. I had the manuscript around but avoided referring to it, and discarded it unread once I'd completed *Eight Million Ways*.

I probably put four months into those 185 pages. Maybe even six months, counting all the research time. So if we add those months to our score sheet, *Eight Million Ways To Die* took twenty months, which isn't all *that* long, I suppose, but . . .

Hang on a minute.

Is that the right way to count it? Or is it more accurate to look at total elapsed time, figuring that a book develops in the author's mind from its conception to its completion, and that one might then say I'd been working on the story from the fall of '76 when I first met with Bill Grose to the completion of the book in late February of '82.

I make it five years and four, five months. Something like that.

The character of Chance drew some strong positive response from readers and critics. Several reviewers mentioned the pimp favorably. But of course it goes without saying that he wasn't the whole book. Jan Keane, Scudder's girlfriend, appeared previously in *Stab*, and had her origins in a woman sculptor who emerged briefly in a Scudder novel that failed to get written in January or February of '76. I went through a stretch there when I kept starting novels that died after thirty or forty or fifty pages. The prototype for Jan Keane emerged in one such thirty-page wonder.

The character of my hero, Matthew Scudder, is certainly an important part of *Eight Million Ways*, and just as certainly did not emerge full-blown when I sat down to write the book. I'd been writing about Scudder since I first started work on *The Sins of the Fathers* in the fall of '73, and he evolved through four books and two novelettes before he was ready to play his part in this latest book.

Eight and a half years?

The city of New York is perhaps as much a character in *Eight Million Ways To Die* as are any of the people in its pages. That's true to some extent or another in most of my New York novels, but it's particularly notable here because one of the book's central themes is the especially perilous quality of life in the city. I first came to New York on a visit in December, 1948. I first lived in the city in August of 1956.

Oh, why do this inch by inch and minute by minute? There's as much of me as anything else in that book, and I couldn't have written it as I did without everything in my life that preceded it. I was born on June 24, 1938. It took me forty-three years and eight months to write *Eight Million Ways to Die*.

18. Points of Order

I was comparing notes the other day with Michael Rosler, a writer friend of mine. (Mike is also a Dixieland trumpeter of uncommon ability, but the notes we were comparing were verbal rather than musical.) I asked him how his current novel was going.

"It was going beautifully," he said, "and then it stopped dead in its tracks. I've been two chapters from the end for weeks now and I can't seem to get anything written."

"Oh," I said. Or words to that effect.

"It's not as though I don't know what's going to happen in the final chapters. They're perfectly clear in my mind. But when I sit down to write them, nothing happens."

"These things happen."

"Well, I wish they would happen to somebody else. I can accept the fact that I write in spurts. It'll flow for weeks and then it'll cut out. Okay, I can live with that. But I never ran into a wall this close to the end before."

"When I run into a wall," I said, "it's usually because I don't know where to turn. But that's not your problem. You know what happens next in the book."

"Absolutely. I just wish I could get these chapters on paper so I could get to work on the second draft."

"The second draft?"

He nodded. "It's clear in my mind, too. And as soon as I get a full first draft completed, I'll start in on it."

"Why wait?"

"Huh?"

"Why not start the second draft right away? Why beat your head against the wall with these two chapters when you're going to have to rewrite them anyway?"

"Well, I thought I ought to finish one thing before I start another."

"The book's already finished in your mind," I said. "Something in you is evidently resisting the idea of deliberately pointless work, which is why you can't seem to get those two chapters written."

"So I could just start right in on the revision," he mused. "It never occurred to me. I figured I *should* finish the first draft."

"You already did," I said. "You just haven't written all of it down, and maybe you don't have to."

GLANCING BACKWARD

The conversation set me thinking. Had I ever plunged into a second draft prematurely under similar circumstances? In my own case, a second draft has almost invariably meant there was something wrong with the first one, that it didn't go as I'd intended. A first draft is generally all I do on a book. This doesn't mean my writing is slipshod, nor would I want to imply that it's an effortless task for me to turn out final copy in a first draft. It might be more accurate to say that I revise as I go along, that my sentences and paragraphs and pages get restructured and polished in the course of each day's work, and that they're revised and rewritten before they're put on paper in the first place.

Sometimes, though, something goes wrong. Once in a while a book goes completely wrong, so much so that I put it aside and never do get back to it. Other times I see that I have to start over.

My conversation with Mike triggered a memory of one such instance, when I was writing the first Bernie Rhodenbarr mystery, *Burglars Can't Be Choosers*. I wrote it, as I often do, with no advance knowledge of who was going to turn out to be the murderer, or how it had been done, or what would lead Bernie to the solution. This can be a dangerous way to proceed, but it has one great advantage—if the writer doesn't know what's going to happen next, the reader probably won't know, either.

Four or five chapters from the end, I figured out how to end the book. The ending which suggested itself necessitated some extensive changes in what I'd already written. I had to rewrite the opening to make the facts presented therein consistent with the book's solution. I had to scatter clues here and there, and I had to get rid of some false clues I'd scattered in thus far. As I reread what I'd written, I saw that I could tighten the book considerably by cutting a day out of its timespan. All in all, it was clear to me that the book would profit considerably from a first-page-to-last trip through the typewriter.

First, though, I continued onward with the story. I suppose I could have plunged into the rewrite at once, but perhaps I needed to make sure that I knew where I was going and could find my way there. I wrote two or three chapters, and then, when I knew exactly what was going to happen in the remaining chapters, I put the book aside unfinished and began again from Page One. I made the changes that I had envisioned, plus some inevitable additional ones that I hadn't, and I wrote the book right on through to the end.

It's quite common for me to write twenty or forty or sixty pages of a book, then start over from the beginning and write on through to the end. The opening chunk serves to get me into the book, to let the characters define themselves. I may have to write that much before I find out just what book I'm writing. Perhaps it would make sense to regard such false starts not as first drafts but as prose equivalent of the pencil sketches an artist makes before beginning a painting.

By the same token, some of those bold openings never amount to anything more than scrap paper. I've always tended to think of such aborted beginnings as wasted time, but as I see it now they're nothing to regret. Not every sketch turns out to be worth developing into a painting, and every exercise at least improves the skills of the hand and the eye.

*F*iction writing is so utterly linear.

WORDS AND BRUSHSTROKES
I don't know that writing and painting have much in common, but I find analogies and comparisons useful, in spite of the fact that I know next to nothing about painting. One interesting difference, it seems to me, is that fiction writing is so utterly linear. Anyone who reads a book can see how to write it—you start with the first word and put down a word at a time until you get to the end.

You could argue that a painting works the same way, with one brushstroke at a time, but there's no natural sequence to a painting, no clearcut reason to begin, say, in the upper left hand corner and move clockwise. The artist can put a little green here and a little blue there, he can work on a tree in the foreground for a while, then fill in the mountains in the distance, then return to the tree.

Is it possible to write a novel that way?

I suppose it happens. Complicated multiple-viewpoint novels are not necessarily written in the sequence in which they ultimately appear; one can write long sections about a character, then chop them up later and shuffle them around. Some stories carom around in time; *Some Unknown Person*, Sandra Scoppettone's fictional retelling of the Starr Faithful case, interwove several narrative lines occurring at different times. Sandra could have written the book as it appears, or she could have written each story line and braided them together afterward. (She doesn't seem to be answering her phone today, so this may remain one of this column's great unanswered questions.)

Mickey Spillane once told an interviewer that he begins his books by writing the last chapter, then writes the penultimate one, then the antepenultimate one, and so on, until he finally wraps things up by writing the opening. This may be true, but Spillane has had almost as much fun over the years with interviewers as he ever had with Mike Hammer. True or not, I like the point Spillane makes—i.e., that the impact of his work depends upon his finale, and thus everything must be designed to strengthen the climax. I don't know that you have to write a book backwards to achieve that end, but it might be occasionally useful.

Almost twenty years ago I wrote a novel called *The Girl with the Long Green Heart*. It dealt with a confidence game and was set partly in Olean, New York, and partly in Toronto. About 150 pages into it, I got stuck. I spent a certain amount of time just staring at the typewriter, and finally I decided that I knew how the last several chapters were going to go, so I went ahead and wrote them. Then, after I'd brought things to a stirring climax, I dropped back to Page 150 and filled in the thirty or so pages I'd skipped.

This seemed to work well enough at the time. I was working with an outline that allowed me to know what was going to happen in the last few chapters, and I had a better grasp on them than on the chapters immediately preceding them. Writing the ending evidently unblocked the middle and I finished the book with relative ease.

The resultant book is seamless enough. I can't tell, looking at it now, just what pages I skipped and came back to. So I suppose the experiment was a success, but I don't think I'd be inclined to repeat it.

SINS OF OMISSION
Why not?

Because everything in a piece of fiction is influenced by what has gone before it. By skipping around the way I did, I kept the last chapters from coming under the influence of the section I skipped over.

To be specific, there were characters introduced in the bypassed chapters who did not take specific shape until their scenes were written. These characters weren't destined to play a part in the last chapters, but, if the book had been written in the usual order, my narrator might have thought about one of them later on. Something in the closing chapters might have bounced off his recollection of something in an earlier chapter. I can't say what might have happened, obviously, because it didn't, so the auctorial sin is one of omission. I doubt that anything important was lost this way, but I can't think that anything was gained—except for the obvious gain in that I was able to unblock myself and finish the book.

And, if writing sequentially is important, that constitutes another argument for the suggestion I gave my friend at the beginning of this column. ("Notice how deftly the guy gets back to Topic A? These old pros know what they're doing.") Momentum doesn't get interrupted by bringing the story to a conclusion, and the last two chapters, when they're finally written, are of a piece with the revised material that precedes them.

Ultimately, of course, whatever works is the right way. You can shuffle the pages, as William Burroughs claimed to do. The order of approach is up to you.

And isn't writing largely a matter of putting words in order? Prose has been defined by Coleridge as words in their best order (and poetry as the best words in their best order.) Anyone with the price of a dictionary has access to more words than he'll ever need. All you have to do is arrange them properly.

19. Look What They've Done to My Song, Ma

Good morning, class.

Good morning, sir.

Today we're going to leap to a wild surmise. Let us assume that you have not merely written something but that someone has actually arranged to publish it. At this point—are you all right, Rachel?

I feel a little faint, sir.

I guess I can understand that. Take deep breaths, Rachel, and try to think calming thoughts. But let's get back to the admittedly hypothetical book or story which you've just sold. In a perfect universe, your worries would be over at this point. You would receive a congratulatory telegram from your publisher, and half an hour later the contracts would arrive in the mail, and fifteen minutes after you signed them you'd get a check for the advance, and the following morning bound copies of the book (or stapled copies of the magazine) would arrive at your door. Sometime before the end of the week an agent would be calling you to discuss movie offers.

One thing that certainly wouldn't happen, in this perfect universe, is that some son of a—yes, Gwen?

There's an alternative to the sexist expression you were about to employ, sir.

Quite right, Gwen. Thanks for calling that to my attention. One thing that wouldn't happen in this perfect universe is that some child of a dog would want you to change the perfect manuscript you've produced. In what we tend to call the real world, this sort of thing happens all the time. The writer is asked to make certain changes, or to consent to such changes being made by the editor. When this happens, there are two obvious avenues open to the writer, flat refusal and blind obedience.

I suppose, sir, that the ideal course lies somewhere between these two extremes.

Am I that predictable, Arnold? As a matter of fact, let me pick a banality of another color and suggest that the ideal course varies enormously with circumstances. The significant variables include who you are, who they are, what you've written, and how they want you to change it.

John O'Hara has said that the only way to improve a manuscript once you've written it is by telling an editor to go to hell. I think it's worth noting that you stand a better chance of getting away with this sort of thing if you happen to be John O'Hara. When you're an established pro, you're in a better position to judge when an editorial suggestion is unwarranted and your view of the matter is more likely to be respected. When you're starting out, the editor is quite naturally an authority figure, and both you and he are inclined to assume that his opinion is of more import than your own.

Curiously enough, this sometimes works out badly. In the past few years I've read too many books by Big Names who would have profited greatly by some editorial guidance. But when you get to be emperor, nobody tells you you're naked.

On the other hand, new writers, desperate to please, often consent to changes that utterly gut their work. Patrick Trese's first novel, based on his experiences with a television crew in the Antarctic, had a change of editors in midstream; the new editor advised Pat to cut the book in half and change it from a novel to a nonfiction memoir. He did, and the book was duly published as *Penguins Have Square Eyes* and vanished without a trace.

I suppose the trick is to know whether or not a proposed change is to the book's ultimate advantage, and that's a neat trick. I've always found this sort of situation problematic. On the one hand, my colossal auctorial ego puffs itself up with the certain knowledge that what I've written is perfect just as I wrote it, and says things like "Don't they know who I am?" On the other hand, a secret reserve of self-doubt nags at me with the thought that anybody, even the kid who delivers the lunches, knows more about my work than I do, and that I'll neglect his advice at my peril. Finally, the urge to make people like me by doing what they want wars with the slothful impulse to avoid rewriting because it's just another form of work.

It helps at such times to have friends and associates whose judgment one respects, who can provide a little more perspective on the situation. Even if they do no more than serve as a sounding board to enable you to determine your own feelings, they play a useful role. In the end, though, the decision is yours to make.

When my novel *Ariel* was seeking a publisher, one editor liked it but wanted a variety of substantial changes. Many of them struck me as wholly sound. One, however, did not. One plot element concerned a nineteenth-century portrait which young Ariel finds in the attic, and to which she bears (or fancies she bears) a strong resemblance. The editor wanted this eliminated because the house she worked for had recently published a book in which resemblance to a painting was an element of the plot.

On reflection, it seemed to me that this coincidence did not warrant my changing an otherwise successful component of my book, and I showed the manuscript elsewhere. I should add, however, that the editor had wanted me to revise the book on spec; if she'd come to me with contract in hand, I can't be sure I'd have displayed an equal measure of artistic integrity.

The story ends happily. After himself suggesting revisions that I could live with, and that improved the book immeasurably, Don Fine at Arbor House published *Ariel.* I can't tell you how glad I am that I didn't make the changes that first editor requested.

> *When you get to be emperor, nobody tells you you're naked.*

I did make changes against my own inclination in some of my earlier books. In retrospect, I can see that some of those changes were for the better and others were not. That's okay. My primary purpose at the time was to get published, and I would have done almost anything toward that end. Nor was I writing on a level where artistic integrity was a useful concept.

I wrote a slew of soft-core sex novels for Beacon Books, and when the first of their number came out I was astonished at what they'd done to it. Almost every sentence had been rewritten, and to no apparent purpose. If I had written, say, "With a mighty leap he jumped out of the pit," it would be changed to, say, "He jumped out of the pit with a mighty leap." No exaggeration. More sentences were tampered with in this fashion than were left alone. I subsequently learned that this particular publisher edited everything this way. The head of the company had a pulp magazine background and assumed that all manuscripts required this sort of treatment. God knows what it cost him to do this, as he evidently had several people on salary doing nothing but screwing up manuscripts, but I guess he thought he had to do it. For my part, I simply ceased looking inside the covers of the books I wrote for Beacon. They were published under a pen name, and they were insignificant to begin with, and I just decided that once those manuscripts left my typewriter they ceased to matter to me. Whatever the publisher did to them was his business, just so I never had to read the result.

I take a far different attitude with the books I write nowadays. I've always had problems with copy editors. It seems to me that they exist only to shift commas from where I want them to where I don't want them. I've come to understand their position—they do have to deal with a lot of writers who don't write smoothly or punctuate effectively, and many of them are freelancers and feel they have to make a lot of editorial changes in order to demonstrate that they've actually done something. And I try to keep an open mind, because sometimes (hard as it may be to believe this) they're right and I'm, uh, wrong. But unless I really believe this, I change things back the way I want them.

In books, that is. In magazines the rules are a little different. Magazines have specific space requirements and particular taboos and God knows what else, and magazine editors generally feel free to make arbitrary changes without consulting the author. Here at *Writer's Digest* I get to see galleys of my column before it goes to press, but that's extraordinarily rare. Even so, sometimes a paragraph has to be chopped at the last minute in order to make the column fit into the space available for it.

But that's nothing compared to the editing most magazines feel free to do. It's occasionally painful to see a story mangled editorially, especially if it's a story you particularly liked, and especially when it happens early in your career. When this sort of thing happens, you can take some of the sting out of the whole business by reminding yourself that magazine publication does not have the permanence of book publication, that you will set things right when your collected stories are published.

(And sometimes you get the chance. I was able to restore some excised material when my *Writer's Digest* columns were gathered together as *Telling Lies for Fun and Profit*, and on a couple of occasions I've had the opportunity to undo an editor's contribution when a short story of mine was later anthologized.)

Mystery editor Lee Wright once told a friend of mine not to worry about editorial interference. "Nothing you publish in a magazine will hurt you," she assured him. I remind myself of her words when I pick up a magazine and discover that someone has rewritten a last line of mine, or "fixed" a particularly felicitous phrase. At least I can tell myself that it's even worse writing for newspapers, where one learns to write less important paragraphs as one goes along, so that an editor can cut from the bottom without even having to read the story.

Anyway, these are some of the problems that—yes, Arnold?

We should all have such problems, sir.

A good point, Arnold. When it's all we can do to get our current project written, let alone find somebody to publish it, it may be hard to take this sort of problem seriously.

I mean, you might as well tell us about the poor writers who don't have control over the blurb copy and the cover art and the ads.

That's next month, Arnold.

I can hardly wait, sir.

20. Reporters and Imaginers

Where does your fiction come from? Are you reporting your stories? Or do they flow out of your imagination?

I raise the question because someone raised it for me. This past July I spent a happy week in Yellow Springs, Ohio, at the Antioch College Writers' Conference. A colleague at the conference was Arno Karlen, once a classmate of mine at Antioch, more recently a neighbor in Greenwich Village. Arno published a well-received volume of short fiction shortly after graduation, and has since mostly written nonfiction; *Napoleon's Glands*, a medical investigation of history, is his most recent book.

Arno's lecture one afternoon concerned the thin and sometimes imperceptible line between fiction and nonfiction; specifically, he discussed Mailer, Hemingway and James Baldwin as reporters in the guise of novelists. What most captured my attention during his talk was his remark that all writers, whether of fiction or nonfiction, could be divided into two categories—those who were functioning essentially as reporters, and those who were working out of their imaginations.

My first reaction, of course, was to recall Robert Benchley's observation that the world can be divided into two classes of people—those who divide the world into two classes of people and those who don't. My next response, predictably enough, was to wonder where I myself fit into the picture, and I didn't have to spend a great deal of time wondering. It was immediately evident that I was not a reporter but an imaginer.

What does this mean? Not that my writing is not autobiographical; I can point to aspects of myself in virtually every character I've created. Nor does it mean that my books are unrealistic. (Some, to be sure, are more realistic than others. The Tanner books are particularly fanciful, the Scudder books quite realistic, but both sorts are equally creatures of the imagination.) What it means, I suppose, is that my books do not seek to tell you what has happened in what we insist on calling the Real World, but report instead on the imaginary doings of imaginary people.

My characters are only rarely based on people of my acquaintance. When I do actually have someone in mind as the starting point of a character, I invariably wind up with a copy that has precious little in common with the original. In the broadest sense, of course, all of my characters are drawn from life, in that my unconscious mind has spent a lifetime synthesizing the people I've known and my made-up characters are drawn from the resultant reservoir. But this means only that reality has served to stock my imagination—but so has everything I've read and everything I've dreamed.

An awareness of this division of writers has helped me to a fuller understanding of the writer I am, and of the problems I create for myself when I try to be another sort of writer. I have always had an untoward amount of difficulty writing nonfiction, and I have never before understood why. It has always seemed to me that it ought to be easier to write nonfiction than fiction, and, for most people, it evidently is.

(Arno made the point, or at least argued the point, that it is more difficult to write meritorious nonfiction than fiction. On the one hand I disagreed; the world, after all, overflows with writers who have had some success with nonfiction and even make a decent living at it, and would give almost anything if they could once in their life get a novel or short story published. I know of not a single successful fiction writer who experiences comparable frustration. On the other hand, I cannot deny that it is infinitely more difficult for *me* to write meritorious, or even acceptable, nonfiction.)

I haven't done much nonfiction over the years, and what little I've done has been difficult for me. (I should point out that I am not talking now about *this* kind of nonfiction, this writing-about-writing I've been doing in *WD* for the past decade. These columns of mine aren't fiction *or* nonfiction. They're letters to friends, the great majority of whom I haven't met and don't know by name, and they have consequently been the easiest writing I've ever done. And why not? What's easier than writing a letter to a friend?)

I wrote a couple of personality profiles for *New York Magazine,* one of a private detective, another (never published) of a jazz pianist. I interviewed Robert Ludlum for *WD.* Having acquired a smattering of ignorance about burglary in the course of chronicling Bernie Rhodenbarr's fictional adventures, I wrote pieces about the burglar's art for a couple of periodicals. With all of these pieces I had more trouble than I expected to have, and put in rather more effort than the finished articles would have led one to suspect. The problem, I suppose, is that I don't know *how* to report. I know the sort of things one can learn, but I don't have the intuitive knowledge that a real reporter has. All writing, fiction or nonfiction, reportorial or imaginative, involves innumerable decisions. Any art does, and perhaps any human activity does. Years ago a half-drunk flautist told me he couldn't fathom how I did what I did. "How," he demanded over and over, "do you know where to put the commas?" I know, I could have told him, because I am a writer, and prose flows in me just as music flows in him. There are innumerable decisions I make as a writer, and I make them in every sentence I write, and I make almost all of them intuitively and automatically, without giving them much thought. Similarly, he as a musician makes constant decisions about phrasing and stress and loudness and God knows what else, and gives them as little conscious effortful thought as I give the placement of my commas.

*A*ll writing, fiction or nonfiction, involves innumerable decisions.

Those decisions come more easily for me in fiction than nonfiction, and I have infinitely more confidence in them. At the moment I'm involved in a collaborative nonfiction work. I'm writing the life story of a friend of mine, and it is an adventurous life indeed. My friend has been a soldier of fortune, a professional criminal, and an undercover agent for the Drug Enforcement Agency. I am having a damnably difficult time deciding whether to tell his story in the first or third person, and to what extent I should allow my own voice to be present in the narrative, and what incidents to include or omit, and how long the book ought to run, and in what order the material may best be presented. If I were writing the same kind of story as imaginative fiction rather than reportorial nonfiction, I would not have trouble with these decisions. I would make them easily, intuitively, automatically, and I would be comfortable with my decisions. They might not be indisputably correct—another writer would scatter his commas elsewhere, with equal justification—but they would be valid decisions, and I could live with them.

The more I found myself thinking in terms of these two classes of writers, the more evidence I found in my own writing. Two examples stand out, one in fiction, one in nonfiction.

The Thief Who Couldn't Sleep, my first book about Evan Tanner, had scenes scattered across Europe and Asia Minor. In his peripatetic quest for a hoard of gold coins, Tanner is jailed in Turkey, escapes from his jailers in Ireland's Shannon Airport, and makes his way back to Turkey via Ireland, England, Spain and the Balkans. At the time of writing, I had been in Ireland and England for about two weeks and in the other described countries not at all. I found it much more difficult to write the secenes set in Ireland than those which took place in Yugoslavia. My Yugoslavia was a pure creature of my imagination, and I'm sure it bore precious little resemblance to the real Yugoslavia, but I had no trouble writing about it. I knew a little about Ireland and was anxious about getting it right, and thus it wound up coming off paradoxically less convincing than Yugoslavia.

An even better illustration can be drawn from a nonfiction book I wrote ages and ages ago, consisting of extended interviews with members of the sexual demimonde. I did one actual interview for the book with a call girl. The other dozen or so chapters I fabricated completely, just making up the lives and personalities of each subject much as I make up the life histories and personalities of my fictional characters. The one chapter drawn from an actual interview was the most difficult to write; more to the point, the publisher, while extremely well-pleased with the book as a whole, pointed to the one real chapter as the weakest of the lot, and the least convincing. (The publisher, let it be said, did not know that the chapter in question was the only real one. He thought they were all real.)

Having looked at oneself, one looks at other writers. All of us are either reporters or imaginers, although every reporter makes some use of his imagination and every imaginer does some reporting. Many reporters write nothing but fiction. The novelist Leon Uris comes to mind as a good example; his books seem to me to be strongest when their fiction is a vehicle for the reporting of factual material, weakest when they concern characters and events of the author's imagination. *Exodus*, for example, was positively gripping when it dealt with real people engaged in real events, while the fictional characters Uris created to carry the story were considerably less convincing, and their fictional lives of less interest.

At the same time, there are writers of nonfiction who work best when they give their imaginations free rein. A few years ago journalist Gail Sheehy was roundly criticized when it came out that some of the characters in what was purportedly reportage were actually composite personalities and, to a greater or lesser degree, the outgrowth of the author's imaginative faculties. "You can't trust a thing the woman writes," I recall thinking at the time, but now I might soften that judgment. For the writer who is more imaginer than reporter, truth is better served sometimes through a willingness to depart from facts.

And why am I telling you all this?

Because it's been on my mind, and I've found that the aspects of writing which intermittently concern me tend to resonate for most of you to a greater or lesser extent. If you've read this far, you've probably already begun considering the questions posed at the beginning of the column and have at least tentatively classified yourself as either imaginer or reporter.

And what will it profit you to do so?

Perhaps it will make it just a little easier for you to find the books and stories you are best suited to write. Perhaps it will facilitate your writing from strength, and perhaps it will allow you to be a little more forgiving of yourself for being less capable in other areas.

I hope it will do as much for me. I have most erred as a writer, it seems to me, when I have undertaken a project because it ought to be written and have lost sight of the fact that it perhaps ought not to be written *by me*. My errors of this sort have not always stemmed from my having mistaken myself for a reporter, but that has sometimes been the case. I suspect I am a little less likely to make that particular mistake for having heard Arno's talk.

And that would please me. Because, after all, that is how one grows—as a writer, and in other areas of life. By ceasing to make the same mistakes, and by thus allowing oneself to make mistakes of another order altogether.

Perhaps it will have the effect, too, of stirring up other thoughts for you as it has for me. Thoughts about the nature of truth and fiction, of subjective and objective reality. The thoughts of youth, Longfellow tells us, are long, long thoughts, and so are these, but you may find them worth the thinking.

21. Sorry, Charlie

Couple of years back, Ross Thomas wrote a book called *Protocol for a Kidnapping*. It was the second or third volume in a suspense series written under the name Oliver Bleeck and featuring professional go-between Philip St. Ives, and the plot, which has largely slipped my mind in the intervening years, concerned getting somebody out of Yugoslavia.

Henry and Park, two charming cronies of St. Ives, were introduced in *Protocol*, and the three of them devil-may-cared their way through Yugoslavia, tossing sparkling repartee back and forth and winning the hearts and the minds of the readers, if not of the local inhabitants.

And then, right near the end, with the Yugoslav rescued and the forces of justice triumphant, there's some gunplay with the bad guys and a bullet comes from out of nowhere and whacks out Park. Kills him deader'n vaudeville. One flat sentence and he's gone.

I'll tell you, it was shocking. I talked to several other readers, fans of the series, and they all had the same reaction I did. We were bloody-well outraged. Park's death was a surprise, but that wasn't the point; we didn't mind surprises in our fiction, and in fact even welcomed them. But this was rather more than a surprise. It was a bitter disappointment. We did not want Park to be dead and we were angry with the author for having killed him off.

I can recall a similar reaction in the late fifties to one of Ed McBain's early 87th Precinct mysteries. The author had introduced rookie cop Bert Kling early in the series, and readers had watched Kling develop as a character and as a cop, and had participated vicariously in his burgeoning romance with Claire Townsend. (I think that was her name. I last read this book more than twenty years ago.)

Well, Claire got killed, as arbitrarily and, yes, as unfairly as Park. All over the country, McBain's fans threw a fit. They flat out did not want the woman dead. They wanted her to marry Bert and live happily ever after.

Writers generally have their reasons. McBain's purpose was to let the reader know that we were playing hardball in this league, that human lives in his books were up for grabs, that you could never take a happy ending for granted. He made his point.

When I became acquainted with Ross Thomas, one of the things I asked him was why he'd killed off Park. I was not the first person to raise the question. "I could just see myself stuck with those three guys forever," he said, "and having to write that happy patter for them, and I thought, hell, I don't want to do that, so I killed Park."

While they don't often follow through, writers have an urge to do in their series characters that makes you ready to believe in the concept of a death wish. Dorothy Sayers reportedly told Agatha Christie that she was aching to do in Lord Peter Wimsey, whereupon Dame Agatha confided that she herself had wanted to kill Hercule Poirot for years. Conan Doyle did kill off Sherlock Holmes and for a reason not unlike Ross Thomas's; he wanted to be spared having to go on writing about him. The public felt otherwise, and Sir Arthur was compelled to resuscitate his detective.

More recently, Nicholas Freeling shocked a large readership by slaying Inspector Van der Valk. He was thus able to write a book in which Van der Valk's widow turns detective, and subsequently to turn to a new detective series altogether.

From a dollars and cents standpoint, killing a series character is a mistake; it has a pronounced adverse effect upon the sales of the series as a whole. I'm not interested in reading the early Van der Valk books now, much as I liked them first time around. Why? Because I don't want to waste my time reading about a dead detective.

Does that sound silly? I can't help it. And I'm not the only quirky type around. When Ben Gazzara's *Run For Your Life* show was finishing its network run, there was the question of whether the last episode would end with the death of the lead character, who had presumably been suffering from an incurable illness since the series inception. I don't remember what course they followed—I don't think I *saw* the final episode— but the argument which I think prevailed held that killing off the Gazzara character would cripple the series for syndication. Oddly, it doesn't seem to matter if an actor dies; viewers will still watch reruns forever. But kill the fictional character and the viewer's tie to that character's fortune is cut.

HAPPY ENDINGS

But there are more ways to disappoint a reader than by killing a popular character, and it's the propriety of disappointing the reader that's this column's concern. The more I read and the more I write, the clearer it becomes to me that when I pick up a book I care how it turns out. If I enjoy what I'm reading, I identify with one or more of the characters and want good things to happen to them in the end.

And it bothers me when I'm disappointed.

That means I'm a lot less sophisticated than I used to think. I'm afraid I have a great deal in common with the kid hearing a bedtime story and demanding reassurance in advance that everything will turn out all right in the end. Like that kid, I don't want bad dreams. I don't want to feel let down or betrayed. I may not demand a happy ending in the full sense of the word, but I want an ending that's emotionally satisfying to me.

A tragedy can be emotionally satisfying. *Hamlet* wouldn't work if the Danish prince went off into the sunset with a resurrected Ophelia on his arm, whistling a happy tune. But there's a difference between a tragic denouement and an ending that leaves you feeling like Charlie the Tuna.

Remember Charlie? He starred in all those commercials, and he wanted to prove he was cultured so that the Star-Kist people would chop him up and can him. Each time the hook was jerked away from him and he was rejected. "Sorry, Charlie," they told him. "Star-Kist doesn't want tuna with good taste. Star-Kist wants tuna that taste good."

> *There are more ways to disappoint a reader than by killing a popular character.*

I read a story the other day that was disappointing in a way that might prove instructive. It was called *Competition*, by David Clayton Carrad, and it ran in the June issue of *Running Times*. And it was a good story, a very well written and provocative story.

Here's the plot: Michaelson is a runner. He's been highly competitive for years until a revelatory moment when he almost ruins himself physically trying to outperform his own capacity. Now he has turned from competition altogether, avoids races, and drifts around the country running in the early morning hours for his own enjoyment. He has stopped keeping records and, in the course of the morning's run chronicled in this story, decides the next thing he's going to do is throw away his stopwatch altogether, so that he'll be able to avoid timing himself.

He has also discarded all his old race tee-shirts, and occasionally sends away for cut-price production overruns. He's wearing one of these shirts this morning, a purple one with some numbers on it that don't mean anything to him. He likes the shirt because he's crazy about the color.

He runs on a causeway that goes to an abandoned island. The causeway's closed to traffic and he's breezing along with the breeze, enjoying the run, when a van comes up behind him and hits him, brushing him to the ground. This is the first round of a duel to the death between Michaelson and the driver of the van, who drives back and forth between island and mainland, trying to kill Michaelson, who can only dodge the van each time and try to make his way over the dangerous causeway to the safety of the island.

This drama is very artfully rendered. Michaelson's struggle against the evil black van is a desperate one, and we're pulling for him to make it, to find some way to beat the driver. He tries a variety of tricks, but in the end the van runs him down and kills him.

And we cut to the driver, who returns to the mainland and gets out of the van wearing Michaelson's shirt, which had made him an unwitting competitor in this death race. The driver—a runner himself now—goes up onto the causeway in the purple shirt, and another character takes his place in the van and gets ready to drive off in pursuit.

As I said, it's a good story. It's an exciting read on the level of pure story, and it has interesting things to say about competition.

But it's also disappointing.

Because we identify overwhelmingly with Michaelson during his duel with the van. We want him to win. We care what happens to him. Fundamentally, most fiction consists of a character's attempt to solve a problem. Michaelson's problem is survival, and if the story is to be emotionally satisfying to us he must resolve this problem. We hope he'll resolve it successfully, but in any event we insist that he be the instrument of its resolution.

But that doesn't happen. He gets killed, and at that point the story's over for us and we've been let down. What follows, the explanation of the inexplicable duel and the irony of the killer's setting himself up as the next target, is interesting but not involving. Our involvement ended with Michaelson's death.

Does this mean Mr. Carrad made a mistake writing the story as he did? No, I don't think we can say that. As readers, we have the right to want stories to satisfy us in certain ways. As writers, we have the right to make those stories come out as we damn well please, whether the reader is disappointed or not. And yet a story is most effective, most enjoyable, and possessed of the most impact insofar as it satisfies the reader's hopes and expectations.

The more I write, the more I find myself trying to write the sort of thing I prefer to read. It is essential, certainly, to be true to one's own artistic vision, but if what I call my artistic vision leads me to disappoint a reader in a way to which I as reader would be inclined to object, perhaps I ought to rethink my artistic vision a bit. Perhaps what I've been pleased to regard as my integrity as a writer is more a matter of self-indulgence, or a thumb in the reader's eye. It's not so much that I have an obligation to the reader—I'm not sure that I do—but that by disappointing him I may be sabotaging my own artistic goals.

22. Midnight Oil

As I've reported previously in these pages, it seems to work best for me to make writing the first thing I do in the day. Although early in my writing career I found considerable romance in the idea of the insomniac writer burning either the midnight oil or the candle at both ends, I learned with the passage of years that I was fresher and more energetic at the beginning of the day than at its end. Newly risen from my bed, I was more in touch with my subconscious mind, more able to tap its wellsprings in my work. And too, with the day's work completed early on, I was free to do what I wished with the rest of the day, and with a clear conscience.

And I mentioned, too, that a majority of writers seemed sooner or later to come to the same conclusion. While nightwork might have its appeal early in one's career, the mature professional knew to start the day writing. If peace and quiet was important, one simply got up *before* the rest of the world instead of staying up after it.

Ahem.

For the past several weeks your correspondent has been getting up around one or two in the afternoon, diverting himself with sundry matters until midnight or one A.M., then sitting down and going to work upon the current novel-in-progress. He has been working for as long as it takes to get the day's (or, more accurately, night's) work done, which is to say until three or four or five in the ayem, whereupon he has showered, sipped a last cup of coffee, read for a while, and gone finally and gratefully to sleep somewhere around daybreak.

Now what conclusion do you draw from this? Yes, Arnold?

That you can't be trusted, sir.

You already knew that, Arnold. Edna?

That teachers tell you to do things they wouldn't dream of doing themselves.

Uh-huh. Rachel?

That you finally discovered after all these years that all along you've been doing it wrong.

What a thought. Well, for all of you who have the sort of mixed feeling of disappointment and triumph that you get when you catch your dentist sneaking a candy bar, relax. I can explain everything.

Around the first of the year, after my year-long vacation from novel-writing, I went to work on a new novel. I started off on my usual schedule, going to work immediately upon arising and keeping at it until I'd done as much as I wanted to. For the first two weeks of this, everything went beautifully, and the book leaped off to a good start.

At the beginning of the third week, I realized I'd written at such a pace as to outdistance the book's evolution in my subconscious, like a general who has outrun his own supply lines. I took a couple days off, resumed work, and got into the swing of things again.

But during all this time I was in one respect getting the work done almost in spite of myself. Because I couldn't get to sleep at night, and I kept staying awake until four or five or six in the morning. And I didn't want to get out of bed even when I did wake up, because the day would start and I would have to go to work. Accordingly I wasn't getting to work until past noon, and when I dragged myself to the typewriter earlier than that I was too groggy to write well, and on top of everything I had a conflict between my writing and my seminar business.

The seminars were not to start until spring, but there was no end of detail work to be handled beforehand, bookings to be made, mail to be dealt with, phone calls to be placed and answered. All of this had to happen during business hours, and my day was such that business hours were devoted half to sleep and half to writing. My novel, which I knew had to be given first priority, was turning into something I had to get out of the way as quickly as possible so that I could deal with other matters.

Well, that's no way to write anything.

And believe me, it was taking its toll. I was tired when I finished my work at the typewriter, too tired to be delighted with the prospect of making business decisions and negotiating with some hotel's catering manager and putting tracers on UPS shipments. For all that I worked with the affirmation *Writing is easy and fun for me*, it felt increasingly difficult and unpleasant and left me utterly drained afterward. Then, hours later, I would lie in bed trying to go to sleep—and then, finally, my mind would buzz with plot ideas and scenes and characters, and I could no more fall easily asleep than I could flap my arms and fly.

So I figured what did I have to lose, and I switched my schedule around, and guess what?

Worked like a charm.

I sit down at my desk at midnight or a little after, proof the previous night's work, and have at it. I don't feel pressured to hurry through my writing because there's nothing I have to do after I'm done. I can take my time and enjoy it, and when I'm done and the effort of the writing has left me drained and tired, I can rejoice in the knowledge that drained and tired is a perfectly appropriate way to feel when you're getting ready for bed.

And, when I'm up and about, I can lend myself wholeheartedly to business affairs, or to social life, or to whatever I want, knowing that I'm not shirking my top priority of the novel. It will get its scheduled turn after midnight. Meanwhile, the day is free for other pursuits.

U ltimately rigidity is the enemy, and . . . one must remain flexible in order to thrive.

I was talking about this the other day with a writer friend, and he observed that the most fruitful stretches of writing he ever did were when he kept to a similar schedule, going to work about the time that the rest of his family went to bed. There were, he said, just two considerations that kept him from employing the same schedule now. One was social, in that a more conventional schedule makes him more available to other people. The other, he said candidly, was alcohol; he knew better than to write after even one or two drinks, and since he more often than not had something to drink during the day or evening, night writing didn't work for him.

Since I don't drink anymore, the latter is not a consideration for me. I seem to have plenty of time for social contact in the evenings before it's time to start work. Sooner or later the pattern of working while the world sleeps might leave me feeling isolated, but it is my custom to write books in fairly intensive periods of activity and to take extended periods of time off between them, during which time I'll surely revert to a more conventional schedule. By the time seminar season starts in earnest, I'll be getting up in the morning and going to bed at night, just like everybody else.

And what of the work? Is my mind less fresh at the tail end of the day, and is my work accordingly less inspired? I can't tell just yet; I'm the person who's writing it, after all, and my opinions, favorable or otherwise, are not to be trusted. I know that I've taken a night off here and there because, when midnight came, my mind felt too tired to be capable of my best work. But those nights have been infrequent, and the rest of the time any impairment in my mental function has passed unnoticed by me.

SOLVING PROBLEMS

Well, what's the point of all this? Is he telling us he was wrong, that morning's not the best time to write? What exactly is he driving at?

Simply this—that ultimately rigidity is the enemy, and that one must remain flexible in order to thrive. How any writer schedules his time is a personal matter best resolved through a consideration of personal preferences and personal circumstances. What's important is that he recognize that none of the decisions he makes about writing habits is etched in tablets of stone. It's all subject to change.

Ultimately, any writer is a problem-solver. The lead character's problem is the core of the typical novel, and figuring out how it will or will not be solved is one of the writer's chief jobs. Plotting is largely a matter of the mind's throwing up one possible development after another. One sifts these alternatives, selects what will work, and runs with it.

If it works, they say, don't fix it. For quite a few years a particular writing schedule worked for me, and so I left it unchanged. That was all to the good, but the attendant risk lay in the possibility that I would think that what worked was the only thing that could work, that if I did not make writing the day's first activity I could not write at all.

It's so easy to let this sort of living rigor mortis set in. If one thing works for us, and works well, we think that nothing else will work in its stead, that we'd be lost without it. I have long made this assumption about the typewriter. While I had proved to my satisfaction that I could write anywhere, and under all manner of conditions, I did need, I used to say, a typewriter and a flat surface to rest it on. (My particular typewriter demands an electrical socket as well, but I've never doubted that I could perform once again on a manual if I had to.)

Two years or so ago I was in Manhattan and my typewriter was in Brooklyn, and I felt like writing this column. (Well, no. Not this column, not the one you're reading. The one that was in this magazine two years ago. You did know what I meant, didn't you?) I bought a spiral notebook and went to a coffee shop, and a couple hours later I had my column written. I had to retype it if I expected it to be read by anybody other than myself, but it was written, and it was sort of fun writing it that way. I've repeated the process several times since, when I did have access to a typewriter, because writing by hand seems to suit me when I'm writing short nonfiction, especially if I'm not all that certain at the start how I'm going to order my thoughts. It's easy to cross things out, move things around, and otherwise keep the thing loose when I'm scribbling in a notebook.

I can't remember if I've ever written fiction that way. I wouldn't want to try a novel like that, but you know something? It might be fun to write a short story that way. One of these days I'll have to try it.

And what time is it now, sir?
Now? Ahem. Well, it's 3:09, Arnold.
In the morning, sir?
Uh, no. It's 3:09 in the afternoon.
Does that mean you've been writing this column for the past fifteen hours, sir?
Uh, no, Rachel, it doesn't. I woke up four hours ago, and after breakfast I realized that I felt like writing this column. And it was Sunday, so there was no seminar business to contend with, and Lynne was still sleeping, and I didn't have anything special to do until six, and I thought sitting down at the old typewriter and batting this out might be easy and fun for me.

And so it was. See how it works?

PART THREE

Spider Love
The Inner Game of Fiction

W hen the male matures considerable effort is put forth in locating the female; which means in the case of snare-building species that it now becomes a wanderer like the hunting spiders. When the female is approached certain preliminaries are usually engaged in before mating takes place. As a rule, in the web-building species the male signals by tweaking the threads of the female's snare. In addition there may be movements of palpi and abdomen, a sort of dance that varies slightly with the species. It is in the wandering spiders that courtship is most marked. This is particularly true of those families with relatively keen eyesight. Here the males may dance before the females, wave their palpi, or legs, or both, and strike peculiar attitudes. It has been assumed that all this serves to gain recognition by the female, as well as to stimulate her. The male's behavior eventually leads to a lulling of the female's normal instinct to consider him as a possible morsel to be eaten and she submits to his advances, subdued by the ardor of the sexual impulse. . . . It is a popular misconception that the male is always killed by the female after the mating act is over. Actually, in only a very few species can this be considered the general rule.

—*B.J. Kaston & Elizabeth Kaston*
How to Know the Spiders

23. *The Beginner's Mind*

A point frequently stressed in books about writing is the need for the new writer to become professional as quickly as possible. This business of turning pro has less to do with throwing up one's job and becoming self-supporting through one's writing than it does with matters of behavior and attitude. We turn professional by becoming professional in our work habits, by being self-disciplined and productive, by using our time and energy to our best advantage. As important, we turn pro by developing the assurance and self-confidence of the professional writer.

I wouldn't dream of decrying the value of professional work habits or a professional attitude. But I think it is at least as important for us to remain forever beginners, retaining the beginner's capacity for growth and development.

Because, while assurance and self-confidence are unquestionably assets, arrogance is a towering liability. And it's very easy for us to bind ourselves up with arrogance in the belief that we need it if we are to survive.

It's not hard to see why. After all, what could be a more arrogant act than to sit down at a typewriter spinning out imaginary stories about imaginary people, sustained in one's task by the belief that utter strangers will voluntarily spend their time reading what we have written, and will actually go so far as to care what happens to these imaginary people?

The whole process of writing, and of breaking into print, generally involves armoring oneself against one's own doubts and the world's rejections. It's very natural for this armor to calcify into arrogance. And there's nothing like a little success to hurry this process. "I've been published," we tell ourselves. "I've been paid for my writing. I'm a professional. I'm not an amateur anymore. I don't have to learn anything, because I already know it all."

I can see some of the ways this operated in my own career. When I was first starting to write, I read *Writer's Digest* with fair regularity. (Yes, the magazine was published way back then. You could find it on the newsstand between *Colonial Times* and *Poor*

Richard's Almanac.) Then, once I started selling a few stories to the cent-a-word crime pulps, I stopped reading *WD*. After all, I was a pro now. And *WD* was for people who were trying to be what I already was.

Now who was I kidding? Obviously, I hadn't learned all there was to learn about writing. And I realized that. I knew that I had a great deal to learn, and regarded my own writing as very much a part of the learning process. Similarly, I saw myself as educating myself whenever I read other writers' fiction. But I resisted the idea of learning by reading what somebody else had to say on the subject of writing; that put me altogether too close for comfort to the role of student or apprentice, and such a role threatened my image of myself as a professional writer.

At first glance, this arrogance may look like self-esteem. Actually it's just the opposite; we manifest arrogance in order to hide our lack of self-esteem.

I've seen this operating in my travels in the past few years. At writers' conferences, I've noted the extent to which instructors seek to differentiate themselves from the writers in attendance, as if it's important that everyone (their own selves included) realize that they're here to teach, not to learn. When staffers do attend one another's lectures, they often take pains to distinguish themselves from the rest of the audience, showing up late, making a point of chatting about extraneous topics with the lecturer, and making it clear that they're only on hand to catch a fellow performer's act, not (God forbid) to pick up something useful.

At my "Write For Your Life" seminar, I've seen arrogance in one form or another limit some people's participation—after they've paid good money to come. And, at the same time, I've seen other writers whose high self-esteem has enabled them to be more completely open to what the seminar has to offer.

The seminar in New York in March of '84 was an excellent case in point. One of the early exercises is an automatic writing process. I supply an opening line for the group, and everyone writes nonstop for ten minutes; the process helps free up everyone's creative flow for what comes next in the seminar, and it's a very valuable technique in and of itself, and very effective in this sort of group situation.

At this particular seminar, one woman in the middle of the room just sat there and didn't write a word. After a few minutes I thought she might be upset or confused and went over to ask her if there was a reason why she wasn't doing the process. She replied that it was too basic and fundamental, that she had done this sort of thing years ago, and that she didn't need to do it. Afterward, during the sharing, she repeated this assertion and informed the group that she was too advanced for this sort of beginner stuff, that she was a published writer.

Just out of curiosity, I asked for a show of hands: how many of our trainees that day had been published? A majority of the hands in the room went up. (Actually, that's inaccurate. A majority of the people in the room raised their hands, but they only raised one hand apiece, so a minority of the total hands went up. Oh, never mind.) "I'm a real writer," the woman protested, implying that her colleagues had published nothing more impressive than a classified ad in a local pennysaver. "I've had a book published!"

I didn't ask how many of the rest had had books published, although I knew of several. But I may have smiled, because one of the writers in attendance had appeared on the fiction

> *Writing generally involves armoring oneself against one's own doubts and the world's rejections.*

bestseller list a couple of times, and he'd participated wholeheartedly in the automatic writing process, and indeed in all of the seminar. His self-esteem was sufficiently high that he didn't have to prove anything to himself or to the rest of us; consequently, he was available to whatever benefit the seminar might have to offer him.

At that same seminar, another trainee was my friend Bob Mandel, who has himself been an extremely successful seminar leader in the field of personal growth. I was afraid to have Bob in the room, sure that he'd sit there in judgment, sure that I'd be so self-conscious with him present that I'd have trouble making the seminar work for everyone. But Bob came to the seminar not to compare my teaching with his, not to reassure himself that he already knew everything he needed to know, but to get the maximum out of the day for himself. He participated eagerly in every process, raised his hand to share at every opportunity, and displayed throughout what Zen Buddhists call the beginner's mind. He not only did the automatic writing but went home and did it for ten minutes every day for the next month. After a long period of being unable to complete anything, he wrote and published two books within a year. I mention this not to suggest that my seminar was wonderful, but that Bob was a wonderful student—because of his ability to get his ego out of the way and be completely open to the day's experience.

If it's arrogance that so often prevents us from approaching writing with the beginner's mind, the source of that arrogance is almost invariably fear, the self-centered fear that we will appear worthless if we let the world know we still have something to learn. A mystery writer who took my seminar in Minneapolis confessed that he'd had trouble working up the courage to come; he himself had recently participated in a symposium, and he was afraid what members of his audience might think if they encountered him on the other side of the lectern. I can understand his fear easily enough. I've felt much the same thing myself on similar occasions.

As I said, I myself stopped reading writing magazines when I started publishing my own stories. I resumed reading *WD* some years later when I started writing this column, and of course I read each issue cover-to-cover. It's hard now to believe that I willfully denied myself such a useful tool for so many years.

I handicapped myself in other ways through the same sort of fear-based arrogance. I published mystery and suspense fiction for over fifteen years before I got around to joining Mystery Writers of America. I wanted to belong to the organization, but I was waiting for an invitation. Through some oversight or other I didn't get an invitation, and I was damned if I'd actively seek membership. (Perhaps I was afraid it would be denied to me.) When I did finally join MWA, I realized I had deprived myself of the pleasures and benefits of membership for reasons of ego and nothing else.

I still have trouble reading how-to-write books, perhaps out of fear that I'll find out I've been doing it wrong all these years. But I try to attend other writers' talks at conferences, not just to "catch their act" but to learn what they have to teach me. And I'm looking forward this season to taking "Write For Your Life" myself. Roy Sorrels and Donna Meyer will be leading half the seminars, and at least once I want to be in the audience—not to see how they're doing, but to see what I can get out of the experience. A couple of times this past spring they led sections of the seminar, and at first I distanced myself by focusing on how they were doing. In Minneapolis, however, I let myself participate wholeheartedly in the character-creation process while they were leading it, and by so doing I learned a great deal about myself and about that particular process. I expect it will be quite a confrontation for my ego, trying to forget while I take the seminar that I created the thing in the first place, but my original motive was to produce the sort of seminar I myself would like to take, and I hope I'll be able to develop enough of a beginner's mind to do just that.

What would you do differently—if you had a beginner's

mind? What don't you do because you're too far advanced for it? What would you like to do that you pass up for fear of what people would think of you?

These are good questions to ask yourself, and the answers may suggest actions for you to take. The minute I stop learning, I immediately stop growing as a writer. That never has to happen—but it will as soon as I let myself believe I already know it all.

24. *Apples and Oranges*

The other night my friend Roy Sorrels told me he'd been depressed. He had met Carolyn Wheat a week or two previously, and her first novel had just come out in paperback, and a few days ago he'd read it, and ever since then he hadn't been feeling too hot.

"Oh?" I said, or words to that effect. "You didn't like it?"

"I thought it was terrific," he said. "That was the trouble."

The book in question, *Dead Man's Thoughts,* is indeed a fine piece of work and was nominated for an Edgar Allan Poe award as Best First Novel of the year. Carolyn is a fine writer. And so, for that matter, is Roy, the published author of several novels and short fiction and a very capable and thoughtful instructor in Writer's Digest School.

So what was the problem?

"I read her book," he said, "and I was struck by how good it was, and how well she brought it off, and I thought that I could never have done what she did there, and this is only her first novel, and I felt, well, fraudulent. Inadequate."

Uh-huh.

"I can handle it when I have that reaction to the work of somebody who's been writing since the Boer War, somebody with a dozen books on the shelf. But Carolyn's had less writing experience than I have and her book was so good, and, well—"

Uh-huh.

I know the feeling. I have it all the time.

If you're looking for a way to make yourself feel hopeless, I don't know of a better way than to compare yourself with another writer. It's just about foolproof. All I have to do to induce depression is to read any book I find admirable and focus on the fact that I couldn't have written it. In no time at all I'm ready to stick my head in the oven, and that's not a great idea; those microwaves can't be good for you.

Of *course* Roy couldn't have written *Dead Man's Thoughts.* Neither could I. It was Carolyn's book to write, and she did so, and quite capably indeed. Why should I flagellate myself for my inability to have written someone else's book? It's remarkable enough that I can occasionally write my own.

When you compare yourself to another writer, you're just comparing apples and oranges, and—what is it, Arnold?

Why apples and oranges, sir?
It's just an expression, Arnold.
I mean why not apples and pears, sir? Or oranges and lemons?
Either would be fine, Arnold, and—what is it, Rachel?
It has to be apples and oranges, sir. Apples and pears is Cockney rhyming slang for stairs, and oranges and lemons is what the bells of St. Clement's say. In the nursery rhyme, sir.
Oh.
So it has to be apples and oranges, sir.

I'm glad you explained that, Rachel. Because the only thing demonstrably sillier than this conversation is comparing oneself to another writer.

Any book I like well enough to read clear through to the end can—if I let it—convince me of nothing so much as my own inadequacy. One writer will tell stories with more complicated plots than mine. Another will create characters that mirror a reality I don't find reflected in my own work. Someone else will create suspense that has me glued to the page, and my own scenes will strike me as rather suspenseless in comparison. Still another writer will write in a clean flat style alongside of which my work seems flabby and flowery, while the next book I read may be couched in such eloquent prose that it makes my stuff look less like writing than typing.

I can even wind up telling myself that I'm writing the wrong books altogether. I can look at what someone else has done and decide that's the sort of thing I should have been doing all along, that my books cover too brief a span of time, that they lack a sense of history, that they exist without a social context, that . . .

Astonishing, isn't it? Simple admiration for a piece of writing it would never have occurred to me to undertake can lead me to invalidate my own work altogether.

And there's no point to this sort of invalidation. It doesn't make me a better writer. It doesn't make me more aware of my own options. All it does is make me feel worse about myself and my work—which in turn makes me less inclined to do work in the first place and less confident of my work when I do manage to get it done.

Most of us manage to be somewhat selective in our self-invalidation-by-comparison. Roy, for example, was vulnerable in this particular instance because the book he admired was a first novel, not the work of an established master. Similarly, I once knew a science fiction writer who was able to read work he regarded as "better" than his own with equanimity—as long as the admired writer was older than he. "I can make an exception for Chip Delaney," he told me. "He's younger than I am, but he's a genius, so that's different. But when I read somebody who writes better than me and it turns out he's younger, too, man, that really burns me."

It's a problem, too, that would seem likely to get worse instead of better with the passage of time. Because every year will see a higher percentage of writers younger than oneself. I hope the fellow has changed his attitude since we had this conversation; otherwise his choices would seem to be limited to hating everything he reads, hating himself, or labeling everybody a genius.

A ll writers are one of a kind.

Comparison works in a couple of ways. First, it allows me to confirm any doubts, fears, and negative feelings I have about my work and myself as a writer. If I'm personally committed to the notion that I'm not good enough, everything good in another person's work can strike me as proof of that initial presumption.

At the same time, comparing my work to another's can be based on the perception that I am locked in competition with every other writer on the planet, that I gain at their expense and they at mine, that we're all fighting for crumbs at a zero-sum table where every person's victory is someone else's loss. "Every time a friend succeeds," a major contemporary writer is supposed to have said, "I die a little." Writers are generally less given to this view of the world than are some of our fellow artists. Actors in particular are apt to see themselves as competing one with another; several actors will find themselves up for a particular part, and one will get it while the others will not. It doesn't happen quite that way with writers. Our books are published or not more on their own merits than because they have been weighed against a competing manuscript. Once published, the readers do or do not buy them because they do or do not want to read them.

Still, we can perceive the writing world as ruthlessly competitive if we so choose. At my seminars, there's often a person or two in attendance who identifies his greatest problem as the competition he faces. A look at the submission statistics for some of the top magazines—thousands of stories offered every month, a handful pur-chased—can easily reinforce this conviction.

The writer who sees the world this way virtually guarantees himself a lifetime of dissatisfaction. Reading quickly ceases to be a pleasure; the only books that don't induce anxiety and despair will be those he actively dislikes. And success itself will be joyless, be-cause anyone else's success at once looms as a threat to it.

I know a writer, one of the most successful novelists in Ameri-ca today. He called another writer of his acquaintance to boast about the contract he'd just signed and the advance he was getting. The other writer responded by telling him the contract *he* had just signed, the advance *he* was getting. My friend yanked the phone out of the wall, threw it across the room, went into his office and closed the door and wouldn't talk to anybody for the rest of the day.

What's the point of success if it leaves one forced to deny an-other's accomplishments or feeling wretched over them? Where's the joy in it? There are a few thoughts which, if internalized, can straighten out the comparison-competition tangle. Here are some which might be worth pondering:

All writers are one of a kind. Apples, oranges, lemons, pears, persimmons, pawpaws—writers are not to be compared with one another. Our writings reflect our selves and our individual worlds. I can't write someone else's book and no one else can write mine. As a matter of fact, my books aren't even in competition with one anoth-er; they were created at different times out of different parts of my-self. I may like one of my books more than another, and so may oth-er people, but that's just taste, for heaven's sake.

Successful writers are an inspiration. When another writer achieves something, I can extend my realization of what exists to be achieved. I can be grateful for the success I have already attained in various areas and the possibilities that lie open to me. I gain when-ever another writer succeeds.

I can learn something from everything I read. The strengths that I perceive in another person's work are not evidence of my own weakness. They help me find ways to do my own best work, rather than indict me for my failure to do someone else's work. They point out not my own limitations but my infinite potential.

Roy Sorrels is an excellent writer. I don't doubt for a moment that he'll be an even better writer for having read Carolyn Wheat's book. And I'll be better for having read—and known—them both.

That's how it works.

25. Keeping Up with Yesterday

Good morning, boys and girls.

Good morning, sir.

This morning I'd like to say a few words on the subject of procrastination. As a matter of fact, I've been meaning to talk with you about procrastination for some time now, but for some unfathomable reason I keep putting it off.

Did you say something, Arnold?

No, sir.

I could have sworn—yes, Mimi?

He said, "The old boy actually expects to get a laugh out of us with that one," sir.

Thank you, Mimi. I don't know that I expected a laugh, Arnold. A chuckle, perhaps, or a knowing smile. I just thought that a touch of levity might be an appropriate introduction to what is unquestionably a Serious Subject. And procrastination is definitely that. A great many writers, beginners and veterans alike, writers at all levels on the success ladder, believe procrastination is their greatest problem.

Yes, Rachel?

Haven't you spoken to us about procrastination before, sir? And didn't you say it was a good thing?

What a wonderful memory you have, Rachel. Some years ago I wrote a column entitled "Creative Procrastination," which was subsequently collected in *Telling Lies For Fun & Profit*. My argument there was that sometimes we are well advised to put off a writing project until such time as we are genuinely ready to write it. By waiting we allow our subconscious minds to play with the plot elements and work things out, and we may wind up writing a better story that way than if we rush to the typewriter the minute we get the glimmer of an idea.

That's a special form of procrastination, Rachel, and it's a far cry removed from what I'd like to talk about today. It's a positive element of the creative process, while procrastination in general shuts the door on the creative process altogether by keeping us from doing the work we want to do. Procrastination leads us to postpone our writing and to despise ourselves for so doing, and, as I've said, many of us think it's our biggest writing problem.

We're wrong, of course.

We are?

Absolutely. Procrastination is not a problem. It's the result of a problem.

Most of us don't recognize this. We mistake the effect for the cause, see that we are indeed procrastinating, and decide that what we have to do is meet the problem head on. The way to combat procrastination, obviously enough, is to stop procrastinating. Sit down at the typewriter, unplug the phone, bar the door, padlock the refrigerator, and just plain Get Down To It.

This doesn't usually work. Or, if it does work, it only works for a little while. Then it stops working, and we return to the habit of procrastination, convinced that we're really rotten and lazy people after all, and that the difficulty we're having reveals a profound defect of character.

Writers often come to my "Write For Your Life" seminar convinced that procrastination is their chief problem. Because they know that the seminar is inspirational and motivational in nature, they may expect a combination of a pep talk and a tongue-lashing. "I want you to make me write," some of them are apt to say. At the point in the seminar where we try to zero in on our biggest obstacles to writing success, they'll point to their laziness or inactivity or procrastination. And I'll explain that it's invariably a symptom, a result, an effect.

If you were to line up half a dozen writers, each convinced his or her biggest problem is procrastination, you would very likely discover that each procrastinated for a different reason. And each reason, one way or another, would translate into fear.

Suppose, for example, that you believe success would separate you from the people you love. This is a common enough belief among writers, and we've especially found it present in women who fear that success with their writing would cause a rift in their marriage or distance them from their children. Beliefs of this sort often operate on a subconscious level; our conscious mind knows better, but on a deeper level we maintain allegiance to the belief.

How can we protect ourselves from the pain of broken relationships? By making sure we don't succeed. And how can we guarantee this? There are any number of terrific ways—by writing poorly, by not sending our stuff out, by sending it to the wrong markets—but one of the most popular consists of not getting it written in the first place. As long as we can put off writing the stuff, we can postpone the danger of success indefinitely.

Suppose, on the other hand, that you have the deep-seated belief that you're just not good enough. On the one hand you're looking to writing to prove that you are too good enough, but on the other hand you're afraid. If you really make the effort, and if the world throws it all back in your face, then you'll discover that your deepest fear was true all along, that you're really not good enough.

And how can you guard against such an unwelcome and possibly devastating discovery? By not running the risk. By not writing anything. If you don't write it, they can't reject it. (You'll feel even worse this way, because your mind will assure you that you're not even good enough to write the damn thing, but that kind of self-abuse somehow feels safer than taking chances.)

*P*rocrastination *is not a problem. It's the result of a problem.*

Suppose you're afraid to let people know you? This is a very common fear among writers, and indeed among artists of all sorts. For one reason or another we believe that it's not safe to let people know who we are, that if they really know our inner selves they'll dislike us or disapprove of us. We may have selected writing in the first place as a way to win approval of our innermost selves, but this fear keeps us from baring ourselves artistically.

Some people with a strong dose of this particular belief get their work done, but they sabotage themselves by keeping their own selves out of their work. Others may put themselves into their work but avoid marketing their work effectively, or one way or another manage to produce work that will not be published or widely read. Finally, some of us simply put off the act of writing; as in our previous examples, if we don't do the writing, we won't have to face what we're really afraid of.

So what's the answer? Self-discipline? If we just force ourselves to write, won't that straighten things out?

Forget it.

Now there's a lot to be said for a disciplined approach to one's writing. Giving writing priority, scheduling time for it, and managing that time efficiently—these are important. But they won't turn a procrastinator into a productive writer.

In my experience, self-discipline is the most overrated commodity on the market. It rarely works in a meaningful way and it never works for very long. If I've been using procrastination as a way to avoid confronting a fear, and if I literally force myself to write, I'll simply find some other way to avoid facing that fear. It's like stuffing a psychic bulge into a girdle; it'll just pop out someplace else.

Suppose I'm convinced people don't want to hear what I have to say. Suppose I've been procrastinating for fear of confirming this belief by writing something nobody wants to read. And suppose that, by virtue of some sort of mental jiu-jitsu, I'm able to manipulate myself into overcoming my habit of procrastination and literally force myself to turn the work out.

Then what happens?

In all likelihood, I'll just succeed in fulfilling my fear—I'll produce something that nobody wants to read. A part of our mind is sufficiently committed to our negative beliefs to work to prove them out. Or I may sabotage the marketing process by invariably submitting my work to people who won't want to read it. I probably won't have to do this for very long, however, because it will be very easy for me to drift back into the pattern of self-sabotage that served me so well in the past. I'll resume procrastination, and it will once again work for me as well as ever.

Yes, Rachel?

Sir, it sounds hopeless. You're saying that even if we make ourselves write, we'll be just as bad off as if we don't. Is there no answer, sir?

If there weren't an answer, Rachel, I wouldn't have encouraged you to ask the question.

The answer consists not in *making* ourselves write but in *allowing* ourselves to write. If we can do something about the belief that has led us to procrastinate in the first place, it will become easy and pleasurable for us to write. After all, writing is a natural state for writers. It's not a punishment, and there's no reason it has to feel like one.

How do we manage this?

First of all, by having the courage to find out what our fears are. I've written about fear elsewhere and there's a lengthy discussion of fear and how to overcome it in the book version of *Write For Your Life*. When you're not getting anywhere with a piece of writing, when you don't seem to be able to find the time to work on it or to make good use of the time you find, sit down with a pencil and paper and make two lists. First, write down all your fears about that particular project. Then write down all your fears about writing in general.

Be very freewheeling when you write these lists. If you can't think of any fears, that just means you're afraid to let yourself know what they are. Ask yourself, "If I did have a fear, what would it be?" And write it down. If you still can't think of any, make some up. And write them down.

Sometimes simple recognition of a fear will disempower it. I once almost failed to fulfill a book contract because I was afraid I couldn't write that particular book satisfactorily; the fear was irrational in a particularly obvious way, and once I came in touch with the fact that I was afraid (because the fear had operated at an exclusively unconscious level) I was able to dismiss the fear out of hand and write the book with no problem at all.

Other times it takes more work. We have to change our negative thoughts in order to allow our writing to flow. But the whole process has to begin with recognition of the fear, and the underlying negative thought.

In the same vein, boys and girls, here's an assignment for all of you. If you've got a piece of work you've been putting off, sit down and write out a list of everything you stand to gain by *not* doing the work. Some of these benefits will be negative in nature ("I don't have to get rejection slips") while others will be positive ("I can watch *As The World Turns* instead"). Like the other process, this is a way of finding out what the benefits of procrastination are for you, and you have to eliminate the benefits if you're going to convince your subconscious mind that procrastination is not the best course to take. Yes, Arnold?

Would it be all right if I started the list tomorrow, sir?
Do it now, Arnold. Now. Force yourself.

26. *Staying Loose*

Writing is a natural state for writers.

Does that have a familiar ring to it? Don't chalk it up to *deja vu*. You actually have read that sentence before, right here in this space, in a long-planned column on procrastination which I finally got around to writing two months ago. I was holding that procrastination was not a nasty little habit or the sign of a profound defect of character but the outgrowth of some sort of mental impediment to action. In the absence of such impediments, we write. It is normal and natural for us to do so.

At the time that I wrote that sentence which begins this column, at the time that the words flowed from my typewriter like, uh, like . . .

Like water from a cleft rock, sir?

Thank you, Arnold. Like water from a cleft rock. As the words flowed, it came to me that I might have further observations to make on that particular notion. Because, for many of us, writing doesn't seem natural and it doesn't feel natural and it doesn't come naturally. We have to work at it, and we may even think that the more we work at it the better it will be.

I think that's where we frequently make trouble for ourselves. The more we work at our writing, the more labored it becomes. When we fail to stay loose, our writing stiffens up. We take what ought to come naturally and make of it something artificial and unnatural, and our writing suffers for it.

Some seven or eight years ago I was walking home after an hour or so of reading in a coffee house. I was lost in thought and paying insufficient attention to where I was walking, and I tripped over something on the sidewalk. My hands were plunged deep in my pockets—it was a cold night—and I didn't yank them out in time to break the fall. I gashed my forehead and went over to the emergency room at St. Vincent's, where they stitched me up again. For a while I had a lump on my forehead the size of a duck's egg. (All I have left now is a stellate scar which, I trust, lends me an air of mystery and romance.)

The point of this is that, for the next five days or so, I had trouble walking. My sense of balance was unaffected and my limbs unimpaired, but my confidence was shattered. Walking was something I had at that time been able to take for granted for four decades. I never had to think about it. It seemed to me that all you had to do was remember to alternate feet, and I seemed to manage that well enough, and that was that.

Now, for the first time in a long time, I found myself thinking about walking. When it came time to negotiate a curb, I couldn't avoid figuring out exactly where I would place my foot, and how I would put weight on one foot before transferring it to the other. I saw right away that this was making things more rather than less difficult, and I tried to stop, but I couldn't. I had gotten into trouble taking walking for granted, and now I was damned well going to be careful about it.

By being careful and deliberate about it, by not taking the process for granted, I was inescapably awkward. I didn't fall down, but I came close. Gradually the days passed, and the shock of having fallen the first time wore off, and I was once again able to walk without thinking about it. I was able to take it for granted. I was able to walk not deliberately but naturally.

We all start out as natural writers because we all learned first to talk, and learned that naturally. In a sense, writing is just talking on paper. We are apt to craft and shape our writing more than our conversation, perhaps in part because we don't have body language and inflection available to help us get our point across in writing. And we are more apt to allow ourselves grammatical lapses in conversation than in print. Our words are in a more permanent form when we've written them down, so it is to be expected we are a shade more formal when we are writing.

All too often, however, we do more than clean up our grammar when we take a pen in hand.

We tighten up.

We realize that we're writing, that we're performing a difficult and dangerous act, and instead of just doing it we find ourselves thinking about it. We calculate the distance to the curb and try to figure out just where we'll place our foot, and immediately we've gone stiff and awkward.

Years ago I received a manuscript from a sort of cousin of mine. Several members of the family had remarked that he'd written the most wonderful letters home when he'd served in the Army. Now he had written a short story, and I read it, and it was terrible.

Reading it, you wouldn't have thought the man could write his name in the dirt with a stick, let alone anything that anyone could read with pleasure.

At the time, I figured that his letters hadn't been all that great either, that his relatives had loved him and were thrilled to hear from him, and that their feelings led them to think his letters were better than they were. Now, thinking back, I'm not so sure. I'm perfectly willing to believe now that my cousin's letters were excellent ones, well-written and amusing and entertaining. Because all he'd been trying to do at the time was write a letter, and he could perform that sort of natural act without tensing up. He could simply put on the page what was in his mind—and, since he had a good mind, it was a simple matter for him to write a good letter.

F *or a writer, learning is an endless process.*

Then, when he decided to write a story, he had to think about what he was doing. He wasn't just putting the thoughts in his head on the page in front of him. He was Doing Something Serious. He was Writing Fiction.

As a result, what he wrote came out stilted. The spontaneity was leached out of it, replaced by awkwardness and self-consciousness.

I don't know what made him decide to write a story. Perhaps he'd had a story in mind and wanted to get it out. Perhaps he'd simply wanted to write something. It doesn't matter. Whatever his motive, he'd sabotaged it by not writing naturally.

Some time ago William F. Buckley wrote a piece in the *New York Times Book Review* in reply to a critic who had called him to task for, among other things, occasionally writing his newspaper column in twenty minutes flat. (I clip these things and I put them somewhere, knowing someday I'll want to refer to them, and they disappear. I *think* it was twenty minutes. If I'm wrong, don't tell me.)

Mr. Buckley took exception to the implicit assumption that a piece of writing is estimable in proportion to the amount of time devoted to its composition, and that anything written quickly must perforce be worthless. He pointed out that, when one knows what it is one wants to say, it is perfectly natural to write it quickly rather than slowly. The mind, he argued, is capable of moving that fast;

any number of people routinely speak extemporaneously, and do so at a faster pace than anyone might type a column. If we are not astonished that people can speak, why should we be astonished that they can write rapidly?

I was particularly delighted to see Mr. Buckley speaking up for fast writing, as one could hardly point to him as an exemplar of slipshod grammar or diction. Indeed, the man would appear to have practiced lexicophagy from an early age. His erudition notwithstanding, Mr. Buckley writes naturally, even as he speaks naturally; thus he is able to do it quickly, and with some ease.

My own writing is best when it flows, worst when it must be worked at. This is not to say that there is no craft involved in what I do, or that there is little I have had to learn over the years. I have spent years learning what does or does not work on the page, and I continue to learn more every time I read or write something. For a writer, learning is an endless process, and that is one of the reasons why we have the opportunity to get better and better at what we do.

This sort of learning, however, is ultimately internalized. When I have truly learned something, I don't have to think about it. I perform it automatically. I can take it for granted.

I think this is why the very best time I spend at the typewriter feels virtually effortless. My fingers fly over the keys. The words come as quickly as I can transcribe them, automatically punctuating themselves and organizing themselves into paragraphs. I don't know that it is proper to describe the process as effortless, as I am generally drained and exhausted after a stint of this sort of writing. Some mental muscles have obviously been used, or they wouldn't be tired. It may be more accurate to say that such writing is without *conscious* effort.

If my conscious mind gets in the way, picking at the writing, worrying it as a dog with a bone, I don't allow the writing to flow. I think about writing, and it's about as useful as when I found myself thinking about walking.

I should point out that most of the time my writing fits somewhere between the two extremes. Now and then it does flow like water from a cleft rock, and now and then it spurts like blood from a turnip, but most of the time it flows and stops, flows and stops, as if some mischievous small boy is mucking about with the garden hose. Sometimes I have to go into the other room and lay out a hand of solitaire in order to nudge the conscious mind out of the way and let the flow resume. Other times I can stay at the typewriter and wait a minute or two.

There are ways to make writing more natural.

Many of us find them without looking for them. Typically our sentences are stilted and self-conscious when we start out as writers. They smooth out as we keep at it. We grow more comfortable with what we are doing, we learn to take the process somewhat for granted, and much of that awkwardness goes away. It is not so much that we learn how to write as that we learn to trust ourselves.

Automatic writing is a wonderful way to allow writing to be a natural process. By writing without pause, by putting words on the page as quickly as we can move the pen, we learn to bypass that part of the conscious mind that wants to pinch the garden hose and cut off the creative flow. I've written at some length about this process in *WD* and in *Write For Your Life*, so I won't describe it here beyond saying that, as long as the pen is moving, you're doing the process correctly.

At the same time, it's important to get past the delusion that writing has to be difficult to do if it's going to be worthwhile. So many quotes from famous writers stress how hard the whole business is that we often assume it has to be that way. If it flows, we don't trust it. Some of us who are blessed with a naturally lucid and limpid prose style labor to make our sentences more convoluted and difficult; we have bought into the idea that a clear style is no style at all, and that writing which is easy to write and easy to read is inconsequential and immaterial.

Writing is a natural process and we do it best by doing it most naturally. It's okay to let it come easy.

It's even acceptable to enjoy it.

27. Goal Tending

What do you want to accomplish as a writer? What do you want to write, and what sort of reception do you want your work to be given? What and where do you want to publish? How much money do you want to make?

Or, to state it as one might were one not in the habit of being paid by the word, what are your goals?

Maybe your answer is that the sky's the limit. You want to write a major bestseller in the next three months, you want a mighty river of words to stream from your pen, you want your book to sit atop the bestseller list for fifty-one weeks, and then to go through twenty-two paperback printings after having been snapped up in a spirited subrights auction for a hearty seven-figure price. You want a film studio to pay a comparably respectful sum for movie rights, you want Robert Redford or Jane Fonda to play the character patterned upon your adorable self, and you want to write the screenplay and, in the course of time, collect an Oscar for your contribution. Meanwhile you want to work the tube mightily, topping Johnny's one-liners on the "Tonight Show," going heart-to-heart with Merv, and being offered your own network talk show as word of your combined wit and warmth makes such an offer inevitable.

Sounds good? You bet it sounds good.

Or perhaps you're a whole lot more laid-back about the entire business. You're not into an excessive concern with the outcome of things. You just want to write, a paragraph at a time, a page at a time, a day at a time. If those pages someday add up to a book, that's nice. If someone wants to publish the book, that's nice, too. If other people want to go to the stores and buy the book, that's also nice. And whatever else happens is nice, too, but you don't want to get hung up on it now, because you're taking it a paragraph at a time and a page at a time and a day at a time, and that's a fine pace, thank you all the same.

Which of these two approaches involves a sound method of setting goals for oneself? Now let's not see the same old hands, class. Yes, Arnold?

The first one, sir. He knows what he wants and goes right for it.

I see. Do you agree with that, Rachel?

No, sir.

Why not?

Because it sounds like a pipe dream to me, sir. The second person has attainable goals. Each day she can do what she sets out to do, without losing her head to unrealistic reveries. And someday, for all we know, she just might wind up on the top of the bestseller list with a big movie sale and a great paperback deal and, who knows, maybe an Oscar and a talk show and . . .

And all the goodies, eh, Rachel?

Well, why not, sir?

Why indeed? Would you like to vote with a show of hands? How many of you agree with Arnold? Edna, are you raising your hand or scratching your head? That's better. All right, now raise your hands if you agree with Rachel. Arnold, why are you voting for Rachel?

Just playing it safe, sir.

I see. Well, the votes are about evenly divided, but I'm afraid there was no way to play it safe on this one, Arnold. Because neither of the approaches represents an effective use of goals. Both fall short, albeit in very different ways.

Rachel's selection, despite her mastery of the fine art of keeping it in the Now and living in the moment, has only the shortest of short-term goals. It's almost as if she's afraid to set more distant goals out of the superstitious fear that to admit wanting something is somehow to sabotage one's chances of getting it. If she literally has no goal beyond each day's writing, how can the pages add up to anything at all cohesive?

Arnold's choice, on the other hand, knows exactly what he wants. He wants the moon and all the stars, and there's nothing wrong with wanting it. But he doesn't have genuine goals here. Rachel was on target when she said it sounded like a pipe dream, because what we're dealing with isn't a batch of goals at all. It's a fantasy.

What, you may ask, is the difference between a goal and a fantasy. Go ahead, Andrea. I just said you may ask.

What's the difference between a goal and a fantasy, sir?

I'm glad you asked me that. A goal is something you want and are taking realistic steps to attain. A fantasy is something you want. Period.

Perhaps you have a dream of winning a million dollars in a lottery. That's okay—you can have any dream you want. Dreams are free, and nobody's yet figured out a way to tax them, although I'm sure someone's working on it even as we speak. But if you sit around every day thinking of the things you'll say to the press and the trips you'll take and the goodies you'll buy, but you never even buy a lottery ticket, what you've got is a fantasy.

Suppose you have the same dream, but you invest a significant portion of your surplus income in lottery tickets. Suppose further you work on your own subconscious mind, implanting the idea that you are now ready and willing to win the lottery, that you deserve to win it, that you have nothing to fear from sudden wealth. You might still go the rest of your life without winning a dime, but you'd be operating with a goal rather than a fantasy, and you'd certainly have a better chance of winning than if you never bought a single ticket in the first place. (You'd also have a great chance of losing, and I'm certainly not touting lottery tickets as the soundest investment going, but all that's beside the point.)

When you set a goal and acknowledge it, you send the thought out into the universe.

Perhaps I can give you an illustration closer to home. For years I thought I would enjoy teaching writing in a college or university. The fact that I myself had never graduated from college made the prospect doubly sweet. A week teaching a summer seminar at Antioch College provided assurance that I enjoyed teaching and that I was quite good at it.

And the years passed, and I wondered why nobody knocked on my door and invited me to teach a course somewhere. I clung to the fantasy, and fantasy was what it was, because I wasn't putting any energy into bringing it about.

Then one day I went to the library and compiled a list of area colleges and universities. And I went home and wrote up a resume, and worked up a letter announcing my interest in teaching a writing course. I sent out twelve or fifteen letters and sat back to see what would happen.

What happened was that I interviewed at two of the schools I'd written to, got polite turndowns from a couple more, and never heard from the rest. One of my interviews led nowhere, while the other led to a course listed for the winter intercession and cancelled at the eleventh hour when too few students enrolled.

So what does that prove?

Patience. I'm not finished yet.

Because what happened next was that I was invited out of the blue to teach writing at another college, one to which I had not submitted my resume. And I did teach there for a semester, and it was valuable experience, and I somehow know I never would have heard from that school if I hadn't put some energy into writing to other schools.

Similarly, I decided more recently that I loved to travel and would be a great speaker at writers' conferences, and that I hardly ever got asked to any except through personal connections. So I sent out a mailing announcing my availability and I immediately received several letters of inquiry, a few of which led directly to teaching and speaking engagements.

And I also immediately began to receive invitations from conference directors to whom I had *not* written, and if you want to call that a coincidence, go right ahead. But don't expect me to nod in agreement.

How do goals work?

I think they work in a couple of ways, on the conscious mind and on the subconscious mind. On a conscious level, when you make a list of what you want, you can then stop to figure out what steps you can take to manifest your goals. If you announce to yourself that you want to write a particular novel, you can begin doing the necessary research, making useful notes, and taking all those first steps with which a journey of a thousand miles is alleged to begin.

At the same time, you're telling your subconscious mind that you want to achieve this end and take these steps to do it. When your eyes hit a newspaper article that might give you a valuable lead, your programmed subconscious keeps you from skipping right over it. When a plot or character idea bubbles around below the conscious level, your subconscious sends up a red flag and brings the useful notion to your conscious attention.

And I think there's even more to it than that. In *Write For Your Life* we put a lot of stress on the power of your thoughts. When you set a goal and acknowledge it, you send the thought out into the universe.

For the longest time I told myself that I didn't care about money. Now this was not true, and a good thing, because if it had been true I probably would have starved altogether. But I told myself and I put the thought out into the ether, and it set about limiting the results of my work.

Then I started admitting to myself that I did want to make more money, and what do you think happened? My income went up. I let myself concentrate on the idea that I wanted my earlier books back in print, and they started getting reprinted. Good things began to happen—because I set goals, and because I put a little of my energy into them rather than let them remain on a pipe-dream level.

I still write a paragraph at a time, a page at a time, and a day at a time. Because that, as far as I know, is the only way to get the work done. And I still concentrate more on the piece of paper in my typewriter than on the trip I'll take with the money it brings me. But I know that just listing and acknowledging my goals immediately brings them immeasurably closer to completion, and that, when I unite my thoughts and my efforts toward a stated objective, my powers of attainment are exponentially increased.

And that strikes me as a far better buy than lottery tickets.

28. An Investment in Pots and Pans

Hi, there. Despite what your calendar may tell you, it's the end of May where I am, and I just got back from Washington, where I attended the annual convention of the American Booksellers Association. This was my first ABA, and it was quite a production, with hundreds of publishers assembled to offer their lines to thousands of booksellers.

They give away a lot of stuff at the ABA—catalogs, buttons, souvenirs, posters, and, inevitably, books. I came back laden with a ton of posters, highlighted by one from the Mysterious Press featuring Modesty Blaise attired in less leather than it would take to make a pair of mittens. And a chap from the Fleming H. Revell Company gave me a copy of *Secrets of Closing the Sale,* by Zig Ziglar.

Now what, you might wonder, would I want with that? A writer, after all, is a verbal alchemist, transmuting the dross of imagination and experience into art itself. What does that have to do with anything as crass as salesmanship? Why would I bother to bring Mr. Ziglar's book home with me? Why, having done so, would I ever choose to open it?

I've got news for you. Writing is a sales job, and every successful writer is, consciously or unconsciously, a salesperson.

"Not me," you might say. "I have an agent who takes care of the selling." Or you might argue that selling is not a part of your work as a writer because you're honestly unconcerned with the monetary fruits of your craft.

Makes no difference. I'm not just talking about marketing. I'm talking about what goes on when you sit down at the typewriter. Selling is an integral part of writing itself.

Consider what you're doing when you write a piece of fiction. You're asking a reader to give you his time and attention, two very precious commodities. You're demanding that he believe your characters exist and that he make an emotional investment in what happens to them. You're asking a lot, and you're trying to close the sale with nothing beyond some words on a piece of paper.

Early on in Mr. Ziglar's book, he touches upon a point that is by no means original with him—the need for a salesman to believe wholeheartedly in what he is selling. He uses an anecdote I found instructive.

Some years ago it seems a friend of his was selling a line of high-quality cookware and not doing terribly well with it. Ziglar went over to his house and told him he wasn't selling the product because he didn't believe in it. The man insisted he *did* believe in it, that it was the best cookware on the market and an excellent value for the money, and went on to give his whole sales pitch.

Ziglar pointed at the stove. "If you believe in it," he asked, "why aren't you using it yourself?"

The salesman replied that he had mountains of bills to pay, that he had had very hard times of late, that he fully intended to buy a set of his own cookware as soon as he got a few dollars ahead, but that in the meantime he really couldn't afford it.

"That's the same answer your potential customers give you every day," Ziglar told him. "How can you refute it when deep down inside you subscribe to it yourself? If I were you, I'd go out and mortgage my furniture in order to buy a set of the cookware I'm selling."

The man bought a set of cookware from himself, and his increased sales paid for it the first week.

Now how does all that relate to writing?

I can think of a batch of ways. The first thing that comes to mind is the whole process of deciding what to write. The greatest liability you can saddle yourself with is to attempt to write something you don't believe in. Your own lack of belief will almost inevitably do you in. You won't be able to close the sale.

Suppose you decide to write an adult western or a romance because you understand it's easy to sell books in those categories. If you have contempt for the type of book you're trying to write, your attitude will turn up in your work. It will somehow come off as cynical and unconvincing. You may get published—a certain number of books are indeed written and published by writers who are contemptuous of them. But you won't do terribly well. The most successful writers in any category are those who believe in what they're doing.

Similarly, you have to believe in your own ability to write a particular piece of fiction. For example, I just don't feel qualified to write historical fiction. If I did write something set in the past, I strongly suspect readers would fail to buy it. No matter how good a job I did with my research, my own inner lack of conviction would somehow communicate itself to whoever read the book. "He doesn't know what he's talking about," they'd think. Another writer, with twice the conviction and a fraction of the researched data, would get across to the reader far more effectively.

There are other ways in which we can sell ourselves a set of our own cookware. I was doing just that this past weekend when I went to Washington for the ABA. Not that many writers go, because there's not a whole lot for them to do. A handful of writers, most often celebrities in other fields who have a book to promote, are brought to the convention by their publishers to sign autographs and smile a lot. I don't have a book coming out that would lend itself to that sort of promotional effort, but I decided that it wouldn't hurt me to say hello to some people, that I'd like to find out what an ABA was like, and that my career was worth the investment of a couple of hundred dollars to attend the thing.

S elling is an integral part of writing itself.

As it turned out, I did some helloing and handshaking at several publishers' booths, and signed autographs for an hour at another. I went to a couple of parties and had a dozen or more useful conversations. And, perhaps most important, I had bought myself a set of that cookware we've been talking about. I was committed enough to my career and my current worth as a writer to attend the ABA at my own expense.

A variety of investments can pay off in heightened self-esteem, which in turn pays off in better writing and a better reception for it. Some years back I started buying the best typing paper available and using it for all my work. Not the kind of 100 percent rag content stuff guaranteed to outlast the pyramids, but a high quality 25 percent cotton 20-lb bond with a nice heft to it. That paper now costs me close to $15 a ream, and I could get by for less than a third of that amount with no trouble. And I could argue that the money I spend on paper is a waste, because more often than not I keep the original manuscript at home and send photocopies to my publishers, and the photocopies are identical regardless of the kind of paper I've used for the original.

Well, I'll tell you something. I *like* using good paper. I like rolling it into the typewriter and I like taking it out covered with words.

I think I write better with good paper in the carriage; cheap paper encourages me to think of my work as first-draft copy, and to be sloppy in mind and fingers. If good paper costs me an extra fifty bucks a year (and I doubt it comes to that much) I'm happy to pay it. Isn't it worth a dollar a week to feel that much better about my work and my worth as a writer?

More recently, I stopped making carbon copies. It's expensive to have everything photocopied, but it saves time and effort and aggravation, and it's worth it. It's also inconvenient, because I have to run out to the copy shop whenever I want a copy of something, and my next major investment in convenience and self-esteem will be a copying machine.

My mind keeps telling me it's a luxury I don't need, and one I can't afford. Well, Ziglar's friend kept finding reasons why he couldn't afford the pots and pans. By the time this column's in print, I intend to have a copier in this house.

You may not *want* a copier, or more expensive paper—if you do a lot of drafts, it could have an inhibiting effect. But why don't you take a moment to make a list of the investments you could make in your career that you haven't made—not because you honestly can't afford it, but because some sort of self-sabotaging mechanism inside you tells you that your writing isn't worth it?

Here are some of the things that might be on your list:
1. Subscriptions to writers' magazines.
2. Annual attendance at a writers' convention.
3. A library of essential reference books.
4. Membership in local and national writers' organizations.
5. Hardcover books on your shelves—it always amazes me that writers who publish their own books in hardcover decide they can't afford to buy other writers' books in hardcover. Granted, sometimes you'd just as soon wait for the paperback, but suppose it's something you really want to read now?
6. A good place to write. I once owned a house in the country with about twelve rooms, and I never did manage to turn one of them into a permanent work area.
7. Whatever equipment enhances your writing. A word processor, if you want one. A good typewriter, a copying machine, a $200 fountain pen, a whole boxful of sharpened pencils, a tape recorder, whatever works for you.

Selling, according to Mr. Ziglar, is essentially a transference of feeling. When everything works, a belief in a book's worth is transferred from its author to and through his agent, his editor, his publisher's sales reps, and the booksellers themselves, until it reaches the reader.

Some writers have the sort of belief system which supports an immediate aim at the top, commercially and artistically. Others of us begin by believing in our capacity to achieve more readily attainable goals; fueled by success, our self-esteem grows and allows us to believe in progressively greater levels of achievement.

Let me emphasize one final point. This whole business only works if your belief is justified. If Mr. Ziglar's friend didn't really like that cookware, owning a set of his own wouldn't have made him a better salesman. If that were the case, he would have been better advised to sell something else.

Same goes for writing. You can't simply adopt a belief system by sheer force of will. And, if you can't sell yourself the pots and pans, if you can't really believe in what you're writing, maybe you're writing the wrong thing.

29. Take Courage

Somehow one rarely thinks of writing as an occupation that calls for courage. High-wire walkers, lion tamers, double agents, soldiers of fortune—such folk would seem to require more in the way of bravery than it takes to sit at a desk and make up stories.

Oh, some kinds of writing entail obvious hazards. War correspondents are always getting shot at, sometimes with accuracy, and now and then an intrepid investigative reporter gets his car blown up or his throat cut. But what comparable perils lie in wait for the writer of fiction? Short of dozing off and falling out of his chair, his workday would look to be relatively risk-free.

My characters, on the other hand, lead unquestionably dangerous lives. Bernie Rhodenbarr, the burglar hero of several mysteries of mine, has a calling which demands nerves of steel. I almost entitled his second adventure *The Guts of a Burglar*. (Wiser heads prevailed, as they occasionally do, and the book saw print as *The Burglar in the Closet*. Imagine, if you will, what the cover might otherwise have looked like.)

Consider, though, the source of my original title. According to Dr. Samuel Johnson, "Sir, he who would earn his bread writing books must have the assurance of a duke, the wit of a courtier, and the guts of a burglar."

Can that be true? Even allowing for a dash of Johnsonian hyperbole, can it even approach the truth? Is courage an essential item in the writer's personal inventory? If so, is it something he can develop?

It seems to me that it takes considerable courage to become a writer in the first place. The odds against even a small measure of success are at least as prohibitive as those one faces in a lottery, yet the writer wagers not a couple of dollars for a ticket but months or years or a lifetime of hard work. To attempt to carve a place for oneself in such an intensely competitive field, and to do so on the presumption that one possesses the essential talent along with the ability to extend and develop that talent, is at the very least courageous.

Sometimes it's foolhardy. I think it was so in my own case. I had the advantage of starting young, and I did so with the certain conviction that I would be able to make a living as a writer of fiction. I'm afraid this conviction grew less out of a sense of destiny than from a kind of heroic blindness that would not see the possibility of failure. Perhaps I was blessed with that ducal arrogance Johnson was talking about.

I think it takes courage for any writer, novice or veteran, to begin a piece of work. Every time I start a book or story, every time I spoil clean white paper with my own poor words, I am performing an act of faith. I'm hoping and trusting that my ability will be equal to the task at hand, or at least that it will not strand me unpublishably short of my goal.

I'm also hoping and trusting that my imagination will not fail me. I never have the entire work in mind when I begin writing. Books and stories grow on the page, plots and characters are born in the process of writing. No matter how well I prepare, no matter how detailed an outline I draw up in advance, every book will be a happening, a spontaneous event. And I can't change this. I can't open the parachute until I've stepped out of the plane, and if it won't open—well, all I can do is pull the cord and pray.

It takes courage, I believe, to do the very best one can do—at writing or at anything else. There's a great security in doing less than one's best. For too many years I wrote inferior books, and there was something very reassuring in laboring in those second-growth vineyards. I could show my work to the world without risking judgment. After all, I knew the stuff was crap. If you didn't like it, well, what did that prove? I mean, if I'd given it my best shot, then you'd have liked it fine. Hell, we both knew I could do better than that.

I stayed with second-rate work for lack of another sort of courage as well. Because it seems to me that it takes courage to grow as a writer, to abandon the sure thing and risk the unknown. There are writers who do the same thing over and over for a lifetime, and I wouldn't presume to judge them. Anyone who has managed to achieve a measure of success in such a chancy business has every right in the world to stick with whatever won him that success. "If it works, don't fix it"—if I knew the Latin for that, I'd put it on my coat of arms.

Similarly, a good many writers are cursed by a Peter Principle mechanism that leads them to reject as unworthy of them anything they're able to do well. They persist until they manage to find something they *can't* do well, and devote the remainder of their careers to noble failure.

On balance, I think it's vital for me to have the courage to take chances, and to risk failure in the process. I am more than willing to admit that there are kinds of books I am not meant to write. Unfortunately, I sometimes have to write them in order to find out which ones they are. I get little pleasure and less money out of writing that doesn't work out, and I seem to do more rather than less of it with the passing years. In 1980, I wrote 150 pages of one book and 250 pages of another, and both of them died unborn. Together, they accounted for ten months of the year, and I'll tell you, I'd have preferred spending those ten months at the seashore. But I was trying new things, breaking new ground, and I have come to believe that such action pays off in the long run.

I recently finished a novel, *Eight Million Ways to Die*, which Arbor House published. It's my fifth detective story featuring one Matthew Scudder, and you wouldn't think it would take much courage for me to do something I've done already four times. My research for the book included riding *Is courage an essential item in the writer's personal inventory?* around for a night in the back of a police van while they rounded up street prostitutes in Queens, but there wasn't much risk in that; the most dangerous part of that evening consisted in riding home afterward on the A train.

But the book's twice as long as the other Scudder novels. There's an elaborate subplot, an abundance of characters. I dealt with a couple of themes that I found difficult to treat in fiction. I plotted the book as I went along, with no real assurance that the parachute would open. And I wrote the whole 443 pages without anyone's reading any of it, so I didn't really know if the characters were convincing, if the plot held together, and if the story was sufficient to justify the book's unusual length.

I would submit that there was courage involved in all of this. And I can attest to the fact that courage is not something I was born with. If I'd had any idea that it was going to take courage to be a writer, I'd have set about becoming something else.

Let me amend that. I suspect courage *is* something I was born with, however undetectable it may have been in the scared child I was. I have a hunch that courage is a sort of emotional muscle, that it atrophies without use and develops when exercised. A writer (or, I suppose, anyone else) develops courage by doing the feared thing.

And you don't have to succeed at it to gain from it. My failures—books I've failed to finish, books which I finished but never published—have been enormously valuable to me. They've helped me grow as a writer, because I grow by meeting new challenges whether or not I meet them successfully. And they've helped me to realize that I don't have to be afraid of failure because I can survive it.

"Fear is the mind-killer," Frank Herbert tells us in *Dune*. For a writer, it is as well the stifler of the creative spirit.

It strikes me that many of the foregoing observations on fear and courage apply as well to other fields of endeavor besides writing. I suspect, though, that the fiction writer requires courage of a special sort if he is to produce his best work. He has to possess and exercise the courage to be himself upon the printed page, to expose—through the characters he creates and in the plots he spins—his own nature, his own problems, his own secret self.

For some writers, to whom autobiography in the guise of fiction comes freely and naturally, this is not terribly difficult. Such a writer still requires courage to present himself with warts-and-all honesty, but it is in his nature to transform his life rather directly into his art.

Others of us have chosen to write fiction because it allows us to reveal ourselves and conceal ourselves at the same time. By creating characters and endowing them with some of our traits, by hatching plots that treat some of the conflicts and confusions of our personal mythology, we explain ourselves cryptically to the world. What our unconscious minds do in dreams, so do our conscious selves accomplish through the medium of fiction.

Well, there's a contradiction here. I want to show you my soul but I'm scared to take off my overcoat. I'm afraid, of course, that if you take a good long look at me you won't like me, which in turn stems from the fear that if *I* take that good long look, I won't like me either.

Faith and fear, they tell me, can't coexist. I try to practice my courage by doing what I'm afraid to do, and I manage that (now and then, anyway) by means of faith. Faith that I will do myself more good than harm by the risks I am willing to take as a writer. Faith that the failure of a piece of my writing can never mean my failure as a writer. And faith, finally, that the best service I can do myself is to do the best and most honest work of which I am capable.

I wish I had more of that faith. But it's a funny thing; the more I use it, the more I wind up with.

30. The Solitary Vice

A few minutes ago, I finished the day's work on what I hope will be the fifth book in my series featuring burglar Bernie Rhodenbarr. The book concerns the kidnapping of a cat and the theft of a painting by the modern Dutch master Piet Mondrian, and by the time this column sees print I trust the book will be completed. As of this writing I have 142 pages written, with a hundred or so to go. I've been doing five or six pages a day and working five or six days a week, so I ought to be done in a month.

By then I'll have played thousands of games of solitaire.

This is a habit I thought I'd broken. Five years ago I moved into an apartment on Greenwich Street, and in all the years I lived there I don't recall playing solitaire once. I might lay out the cards now and then while traveling, but I don't believe I played at home, and I certainly never dealt out a hand during my work.

Then, about a year and a half ago, I was out in Los Angeles, where I managed to pick up a quick screenplay assignment. I took a hotel room, set up a typewriter, and bought a deck of cards. Every morning I got up, had breakfast, drank a few cups of tea, played two or three hands of solitaire, and started work. I would write a page or a scene or an exchange of lines, push the typewriter aside, play a couple games of solitaire, write some more, play more solitaire, and so on until I'd done however many pages constituted a day's work.

I came back to New York, changed apartments a few times, wrote some things that didn't work out, and then spent two very intense months writing a book called *Eight Million Ways To Die*. I did each day's work without any interruption, whether from cards or conversation, but at night, when my mental wheels were spinning and I couldn't think sensibly about the book or get it out of my mind, I often sat at my desk with a deck of cards.

Now I'm working on my burglar book, getting to my desk each morning after breakfast, writing a page or so, playing a few hands, writing some more, playing more solitaire, and continuing the process until I've got enough pages done to call it a day.

I still don't know whether the idiot game is a help or a hindrance to me.

Let me explain something. I do not, repeat not, find solitaire interesting. I would prefer that you refrain from writing to acquaint me with your own treasured variations on this unaccompanied pastime. I have, over many years, learned innumerable ways to play solitaire, some quite elaborate, others idiotically simple. They're all boring. The one I play—and I play only one, over and over—is a version of Canfield or Klondike, and I don't suppose it's any more interesting or involving than its fellows.

For years I felt guilty about playing solitaire while I worked. It certainly seemed to go against the grain of the Puritan ethic. Never mind that playing cards are the Devil's press passes, or whatever the hell they're supposed to be. When I was laying out a hand of solitaire, I clearly wasn't working. I was playing. Work ain't play, and vice versa, and solitaire was a self-indulgent way of stealing time and energy and concentration from the important business of writing.

With the passage of time, the nature of this guilt changed. The trouble with solitaire, I decided, was not that it reduced my overall productivity but that it detached me from what I was writing. I would be sitting there, concentrating with all my might, really involved in my work, and then I would yank myself away, pick up a deck of cards, and send all thoughts of the book out of my mind while I moved red queens onto black kings. It's not as though the cards functioned like worry beads, giving my fingers something to play with while my mind played with the problems of the work. On the contrary, my mind would abandon the work entirely while I dealt out the cards.

In recent months, I've begun to look at the solitary vice, so to speak, with a more permissive eye. I've taken to assuming what doctors are beginning to assume about presumably useless organs— i.e., if it's there, it's probably there for a reason. I have, after all, been writing books for an uncommonly long time. I get a lot of work done, finish most of the books I start, and publish most of the ones I finish. If I've so often performed my work with the diversion of a deck of cards at my elbow, is it so illogical to suppose that those cards are there for a purpose? And might it not be more profitable to inquire as to the nature of this purpose than to strive mightily to break the habit?

The most obvious function of solitaire for me is that it gives me a brief break from what I'm doing without getting me really involved. I have to concentrate very hard on writing in order to do it as well as I possibly can. There seems to be a limit to the duration of that sort of concentration. It tires me, and I keep wanting to stop.

Solitaire lets me stop without letting me leave my desk, and without tying me up for any real length of time. If I pick up a book or a magazine, I might put it down in five minutes or I might get engrossed in it and read for the next three hours. But I'm not going to play solitaire for three hours. A hand lasts three or four minutes, and, after one or several, I'm ready to go back to work.

These breaks seem to be essential, as if the mind (or whatever part of the self is involved in the creation of fiction) needs to loosen its hold now and then in order to get a better grip. Paradoxically, the way to hold on is by letting go, and quirks of memory provide a good analogy. Have you ever been blocked on something, unable to call to mind a person's name, a book title, whatever? When sheer force of will won't bring the memory into focus—and it generally won't—the best thing to do is shrug it off and think of something else. Then, more often than not, the forgotten name or title will come to mind unsummoned a little while later, apparently out of the blue.

> *Solitaire lets me stop without letting me leave my desk.*

There are times when I'm writing and I just plain get stuck. I can't think what should happen next, or how to manage it, and I have to let go of the problem to solve it. A long walk might help, or an hour at the gym, but such remedies would also drastically interrupt the day's work, and could hardly be indulged in every page or so. Solitaire provides a brief interruption, a short-term delaying tactic.

Sometimes I think its main function is to keep me at my desk. I like to get up, pace around the apartment, and find one thing or another to do. There's always something to do around here and I can always find a reason to get up from my desk and do it. But my desk is where my work gets done, and there's a direct ratio between the amount of time I spend at it and the number of pages of finished copy accumulating alongside my typewriter.

The cards also play their part on those days when getting started seems almost impossible. Sometimes, when writing the first word on the first page of the day looks to be a more arduous task than scaling Everest barefoot, I'll sit and play one game of solitaire after another, shuffling and dealing far past the point of utter boredom. I can't make myself write, but I can bloody well make myself stay at the desk this way, and sooner or later I may be able to get a paragraph written, and more often than not I wind up salvaging a day's work out of the day.

I suppose solitaire must have drawbacks. There are probably times when I interrupt my writing unnecessarily, simply because solitaire breaks have become habitual. All in all, though, I've come to believe that it probably works to my advantage. I seem to spend more hours at the typewriter and emerge less exhausted when I stop every once in a while to lay out the cards.

On to other matters. I wouldn't bring this up, but a recent column on pen names drew a surprising number of letters all putting the same question. If one should write under a pen name and keep it a secret from editors and publishers, how might one cash checks payable to the pen name? No problem. The simplest way is to endorse the check with the pen name, then endorse it anew with one's own name and deposit it in one's account. If one has a particular reason, paranoid or otherwise, for keeping one's own name undetectable, the check can be endorsed with the pen name, then cashed by a friend who runs it through his own account. Since there's no intent to defraud anywhere here—after all, *you* wrote the story, and the pen name's just one of your own aliases, so it's not as though you were forging someone else's name—the whole procedure is legal, or close enough to it.

A consideration began nagging at me when I kept opening envelopes and finding this point raised within. If you can't figure out this sort of thing for yourself, I found myself wondering, how can you possibly possess sufficient imagination to write fiction in the first place? Alas, it doesn't always work that way. We're rarely as clever as our characters. Bernie Rhodenbarr can open doors and Matthew Scudder can kick them in, but when I lock myself out I'm completely powerless over the situation. I'm a lot cleverer at the typewriter than I am away from it, and I ought to be able to assume as much for all of you out there.

Anyway, that's how you cash a check made out to a pen name. And it gives rise to a suggestion. Next time you're confronted by a similar dilemma, don't try to figure out what *you* should do. Grapple instead with the question of what a *character* might do, a character of yours in a story of yours, if he should be faced with something similar. And, if you're still stuck, try laying out the cards for a game of solitaire.

31. Going for the Gold

Well, class, that's a convenient stopping place for us today. I know a lot of you are anxious to get in front of a television set and watch the Olympics, so unless there are any questions I think I'll dismiss you early and let you watch the world's finest young athletes go for the gold. Fine, then, and I'll see you all—yes, Mimi? Was there something you wanted to say?

That phrase you used, sir. Going for the gold.

A cliche, I know, and one of which I'm beginning rapidly to tire. My use of it was in part ironic, and—

That's not it. I was thinking that just one person in each event gets the gold medal, no matter how many of them go for it.

Why, yes, Mimi. That's true, and—

Well, it's like writing, isn't it, sir? All of us face these insurmountable odds. You can give us tips, and you can tell us the ultimate answer lies within ourselves, but when all is said and done, one of us winds up with the gold medal and the rest of us get little form slips assuring us that our submission doesn't meet somebody's current needs. I mean, sir, we can come to every class and pay close attention and all, and even so not all of us are going to succeed. Isn't that so, sir?

Hmmmm. That's an interesting point, Mimi, and maybe we ought to talk about it right now. In fact—

I'll get you for this, Mimi.

Shut up, Arnold.

He was going to dismiss us, I was halfway out the door, and you had to open your yap. I swear I'll—

Steady on, boys and girls. Mimi, I'm glad you raised the question you did. A young woman named Melinda brought up much the same point recently at a seminar of mine in Plainview, Texas. After we'd all gone through an extended process designed to reverse specific negative thoughts and bolster our self-esteem as writers, she pointed to what she saw as a contradiction in my message. "You're encouraging us to tell ourselves that we can all be successful," she said. "But you don't really believe that. Do you?"

I'm not sure what I told Melinda. I don't think I said much of anything, but later on I had a cup of coffee and thought about her question.

The next morning, flying to Houston, I thought about it some more. On the one hand, I weighed my own commitment to the idea that we can succeed in direct proportion to the strength of our own belief systems. On the other, I looked at the number of manuscripts written vs. the number published, and the comparable ratio of hopeful to professional writers. Was I telling people that all of those hopeful writers can someday wind up on the bestseller list? And was I doing them a disservice in the process?

Let's ask the question again, narrowing its scope to the limits of this classroom. Do I believe everyone in here can become a successful writer?

No. No, I don't.

But I *do* believe that *anyone* can.

Do you get the distinction? All of you in this room won't wind up with the gold medal, any more than all of the hopeful writers in America will get their books published. There are too many people in the race and too few gold medals to go around. Not everybody can have one.

But anybody can.

Which is to say that I don't believe there's anyone here today who is specifically precluded from achieving a full measure of writing success. No matter who you are or what you've written, no matter how much demonstrable talent you possess, you can get what you want in this game. This is not to say that you will, only that you can.

And I'm glad it was you who raised this point, Mimi, because that reminds me of *The Screaming Mimi*, a mystery novel by the late Fredric Brown. One of the characters, a hard-drinking journalist out on a toot, is smitten with a beautiful young woman named Mimi, and confides that what he wants most in the world is to spend the night with her. And—were you saying something, Arnold?

I was just remarking that Fredric Brown must have had quite an imagination, sir.

You watch it, Arnold.

Watch it yourself, Mimi. We could be watching the javelin finals, and instead we're stuck here.

Ahem. The reporter's friend, a philosophical drunk named

Godfrey and known to his friends as God, tells the reporter he can have his wish if he wants it badly enough. "You can have anything you want in this world," he maintains, "if you want it badly enough."

Whether or not everyone succeeds who wants it badly enough, we can see readily that a great many people don't succeed because they *don't* want it badly enough. All of you in this class want to write, and all of you want to succeed as writers, to be published, to be well-received, to make a living, to win whatever your version may be of the Olympic gold medal. You all want it to one degree or another, but not all of you want it badly enough.

Many of you, for example, will explain quite sincerely that you would get more writing done and accomplish a great deal more if you only had the time. Well, I'll tell you something. "I don't have the time" is one of the two most popular excuses ever invented—the other is "I can't afford it." And, while both of these statements make dandy excuses, excuses most people find altogether unanswerable, they are almost invariably untrue.

> *The only reason to write anything, ever, is because you want to.*

Oh, not *always*. If you have five dollars to your name and the rent's due, you can legitimately tell a car salesman that you can't afford to buy a new Cadillac at the moment. If you work a forty-hour-a-week job while taking a full load of college courses, you could with some justification maintain that you don't have the time to run seventy miles a week training for a marathon. Even then, one could argue in rebuttal that you don't want the car or the race tee-shirt badly enough, that if you did you would find a way to create the money and/or the time.

When it comes to writing, almost everyone has enough time to do enough writing to succeed at it. I never heard time better discussed than in a talk by Dennis Hensley, who pointed out a vast number of ways in which virtually anyone could create writing time amounting to two hours a day, five days a week. By going to bed later or getting up earlier or cutting out some time-wasting habits, just about anyone could find those two hours a day.

That comes to ten hours a week, Hensley pointed out, or one forty-hour work week every month, or three months of full-time writing every calendar year. And if you can't produce something substantial in that amount of time, you've got a problem that has

nothing to do with time. (And, please note, you can do all this without even cutting into your weekends.)

If everyone has plenty of time to write, and if lack of time remains such a popular excuse, what does *I don't have the time* really
mean? The answer seems clear enough. It means *I don't care
enough about my writing to make time for it.* It means *I don't give
writing high priority.* It means *I want to make it as a writer, but I
don't want it badly enough.*

Well, why don't we say that? I suppose because our self-image
would suffer. *I don't have the time* sounds overburdened and indus-
trious; *I don't want it badly enough* sounds frivolous, self-indulgent, spineless.

Which is clearly ridiculous. So many of us seem to regard writing as a debt we owe the universe. "I should write more," people tell
me, wringing their hands and avoiding my eyes. "I really should
work harder, should put in more hours, should apply myself more. I
should make the time, I should show some self-discipline, I should
lock myself in a room and throw the key out the window. I should, I
should, I should."

Oh, come on. Why should you? Who besides you cares whether you ever write anything or not?

Let me tell you something. The only reason to write anything,
ever, is because you want to. The planet will keep on spinning at the
same old pace irrespective of anything you or I put on paper. I don't
have to write to save the world, nor do I have to write to justify my
presence on it. And neither do you.

Of all the grim prognostications of ecological disaster, few
seem to involve a worldwide shortage of fiction. We can work ourselves into a frenzy over the prospect of aerosol cans eating up the
ozone layer of the atmosphere, or non-biodegradable styrofoam
cups filling up the Grand Canyon, but it's hard to argue that the
world will come to an end because there won't be anything for us to
read. When I talked about taking a year's sabbatical from writing, a
friend reminded me gently that I'd reached the stage in life where
the highest moral act I could perform was not to write another book
but to spare a tree or two. If I choose to write something, it's for my
own benefit, not the world's.

See what I'm getting at, Mimi? Not everyone in this room will
put in the time, will make the time for writing. But anyone can. Rachel?

What about talent, sir?

Talent?

Talent. Not everyone who puts in the time will succeed. It takes talent, too. Doesn't it?

Indeed it does. I've pointed out previously that it takes more than talent, that natural writing ability is not enough in and of itself to guarantee success. But this doesn't mean that talent is immaterial, that all you have to do to succeed is put in the hours.

So? You said anyone in this room could succeed, but what about the ones who don't have the talent?

And which ones are those? Can you tell? Because I can't.

I can walk around the room and read what you've written, and I can say that certain ones of you have real writing talent. But I can't say with assurance that any of the rest of you don't have comparable talent—*even though it may not show yet.*

I didn't always believe this. I used to think that talent, if present, was always visible. If a person showed you a piece of writing that was utterly without merit, writing in which not a shred of talent was evident, I figured you could tell him to give up, that he could never be a writer.

I have learned different. I have seen enough examples of writers who at one stage displayed absolutely no talent, and who went on to demonstrate abundant talent at a later date, to change my view of what talent is. I find myself coming increasingly to the belief that everyone has talent. For some it lies close to the surface, so that it takes little effort or will to bring it out into the open. For others, it lies deep within, accessible only to those who, as Godfrey would put it, want it badly enough.

I have some more things to say about talent, but I've kept you long enough today. Goodbye for now, boys and girls. Arnold, perhaps you'll be in time to catch the javelin competition after all.

Is Arnold going to catch the javelin, sir? I'd pay to see that. I'll get you for that, Mimi.

Perhaps you will, Arnold, if you want to badly enough.

32. *Try, Try Again*

When is it time to throw in the towel? How much effort does a writer have to make before giving up?

This is a question that comes up all the time. "I've written five novels," a gentleman writes, "and I haven't been able to sell a single one of them. I'm halfway through with my sixth, and if it doesn't sell, that's it for me. That'll be proof I just haven't got what it takes."

"My family saga novel has been rejected by eight publishers," a woman writes. "Is there any rule of thumb as to how many rejections a manuscript should garner before you cease attempting to market it? I don't want to give up prematurely, but neither do I want to invest endless time, postage, and psychic energy in a piece of fiction that may not be good enough for publication. How do I know when to stop?"

Good question—and one that occurs in one form or another to virtually every writer sooner or later. Those of us who are as yet unpublished wonder when we must bow to the inevitable and admit to ourselves that we are never going to be published. Those of us who are successful also try things that don't work, or meet with one or another sort of failure along the way. (A writer who never puts a foot wrong, never meets with rejection, is a writer who doesn't take enough chances. If your reach never exceeds your grasp, you're not reaching.)

How do we know when to stop? What quota of rejections entitles us to retire from the field with honor? How long do we have to do this before it would behoove us to do something else?

For openers, let me say that I don't think anybody has to earn the right to stop writing. A great many of us seem to believe that writing is something we have to do, that we have no right to exist on the planet unless we devote a substantial portion of our time and effort to the business of putting words on paper. Often we exacerbate this belief by our commitment to the idea that writing has to be difficult, and even unpleasant. As a result writing becomes a tedious struggle we voluntarily undertake on a daily basis, convinced that, should we stop, Something Terrible Will Happen.

Well, that's nonsense. The only reason for you to write is because you want to. If you don't want to do it, do something else instead. If you want to write but find it a struggle, find a way to make it less of a struggle and more of a pleasure. But don't keep at it out of a sense of duty to the world. The earth will go on spinning irrespective of what you or I do or don't write. For all the implicit altruism in writing—our work has merit in that we are willing to share portions of ourselves with others—writing remains at the core a fundamentally selfish act. We put ourselves into the work because of what we get out of it.

(Why don't you make a list—right now—of what you get out of writing? List all the rewards, internal and external, material and spiritual. Go ahead and write out your list, and take your time; I'll be here when you get back.)

Having established that writing is ultimately a matter of choice for us, we haven't by any means dismissed our original question. Is there a reasonable quantity of rejections after which one would be well advised to retire a manuscript? Is there a logical amount of failure after which one might sensibly abandon a particular area of writing, if not pack up one's typewriter altogether?

"If at first you don't succeed," we are told, "try, try again." To which W. C. Fields added, "If you *still* don't succeed, give up. There's no point in making a damned fool of yourself."

I wonder.

Where's the line between perseverance and damned foolishness? At what point do we stop resolutely believing in ourselves and our work and face up to reality?

If I submit a manuscript relentlessly, over and over and over, shrugging off rejections and remaining forever optimistic about its chances, will I ultimately wear down the resistance of the Big Editor in the Sky and win the acceptance I've been seeking? Or will my efforts actually become counterproductive, alienating editors along the way and leaving me trying to peddle a story I no longer believe in myself.

On the other hand, how do I know when to stop? Where do I get off assuming that the next thing I write won't be the one that works? How can I be sure the thirtieth editor to see my work won't find something in it that the previous twenty-nine missed? Do I really want to kill myself five minutes before the miracle?

I don't have answers for you this month. I think I'll perform my function best by offering you some questions.

And, perhaps, a thought or two to go with them.

It's easy enough to point to writers who persist too long, or quit too soon. Some years ago I led off a column with the story about a man who had written a short story and sent it to *Harper's*, whose estimable editor kept it for a month or so and returned it with a warmly encouraging letter. The writer, astonishingly enough, never sent the story to another market, nor did he try anything else for *Harper's*.

For an example of a fellow who erred in the other direction, persisting in the face of a complete lack of encouragement, I'll move away from the writing dodge for a moment and turn to the restaurant business. There was a chap I heard of a while back who arrived at retirement age, looked at the amount of his Social Security check, and decided he had to find a better way to make ends meet. He took an inventory of his assets and discovered that the one thing he had going for him was the ability to cook chicken well. So he went around to restaurants and offered them an eminently resistible deal.

> *What quota of rejections entitles us to retire from the field with honor?*

I'll teach you my method for cooking chicken, he said, and every time you sell a piece of chicken, I get a percentage of your take.

You wouldn't believe how many people told him to help himself to a drumstick—and beat it.

If you were in this man's shoes, how many rejections would it have taken for you to realize you were cackling up the wrong tree? A dozen? Fifty? Or would you have been stubborn enough to swallow a hundred straight rejections without a single restaurateur going for your deal?

The man I'm thinking of had one thousand and eight people say no to him before the first person said yes. Can you imagine that? How on earth could he get up the energy to make a presentation after the thousandth rejection? Sometimes all that kept him going was simple hunger; if a restaurant proprietor at least let him demonstrate his cooking skills before turning him down, there'd be some chicken cooked—and that might be the only way he'd get to eat that day.

If you're familiar with the story, you know who the crazy old fellow was. Maybe you've figured it out by now.

His name was Colonel Sanders.

Remarkable, isn't it? If you were serving as a business consultant to Colonel Sanders, wouldn't you have told him to quit after a thousand rejections? If not sooner? And, if he'd done something no one in his right mind could have quarreled with, if he'd bowed to the inevitable and thrown in the sponge after Prospect #100 or #500 or #1008 turned him down, he'd just be another man who tried something that didn't work out, and who gave it a fair shot before giving up on it.

Instead, he kept on trying, and became a multimillionaire and a great American success story.

Does that mean you should send your story to a thousand and nine markets before lining the bottom of the birdcage with it?

Not necessarily.

What's relevant, I think, is that Colonel Sanders didn't stop believing his idea was a good one. He may have had his share of doubts along the way—he'd have had to be at least marginally psychotic not to—but he always had sufficient faith to balance those doubts. And, on sales pitch #1009, he found someone who either shared his vision or was as crazy as he was, depending on how you want to look at it.

How many rejections do you have to get before you retire your story? The trouble with that question, I suspect, is that it's the wrong question. Ultimately it doesn't matter how many rejections your story gets. What matters is how many acceptances it gets, and you only need one of those.

Know something? Once your book or story is accepted, no one will care how many rejections it accumulated along the way.

That's all easy for me to say, isn't it? I'm sitting here, writing my column, reasonably secure in the knowledge that it will be accepted and printed, and even paid for. What do I know about rejection? What did I ever do that was anything like Colonel Sanders's ordeal?

Simple.

I learned to walk.

And so, unless you're quite a bit younger than this column's average reader, did you. Once upon a time, farther back than you can probably consciously remember, after a brief lifetime of crawling, you pulled yourself into a standing position and took a step.

At which point I strongly suspect you fell down.

Most of us do. I don't know a whole lot of little kids who walked clear across the room on their first attempt. Haven't heard of a one, actually.

You wound up walking, didn't you? You wound up walking

because you kept on trying until you could do it. There was no logical way for you to know that you would eventually be able to do it. Everyone—barring victims of illness—learns how to walk sooner or later, but you had no way of knowing that. Still you kept trying, and it probably never occurred to you to abandon the attempt, and then one day you were walking.

Just like that.

Imagine if little kids were blessed with adult minds. "Well, I fell down again. I'll probably never be able to do this. You know what I'll do? I'll try five more times, and if I fall down five more times, I'm gonna say the hell with it. Some people are meant to walk and evidently some of us aren't. Five more tumbles and I'll resign myself to crawling for the rest of my life. Listen, crawling's not so bad. If I crawl all the time, if I sort of specialize in it, I can probably be better at crawling than the average kid. Five more flops, so no one can say I didn't give it my best shot, and then I'll focus my energies on improving my crawling."

Is it really all that simple? Doesn't talent enter into it somewhere? Every child does have an inborn capacity to walk, and who is to say than each of us has a similar inborn capacity to write marketable fiction? After all, one keeps reading stories of people with no experience who sit down and write first novels that get auctioned for upwards of a million dollars. How is one to Try, Try Again while contemplating others who try once and succeed beyond imagination?

Well, I told you this chapter would hold more questions than answers. And remember what I said early on: you don't have to write, and ultimately you're the only one with a vested interest in whether you do or not. Maybe it's not worth the struggle, and the pain of rejection. Maybe you don't have the talent.

But you're walking, aren't you? And the Colonel sold a lot of chicken, didn't he?

It remains to be said that grownups have further to go when they fall, and sometimes it hurts more. I wrote about coping with rejection in *Telling Lies For Fun & Profit*; I find I have some further thoughts on the subject, and we'll look at them in the next chapter.

33. *Surviving Rejection*

Good morning, boys and girls.
Good morning, sir.

This morning we're going to be examining the whole problem of rejection. Now I know this may not be of much interest to some of you, so I thought I'd let you know in advance. If you've never been adversely affected by rejection, and if you've never failed to take chances out of fear of rejection, you probably don't need to hear any of this. If that's the case, just leave the classroom quietly—or, if you're part of our home audience, just turn the page.

Did we lose anybody?

I didn't think so.

The spectre of rejection typically comes into our writing lives very early on, when we first try submitting our efforts to prospective publishers. Some of us spend a long time writing for our own amusement before it occurs to us to try marketing what we've written. Others send out our first poems and stories before the ink is dry. In either case, our initial submissions are almost certain to be rejected; in those rare instances where one of us sells the first piece we send out, we're still likely to reap a rich harvest of rejections later on.

And it really never stops. Highly successful professional writers have to go on dealing with rejection in one form or another all their lives. Not long ago someone was asking me questions about marketing one's wares, and I explained that I'm not much of an authority on the subject, that my novels are all published by the same house, that an agent submits my manuscripts, that I'm no longer involved in the process of mailing things off and getting them back with rejection slips attached.

Does that mean that rejection's no longer a factor in my career? You must be kidding. Rejection is very much a part of my writing life, and I'm certain it always will be. I get rejected all the time—by foreign publishers, by movie producers, by book reviewers, by magazine editors, by reprinters. This would seem inescapable. We are all of us in a field of endeavor where we seek approval of our work—and, by extension, of ourselves. Not everyone will approve wholeheartedly of everything we do.

Suppose you write a book and a million people rush out and buy it. Does that amount to universal acceptance? Certainly not— in that some of those million readers won't like the book, and 199,000,000 will have rejected you by not buying it in the first place. One way or another, every single one of us gets rejected over and over again.

And, if you *never* get rejected, you're probably doing something wrong. I know of a woman who was famous for never having had a short story returned. Her first submission was to a genre fiction magazine. The story was accepted and enthusiastically published. They bought her next story, and the one after that, and so on. They never sent one back, and she was not awfully prolific, and loyalty moved her to submit every story she wrote to the same publisher.

An agent I know of shook his head when he heard this story. "She should be submitting to better markets," he said. "Loyalty's fine, but she's costing herself money and readers by giving them first look at everything she writes. If she's never getting rejected, she's playing it too safe."

At the beginning of my "Write For Your Life" seminar, we play a portion of a tape of affirmations for writers. Several of the affirmations specifically address the problem of rejection; the first one of the group, and a favorite of mine, is "Rejection enhances my self-esteem."

Well, that one always gets a laugh, and the laughter is at once nervous and ironic. The idea of rejection enhancing one's self-esteem tends to strike people that way. Because rejection, as most of us experience it, doesn't enhance self-esteem so much as it crushes it. When we put our hearts and souls into a piece, only to receive it back by return mail with a form rejection slip attached, our self-esteem is such that we could walk under an inchworm without removing our hat.

What happens, of course, is that rejection seems to confirm all of our own worst fears about ourselves. We send out our work, hoping that the approval of others will validate us. When our work is returned to us, it seems to prove that we were right all along, that we're not good enough, that all our secret doubts and fears are justified.

Perhaps it doesn't have to be that way. While rejection may never be a source of unalloyed delight—after all, one sent the thing off in the hope of a sale, and there's no point in pretending that a rejection was what one hoped for—nevertheless, it may be possible not only to roll with the punches but to get some positive value out of rejection.

For openers, you can look on your rejection slips as membership cards in the universal fellowship of writers who are willing to put themselves on the line. During my first year in college, when I first began submitting my work to publications, I papered part of a wall with rejection slips. I did not find myself devastated by rejection; on the contrary, I took it for granted that no one was going to buy what I was writing, and the rejection slips themselves somehow helped assure me that I was indeed a writer, engaged in that mysterious process that would ultimately lead to acceptances and publication. (As soon as I did get a couple of pieces accepted, I took the rejection slips down from the wall and tucked them away somewhere.)

The spectre of rejection typically comes into our writing lives very early on.

More important, I think we have to understand profoundly that we ourselves are not rejected every time a story is sent back to us. Because our work is so much a part of ourselves, it is easy to take rejection personally, and that's what we're doing whether we die a little with each rejection slip ("Ohmigod, here's the proof, I'm no good, nobody wants what I have to offer, I oughta curl up and die.") or reject the rejection ("What do these idiots know, I'm a better writer than the hacks and has-beens they publish, I'm too good for their rag!"). Either way, we're giving little slips of paper unwarranted power over us.

Perhaps it's worthwhile to consider what a rejection is. When an editor sends a story back to me, that editor is not judging the overall merits of that story. The editor is merely declining to buy it. When I buy one brand of soap flakes instead of another, I'm not condemning the brand I don't buy—nor is the manufacturer likely to burst into tears as a result.

The more confidence I have, in myself and in my work, the less likely I am to be bothered by a particular rejection. A month or so ago I wrote a short story and sent it to my agent. He didn't like it much but he sent it to a top market, if only because the editor there deserved first look at my short fiction.

Well, she didn't like it, either, and wrote a rather stinging note to that effect. This didn't bother me much—I still sort of liked the story, and I'd never expected her to buy it anyway, since it didn't strike me as right for her magazine. My agent, however, hadn't liked the story in the first place, so this rejection tended to confirm his feelings, and he promptly dumped the story at a much lower-paying market rather than try it with a couple of better magazines first.

A few years ago, my British publisher declined to publish my new novel. Although his firm was a long way from the top rank of English publishers, he'd brought out quite a few books of mine by then, and his decision against the new one was a surprise.

If my self-confidence had been lower, I might have found the rejection upsetting. Instead my immediate reaction was that this was not a misfortune but an opportunity, that we would almost certainly place the book with a better publisher and be better off for it. This is in fact precisely what happened, and this sort of thing happens all the time. Rejections may well be blessings in disguise, but it's hard to pierce the disguise when you're vulnerable to rejection.

Does this mean rejection should never hurt? That we ought to be able to take it all in stride, and never feel bad when our work gets thrown back in our face?

It might be nice to be so suffused with self-esteem as to remain unaffected by rejection, so laden with optimism as to assume that every bit of apparent bad news is one of those blessings in disguise. Perhaps some day we'll have reached a state of spiritual and emotional growth where we will genuinely respond in this fashion. In the meantime, however, I think it's healthier to let ourselves feel the pain of rejection than to try to sell ourselves a bill of goods by denying its existence altogether.

A couple of years ago, a friend of mine had two plays open on Broadway in the same theatrical season. That was the good news. The bad news was that both shows got roasted by the critics and shunned by the public, and neither one ran more than two weeks. My friend went around assuring everyone that this simply did not bother him at all.

I'm sure he wasn't lying. I'm certain he believed he was speaking the truth. And I'm just as positive that the experience was in fact painful, that he was simply blocking his feelings and remaining blissfully ignorant of them. That was his way of coping with the pain; on some unconscious level, he elected not to feel it.

In *Telling Lies for Fun & Profit*, I have a chapter on handling rejection. I talk some there about the value of submitting your work relentlessly, of getting a rejected manuscript back in the mail immediately. Here are a few other suggestions for lessening the damage of rejection:

1. *See rejection as part of the process.* Everybody gets rejected some of the time. The only foolproof way to avoid it is to publish everything at your own expense, and even then you'll experience rejection at the hands of booksellers, critics and readers. If you want to avoid rejection completely, keep the stuff in a drawer—or don't write it in the first place. Rejection is part of a process, and the ultimate goal of the process is acceptance, and once your story is published, nobody—including you—will give a damn how many rejections it garnered along the way.

2. *Give yourself credit for taking chances.* You have to take a chance in order to get rejected. Instead of dwelling on the rejection, focus on the chance you took, and applaud yourself for your daring. (Now are you beginning to see how rejection might enhance your self-esteem?)

3. *Accept yourself.* Another line on the affirmations tape says, "I accept myself; therefore I can never be truly rejected." The more you do in fact accept yourself, the less of an edge rejection can have over you. And, the more fully you accept yourself, the more acceptance you'll get from others.

4. *Feel the pain—and get over it.* When a rejection is disappointing, let yourself feel the disappointment. But don't wallow in it. Feel it, whatever the feeling is, and then let go of it.

5. *Don't blame anyone.* Don't blame yourself, first of all. But don't make the mistake of trying to affix blame elsewhere. Don't tell yourself that the editor is an idiot, that the market requirements are impossible, that the odds are stacked against the new writer. Don't try to make someone wrong in order to explain the fact that your material has been rejected. Rejections don't require an explanation. Remember, it is very much in the natural order of things that the vast majority of manuscripts get returned from the markets to which they are submitted. It's not somebody's fault when this happens, yours or anyone else's.

6. *Don't overanalyze.* I get a lot of correspondence from writers who go on and on about the language of the rejections they've been getting. "What does it mean, 'Doesn't meet our present needs?' " Well, it means what it says, and I don't think there's much point in paying a lot of attention to the language of a rejection notice. Most of the time we're probably better off with

form rejection slips because we don't knock ourselves out trying to figure them out. All any rejection note ultimately means is that a particular editor didn't like it enough to buy it, and the reasons aren't terribly important. If all your rejection letters seem to be saying the same thing, you might want to take notice, but trying to read rejection slips like a Roman soothsayer reading bird entrails is a great waste of time and energy.

7. *Get used to it.* That, ultimately, is the way to handle rejection. Grow accustomed to it. Send so many things out, and keep at it so regularly, that a rejection ceases to be such a big deal.

Will that happen? Sure it will. But it may take a while, and it's never a hundred percent. I'll tell you, if Bill Brohaugh sends this column back to me, I'll probably have a fit.

Spider Dreams
Living the Fictioneer's Life

They may be found almost everywhere; on or near water, in or on the ground, from underground caves to the tops of mountains. In fact salticid spiders have been taken as high as 22,000 feet on Mt. Everest, the highest elevation at which any animal has ever been taken. Ballooning spiders have actually been collected from airplanes at an elevation of 5,000 feet. Some kinds of spiders live inside human habitations, others frequent the outside of structures. Tall and low plants have spider tenants, as do the dead leaves on forest floors and the curled, dried leaves on trees in winter. Under bark, under stones, under fallen logs—these are only a few of their varied habitats . . .

Many spiders are not only colored like their surroundings but are of a peculiar body form resembling inanimate objects. Some, like Cyclosa, resemble a piece of bird dung; others like Hyptiotes, look like the buds of the plants on which the web is built; and many with elongated bodies and legs resemble pieces of straw and grass. Some spiders resemble other animals and of these mimics the ant-like spiders are most common. Often the mimicry extends not only to the body form but also to the behavior, the spiders moving about with anterior legs elevated like a pair of antennae.

—B. J. Kaston & Elizabeth Kaston
How to Know the Spiders

34. The Guts of a Fictioneer

If the writer of fiction has need of a totem animal, I submit that he might do worse than consider the spider. The humble arachnid spins his web out of his own guts, makes of it a work of art and a masterpiece of engineering, rests comfortably within its confines, and uses it to snare his dinner.

Even as you and I.

For where else does fiction originate? It comes from deep within, and we do not merely spew it forth. No, we construct it with art and with craft. And, if we have done our work well, it shelters and feeds us.

I don't know if others have remarked on the spider as metaphor for the writer. I should be surprised if they haven't; the image is a fairly obvious one, and first struck me over twenty-five years ago, when I was a second-year college student writing poetry that was every bit as sophomoric as I. Just the other day I unearthed an Elizabethan sonnet of mine based on the spider-writer image, and I can't wait to earth it again. The final couplet,

> Letters are digits and a brain a lever,
> Intestines thought-reels that give line forever

strikes me as the sort of thing Alexander Pope might have done if he'd had no talent.

I thought of the spider—if not yet the sonnet—a couple of months ago when *WD*'s Bill Brohaugh first proposed a piece on what it takes to write fiction, and suggested its present title. "You could deal with 'guts' in both senses of the word," he suggested. "The inner workings of a fiction writer and the courage and integrity necessary to make a go of it."

All I could think of was that spider.

My first thought was to be a writer. I didn't know what sort of writer I'd be and I don't recall caring much one way or the other. I was fifteen, an English teacher had found something promising in some compositions I'd written, and writing suddenly struck me as something that I could do and something that was worth doing. My immediate desire was to *be* a writer. I didn't know—or much care—what I'd write or what sort of writer I'd be.

More recently I've had occasion to take a long look backward at my early years. I have come to believe that most of us tend to be shaped in large measure by ideas we pick up about ourselves and the universe at birth or not long thereafter. One notion I seem to have acquired early on was that it was not appropriate for me to gain attention by making a fuss or creating a lot of noise.

I've been told that I didn't cry in infancy, that when I did once howl for twenty minutes my parents called the doctor. "All babies cry," the poor man advised them. "Well, I know that," my mother said, "but he never did before."

What a perfect answer writing was for me! I could get attention—indeed, I could seek attention from the entire world. And I could do so in utter silence, and from a great distance. No one would be near me while I did my silent work, and I would be nowhere around when people read what I'd written, and applauded or hissed.

I talked about this at my "Write For Your Life" seminar last May in Boston, and most of the people in the room were nodding in recognition and identification. I wouldn't be surprised to learn that many writers—and others in the non-performing arts as well, painters and composers and such—have similar ideas about getting attention, wanting it, even craving it, but deeming it unsafe or unwise or unseemly to be open and loud in the seeking of it.

I suppose all art is a cry for recognition, for acknowledgment, for applause. Even the recluse sheltered by a pen name must be sending the stuff out for a reason. Even the secret writer who keeps his poems and stories in a locked trunk has a reason for writing them down instead of keeping them locked in the confines of his own mind. Everything I write cries out something along the lines of *Look at me! See how good I am! See how clever/thoughtful/informed/sensitive/decent/honest/brave I am! For God's sake look at me!*

The cry of the fiction writer is probably a little different from that of the reporter. *Look how knowledgeable I am*, the journalist calls out. *See how much I know, and how good I am at telling it to you.*

The fictioneer carries a somewhat different message. *This is who I am*, he announces, *but it's not really who I really am. I want to show you the real me. But I'm not sure you'll like the real me, so I'm just telling you a story. It's a nice story, isn't it?*

Most of the fiction writers I know have a lot of ambivalence in the area of letting people know who they are. On the one hand, we want to be known. We have a very real need to show ourselves to others. On the other hand, we don't think it's safe. We've got the bone-deep conviction that, if people know who we really are, they'll hurt or reject us.

This is me, we cry out. *But not really!*

In a sense, my own growth as a writer has been largely a matter of becoming increasingly willing and able to reveal myself in my work. This is not to say that I consciously withheld myself from the reader in my earlier work. It's more that I didn't know how to use my own self in my writing. Even when I used characters whose experiences and circumstances ran parallel to my own, I kept myself somehow out of my own work.

Remember the child's rhyme?

> *I put my whole self in*
> *I take my whole self out*
> *I give my whole self a shake*
> *shake shake*
> *And turn myself about*

> *All of my characters are somehow aspects of myself.*

Isn't that precisely what fiction writers do all the time? We put our whole self into our work, then take our whole self out, shake the box and turn ourselves around.

With time, as I continued to write and continued to grow as a writer, I somehow became able to put more of myself into my characters. This is not to say that they are me or that I am them. Indeed, all of my characters are somehow aspects of myself, but with time they have held more of me as I have learned—and dared—to show more of myself.

The first Evan Tanner novel, *The Thief Who Couldn't Sleep,* was a big step forward for me. The book was hardly autobiographical—if Tanner was based on anyone, he was based on a couple of friends of mine. But Tanner's eyes became a pair of windows on the world for me, and I lived in his skin as I had not done in any previous creation.

In the mid-sixties I was for a period of a year or two a compulsive client of Times Square streetwalkers. I did not understand my own behavior, and I don't know that I examined it too closely at the time. But I did use it as the basis for a novel, *After The First Death*, and that constituted an unprecedented show of guts for this particular fictioneer, and in both senses of the word. By letting Alex Penn act out my own compulsions in print, I spun a work out of my own innards and showed uncharacteristic courage in the process.

But not all that much courage, it seems to me now, and not all that much of my inner self, either. I read the book now, and although I like it well enough as a piece of writing, I am struck by how differently I would handle the same material if I had it to do over. I'd let a lot more of my own self into Penn, I'd be rather more honest about the nature of his fears and longings.

This is not to say that I regret the way I wrote *After The First Death*, or that I would welcome the chance to write it again. Just as it has taken me time and practice to learn the techniques of writing, so it has taken time and practice to learn courage and self-revelation.

Sometimes one is able to trace an author's progress within the evolution of a single character. Ross Macdonald's Lew Archer comes immediately to mind. In the first few books, Archer was a sort of kid brother to Raymond Chandler's Philip Marlowe, a wise-cracking cynic whose origins in the work of other writers were not hard to detect.

As Macdonald went on writing, something happened to Archer. The voyages of self-discovery forced upon the author found expression in his creation. More and more of Macdonald got funneled into Lew Archer, and the fictional detective became increasingly his own man and less and less the heir of Spade and Marlowe.

I look for similar metamorphoses in my own series characters and am unable to see them. I wrote seven books about Tanner, and it seems to me that he's not much different in the last one, but then those books were all written in the space of a few years, not over several decades like the Lew Archer books. Still, I went through changes during those years; you'd think Tanner would show some of those changes, and perhaps he does to an eye other than my own.

Bernie Rhodenbarr changed some in the course of the five books thus far written about him. Or perhaps it's more that his life filled out with the addition of a bookstore for him to operate and a best friend to hang out with. Matthew Scudder has undergone great changes in the course of five books, but in his case it seems to me more a matter of the books' constituting a single long novel, in the course of which Scudder is affected by what he undergoes. He's changed by the time *Eight Million Ways To Die* is over, not because I'm writing about a different person but because he's been altered by what he has experienced.

I just read through the last paragraph, then looked over the ones immediately preceding it, and wondered at the way I was discussing fictional characters as if they were real.

And I thought of something a friend of mine, herself a novelist, once said about fiction writers in general.

"Anyone who spends the most meaningful hours of the day in the exclusive company of other people who do not exist, and who are indeed the product of his or her own imagination," she said, "is apt to be a little weird."

Well, I can't argue with that.

In April of 1984, *WD* ran a feature article of mine with the title "Conquering the Ultimate Writer's Block." The title may have been a little misleading, in that writer's block is a term generally used to describe a condition in which one is unable to get words on paper, or to get work finished. My article discussed negative ideas held consciously or unconsciously in the mind which work to sabotage one's writing success. I talked about the manner in which these beliefs get in one's way, and how to unearth them and reverse them, primarily by working with written affirmations.

A major portion of the "Write For Your Life" seminar centers upon this topic. Each participant selects that negative thought which seems to be the most basic impediment to his or her own success and then creates a positive affirmation to reverse it. We then use a couple of processes to help our minds internalize this new positive thought.

At a recent seminar, one woman's complaint was that she had trouble concentrating on her fiction, that the more meaningful a piece of writing was to her, the less likely she was to complete it. In the course of the self-analysis process, it became clear that the negative thought at the bottom of all this was that it was not safe for her to reveal herself to others, that people would not like her if they really knew her.

This woman wrote out several affirmations for herself and shared them with the rest of us. The one she was reluctant to read at first was one which resonated the strongest. It was "To know me is to love me."

I told her I thought that was the one she should work with. "I know it is," she said a little grudgingly. "I got a chill up the back of my neck when I said it."

That section of the seminar continues with a paired process, in which one person says his new affirmation over and over to his partner, who then says it back to him repeatedly.

When her partner said to her, over and over, "Jan, to know you is to love you," Jan couldn't stop crying.

> *It's safe to let people know who I am.*
> *The less I keep to myself, the more I have to give.*
> *The more I reveal myself, the safer I am.*
> *The more I share with others, the more I have for myself.*
> *To know me is to love me.*

These are all powerful affirmations, and all of them address themselves to the negative thought which stood in Jan's way—and which blocks a great many of us fictioneers to one extent or another. One can create infinite variations on this theme, and can use any or all of them to one's profit.

We all have a desire to reveal ourselves in our work, whether we're writing moral fables about kittens and bunny rabbits or shoot-'em-up adventure yarns or romance novels. And we all have some difficulty putting ourselves completely into our work, even those of us who gush autobiographically in the manner of Thomas Wolfe and Earl Thompson.

The more we internalize the notion that it's safe and desirable to reveal ourselves in our work, the more successfully we'll be able to do so.

Am I suggesting that every fiction writer is no more than a frustrated autobiographer? That if Edgar Rice Burroughs had been less neurotic he'd have written his own story instead of Tarzan's?

No, of course not. The fictioneer is concerned with revealing himself and with gaining applause through this revelation, but these are not his sole concerns.

He is also concerned with creation.

"If a poet is anybody," wrote E.E. Cummings in his introduction to *Is 5*, "he is somebody to whom things made matter very little—somebody who is obsessed by Making. Like all obsessions, the Making obsession has disadvantages; for instance, my only interest in making money would be to make it. Fortunately, however, I should prefer to make almost anything else, including locomotives and roses. It is with roses and locomotives (not to mention acrobats

Spring electricity Coney Island the 4th of July the eyes of mice and Niagara Falls) that my "poems" are competing.

"They are also competing with each other, with elephants, and with El Greco."

The fictioneer is obsessed with making up stories. "Once upon a time," he says, and we are off. He may be telling of something that actually happened to him or someone he knows. He may be spinning a plot wholly out of his imagination and setting it in a locale he never visited outside of dreams.

It doesn't matter. It's all very much the same thing. He is fabricating a world out of thin air and inviting you to enter it. "This is all make believe," he tells you in advance, "but I want you to believe it while you're in it."

And so we do. We enter into a compact with him, putting our skepticism On Hold the moment we hear the words *Once upon a time*. Or *Call me Ishmael*, or *Through the fence, between the curling flower spaces, I could see them hitting*. Or *The day broke gray and dull. The clouds hung heavily, and there was a rawness in the air that suggested snow*. Or *Alice was beginning to get very tired of sitting by her sister on the bank and of having nothing to do*.

We suspend our disbelief. We enter this world of the fictioneer's making even though we are well aware of its unreality.

"My husband thinks he's a chicken," said the woman in the old joke, "but I don't know as I want you to cure him, Doctor. Because we get a good price for the eggs."

"All right," we say. "I believe in Madame Bovary, and Mack Bolan, and Rebecca of Sunnybrook Farm. Why not? I can use the eggs."

Truth is stranger than fiction.
Heard that before, have you? Well, then, look at the converse.
Fiction is more plausible than truth.
Because it has to be. The people who write for the newspapers have it a whole lot easier than those of us who turn out novels and short stories. All they have to do is tell the story. It doesn't have to be believable and it doesn't have to make sense. They're dealing with facts, and they can be smug about it.

"This is what happened," they say, and we can like it or lump it.

Now there was a wire service story a while back about a child named Dewey McCall whose father ran over him with a huge piece of earthmoving equipment, a backhoe or something along those massive lines. The kid wound up squashed under the tread of this thing, with nothing but hard-packed earth under him. When the father backed the machinery off of the kid, Dewey was flat as a flounder and, according to an eyewitness, "his little eyes were bulging."

Relax. I am not telling you a horror story. Dewey turned out on examination not to have sustained any serious injury whatsoever. He regained his original shape like a rubber doll trod underfoot, and the only visible evidence of his travails were some treadmarks on his little chest. A few tons of heavy machinery parked on top of him for a few minutes there and he didn't even wind up with a nosebleed.

How'd you like to try to get away with that in fiction?

Oh, you could do it. If you were writing fantasy or science fiction in which you postulated that Dewey was immortal, or under some sort of mystical protection, your readers would readily accept his invulnerability to death by squashing. Heroes from Achilles to Superman have laid claim to our voluntary suspension of disbelief.

You could even get by with it as an inexplicable miracle, if you placed it in the right kind of context. Suppose you're writing the story of a man, and in the first chapter the man's son goes through what Dewey went through, and the father is forever after affected by what has happened. You could get away with that.

But as a general thing, you couldn't just toss off a miracle on this scale and expect the reader to buy it. Miracles and major implausibilities aside, you can't have inconsistent behavior and random chance and coincidence play a major role in fiction without infuriating the reader. We demand a balance in fiction, an inner logic, which we are not always able to detect in life itself.

Years ago I wrote sexually-oriented nonfiction under a pen name. What I did, essentially, was fabricate case histories with the aim of informing the reader in a particular area of human sexual behavior—and, to be sure, of appealing to his prurient interests in the process.

It was a pleasure to write this stuff. The stories were supposed to be true, and they thus were not under the constraints imposed upon fiction. The human lives of which I was writing could take abrupt and unlikely turns. They could have all manner of loose ends and could bear no end of inconsistencies. I had in my arsenal the journalist's ultimate weapon of factuality, against which there is no defense. "You have to believe this," I was in effect saying, "because it happens to be the truth, and I don't care if it makes sense and comes out even. Facts are facts."

Oh dear. Interestingly enough, before I was done writing these books they had begun to evolve into a sort of legitimacy. Readers wrote to me, I engaged in correspondence and conducted interviews, and ultimately a majority of my case histories were indeed based on fact. And it was at that point that I began to get occasional criticism from my editors. In one book, I recall, one case history out of a dozen was drawn from a real interview. It was specifically singled out by my publisher as unconvincing, and less realistic than its fellows.

Sometimes I think it takes guts to write fiction. And other times I think what it really takes is arrogance.

Consider the colossal effrontery of the fictioneer. He sits down at his desk and makes up a story, assuming that the product of his own imagination will keep other people, total strangers to him, interested and enthralled. He invents characters and trusts that these strangers will care mightily what happens to these made-up people.

The flip side of all this arrogance is anxiety and insecurity. Why should anyone waste his time reading my made-up stories? Why should people care what happens to my characters? And where do I get off deciding what happens next? How do I know what my characters think/feel/believe? What entitles me to decide how their fabricated lives will turn out?

It helps if I can learn to operate less on arrogance and more on humility. Most of us find out in the course of time that we've got a lot to be humble about. For all that it seems to demand arrogance in advance, the profession of fiction writing tends to constitute a humbling experience in the long run.

What has served most to humble me over the years has been the increasing realization that my work has so often succeeded not because of me but in spite of me, that it has been most effective when I've taken my own hands off the wheel and let some other driver steer the car. In my very best books, it has sometimes seemed as though I've had precious little to do with the writing, as though the books have largely written themselves. In all of my writing, the most effective dialogue has been that which my characters supplied themselves; I've sat at the typewriter feeling rather like a courtroom stenographer, jotting down lines that other voices have shouted or whispered deep within my mind. I do my best work when I feel least like its source and most like its channel.

Of course I impose a certain conscious control upon what I write. I make sure that it's in grammatical form, that there's a structure and logic to it, that the spider's web is geometrically sound. But the more I let go of trying to figure things out and make them happen, and the more I allow myself to tap into some universal source which I don't presume to understand, the better my work turns out.

Mozart said musical composition was the easiest thing in the world. All he had to do, he explained, was take the trouble to write down the music he heard in his head.

I find my thoughts returning to the spider. "The humble arachnid," as I called the creature in this article's first paragraph.

The word comes from mythology. Ovid tells us that Arachne was a mortal who excelled all other maidens in weaving. Both her finished work and her own grace and skill at the loom brought her admiration. Arrogant as any writer, Arachne challenged the goddess Athena to compete with her. Athena accepted the challenge.

In her tapestry, the goddess wove the stories of those who had dared to compete with the gods and had been punished for their pains. Arachne, undaunted, wove into her web the weaknesses and foibles of the gods themselves. Then, in Jessie M. Tatlock's retelling of the myth:

"Athena herself could not but wonder at the maiden's skill, but her arrogance aroused her resentment. She struck the delicate web with her shuttle, and it crumbled into bits; then she touched Arachne's forehead. A sense of her impiety rushed over the girl; she could not endure it, and hanged herself with a skein of her own silk. But Athena did not wish that so skillful a worker should die; she cut the skein and, sprinkling upon her the juice of aconite, transformed the maiden into a spider, that through all ages she might continue to spin her matchless webs."

Do you suppose there's a lesson there? I have a hunch there might be. Just a gut feeling, you could call it.

35. Scattering Stones

There are times when the best writing a person can do is none at all.

By this I do not mean to imply that there are those among us who would be well advised to beat our typewriters into plowshares and take up some other pursuit altogether. What I'm suggesting is that there are intervals in one's writing career, irrespective of one's relative talent or accomplishment, when not writing serves one better than writing, and when one's writing career is best furthered by covering one's typewriter and putting one's career itself on hold.

The conventional wisdom does not always take this position. Because writers have to generate their own motivation and discipline, many of us raise self-discipline to the level of self-flagellation. Either we write all the time or we beat ourselves up for our failure to do so. The hours we put in and the pages we turn out are the standards by which we measure our commitment to our craft—and, as often as not, justify our existence altogether.

When someone asks us how we are, we tend to reply in terms of productivity. "I'm fine; the book's really moving along." As if one's own fineness and the progress of one's work are joined at the hip.

Most of the people who take my "Write For Your Life" seminar find it an empowering experience, and an increase in productivity and writing-oriented energy is a common effect. But it is by no means universal, and occasionally a graduate will report that the seminar was followed by a period in which he or she wrote little or nothing. More often than not, the person involved feels guilty about this situation. (Guilt is an understandably popular emotion, providing as it does the illusion that we're doing something without requiring any action on our part. If we're not working, at least we're feeling rotten; what more can the world ask of us?)

Initially I reacted to such reports by thinking that the seminar had not worked for those particular individuals, that for some indeterminate reason they had not benefitted as fully from it as the writers who'd rushed home and written three family sagas and an epic poem before breakfast. I no longer feel that way, largely as a result of my own experiences over the past year.

As some of you may recall, I once wrote a column recounting my difficulties at the typewriter. I reported that I had made four consecutive attempts to write a book, three of which ran on for over a hundred pages before I abandoned them, and that I had finally concluded that I was not destined to write a book in 1984. Accordingly I resolved to take the entire year off from book writing.

I thought of it at the time as a sabbatical, and one to which I was very likely entitled after a quarter century of incessant scribbling. It was, let me assure you, a long way from being a year on the beach. I have never put in so many hours in my life, or worked anywhere near so hard. I spent six months enrolled in an intensive seminar-leadership training program. I traipsed all over the country presenting my own seminar, and did all the work, both cerebral and clerical, involved in the creation of a new business.

And I did a certain amount of writing. I wrote this column every month, and I wrote two or three short stories, and a feature for *Writer's Yearbook*.

But no books.

I didn't write a book and I didn't *try* to write a book, and I didn't even do any serious *thinking* about a book. It was sometime in late January of '84 that I decided to take the year off, and I did not go back to bookwriting until January 1, 1985. That's not quite a full year, but it was the goal I set myself, and I think it surprised a few people when I stuck to it.

Let me tell you something.

It was one of the best gifts I ever gave myself. And it was unquestionably one of the nicest things I ever did for my writing career.

What was so great about it?

I suppose the most significant benefit was a subtle one. I had managed to change the rules. I did not have to produce fiction in order to establish my value as a human being.

It's interesting, I think, to note how we tend to believe it's necessary to make our writing a compulsive activity. We're evidently afraid that, if we let writing be other than compulsive, we won't do it at all.

I became especially aware of this when several different writers took exception to the same affirmation on my tape of affirmations for writers. One of the hundred or so positive thoughts on the tape is *I don't have to write*. The idea behind it is that one writes not out of compulsion but out of choice. When we internalize this idea, we're less likely to resent our writing as a duty and more capable of enjoying it as something freely chosen. Another affirmation on the tape, *I'm a success whether I write or not,* has the same basic underlying logic.

But, as I said, some writers didn't like it. They feared that, if they gave themselves the choice of writing or not writing, they might choose not to write. And then Something Terrible Might Happen. The sky might fall, Tinkerbell might die, ontogeny might cease to recapitulate philogeny.

I can understand the fear. I've had it myself over the years. It goes like this: maybe I don't really want to write. So I'd better believe that I *have* to write, or else I might stop writing, and I don't want to.

Never mind the illogic of it. This kind of mental jiu jitsu is not essentially a logic problem. The point is this: once we make a leap of faith and allow writing to be a matter of choice, we become free to choose it. And that leaves us free to enjoy it, and to stop resenting it, and to do our best work all the time.

O ur writing is always a mirror of ourselves.

I think the fact that I was very busy in 1984, that I was working harder than ever, made it a lot easier for me to give myself permission not to write. I was often too busy to notice that I wasn't working on a book. Sometime I would very much like to take a real sabbatical, giving myself a year off from book writing and not filling the gap with intensive work in another area. I think I might learn the great lesson that I'm a success whether I work at anything or not, a mind-boggling notion at the moment, but one I'm sure it would be enormously liberating to believe.

Not just now, though.

Another great benefit of my year off from bookwriting lay in the fact that it gave me a chance to digest and absorb various changes in my life and my outlook that had been taking place in recent years. Most of us are growing and changing all the time, and there are stretches in a lifetime in which these changes are particularly rapid and far reaching.

Our writing is always a mirror of ourselves. As we change, our writing has to change. But sometimes one needs to pause in order to allow this to happen.

"To every thing there is a season," the author of *Ecclesiastes* tells us, "and a time to every purpose under the heaven: a time to be born, and a time to die; a time to plant, and a time to pluck up that which is planted; a time to kill, and a time to heal; a time to break down, and a time to build up; a time to weep, and a time to laugh; a time to mourn, and a time to dance; a time to cast away stones, and a time to gather stones together . . ."

To every thing a season. A time to write, certainly, and a time to fill up with what shall be transformed into one's future work. A time, if you will, to recharge one's batteries. A time to gather stones together.

Ahem.

I don't want to give the impression that my year's vacation was taken after philosophical reflection, that I looked up from a spate of Bible-reading and suddenly realized it was time to gather stones. I took my vacation because I had to. I couldn't get a book written, and I was driving myself nuts in the attempt.

Nor, having resolved to leave off writing for a year, did I remain forever confident of the wisdom of my decision. There were times, to be sure, when I felt rather like a Christian Scientist with appendicitis.

I have a feeling my anxiety was exacerbated in a curious way by the two writing-related activities in which I was involved—i.e., leading my seminars and writing my columns. They say that every time you give a seminar you are taking it yourself at the same time. They say, too, that one always teaches what one most needs to learn—and that the teacher is generally his own worst student.

What irony if, after writing a dozen columns and presenting twenty seminars in 1984, I found myself incapable of writing anything?

Don't think I wasn't afraid of it. Of course I was. And I really had no way of knowing what would happen until I sat down at the typewriter, and I'd resolved not to do that until after the first of the year. It was all well and good to talk liltingly of casting away stones and gathering them together, but I wasn't altogether sure of the propriety of casting the first stone, especially since I seemed to be living in a glass house.

Well. Let's get right down to the bottom line, or the proof of the pudding, or whatever you want to call it. On January 1, I started a new novel, and on March 4, I finished it, and I'm delighted with it, and my agent loves it, and it was a genuine pleasure to write the thing.

So there.

It was also a book I couldn't have written without the time off. I had previously been trying to write a sixth book about Matthew Scudder, and had given up in something not unlike despair. I didn't know until late December that I would wind up returning to Scudder in the new book. I discovered that that was what I wanted to do, and I found a way to do so while at the same time producing a book which represented an advance over previous volumes in the series and used elements of myself I hadn't employed before. I needed a year of nonwriting to gather those stones. I didn't have them at hand before.

Many have written—and I among them—of the virtue of day-in-day-out writing, of keeping at it, of applying the seat of the pants to the seat of the chair and hitting those keys relentlessly.

Sometimes that's what you have to do.

But sometimes what you have to do is *not* write. It may be a little more frightening to let yourself believe that, but in the long run the rewards are great.

36. A Writer's New York

It was 1948, around Christmas. I was ten and a half years old. My father, who'd moved to Buffalo sixteen years earlier when he married my mother, had decided to introduce me to the city in which he'd been born and raised.

And so we rode the New York Central and shared a room at the Commodore Hotel, right next door to Grand Central Station. And, in the course of a single long weekend, my dad showed me New York. We rode the ferry to Bedloes Island to see the Statue of Liberty. We went up to the top of the Empire State Building. On Sunday morning we rode the Third Avenue El all the way downtown and watched drunks stagger around on the Bowery. That same night we were in the studio audience of the Ed Sullivan Show. I alternated between watching the stage and the studio monitor; it was another year before I actually saw television in someone's home.

We spent another evening in a Broadway theater, watching Ray Bolger in *Where's Charlie?* Thirteen years later I brought my newborn daughter Amy home from the hospital, played an old 78 of Bolger singing "Once in Love With Amy," and danced around the floor with her in my arms.

By then I was a New Yorker. I may have become one on that first trip to the city with my dad. The transformation may have taken place later. There was another trip, with my parents and my sister Betsy, when I was around sixteen. I recall little more than that we saw *South Pacific* and *The King and I*, and stayed again at the Commodore. Or I may have crossed the line during those last two years in high school when I knew that I would become a writer, and knew from my reading of other men's novels that New York was where you went to take up that vocation. Even those writers who went first to Chicago, or went to pick fruit in California, or ran away to sea, moved on to New York when they were ready to get serious.

I was unquestionably a New Yorker in the summer of 1956, when I lived on my own in the city for the first time. I was an Antioch student with a co-op job in the mailroom at Pines Publications, publishers of Popular Library paperbacks and a long string of magazines and comic books. I lived in a couple of furnished rooms in Greenwich Village before finding an apartment on Barrow Street. It was there, on the kitchen table, that I wrote my first published short story, and it was just about a year later that I sold that story to *Manhunt* for a hundred dollars. When I wasn't writing, or carrying interoffice envelopes around the Pines offices, I was hanging out with folksingers in Washington Square or sneaking into the second act of *My Fair Lady* or walking all over the city.

I have been moving back and forth ever since. I've lived in Buffalo, in Racine, in New Jersey, in Los Angeles. I've visited forty-eight states, and a handful of foreign countries, and I've had fantasies of taking up residence in every last one of them.

But I always come back to New York. I have loved this city and I have hated it, and I have frequently felt both emotions at the same time. (In her stage show *Applesauce*, my friend Maggie Bloomfield refers to New York as "the place where the phrase 'love-hate relationship' originated.") I've lived here continuously for the past eight years, and am about to move for the seventh time into an apartment I hope I'll get to occupy for the next fifty years.

It's possible, though, that I'll leave New York in a year or two or three. I may want to get out; God knows the city gives all of us plenty of reason. I know, though, that I'll come back. I'll always come back. I've precious little choice in the matter.

I'm a New Yorker.

Do you have to come to New York to become a writer?

No, of course not. Writing, as we all know, is something anybody can do anywhere. All I really require is a flat surface for my typewriter. Once the work's written, it speaks for itself. No editor ever turned down a story because it came in an envelope with a faraway postmark. You do not have to come to New York to become a writer.

Unless you're like me.

Because I *did* have to come to this city to become a writer. More fundamentally, I think I had to come here to become myself. The city's extraordinary energy level made it impossible for me to remain the shy and passive person I'd been. I found, in the teeming anonymous tumult of New York, the space and safety to grow and unfold.

Other people find that particular acre of diamonds in their own backyard. They are rooted firmly in the towns in which they grew up and draw personal and artistic nourishment through those roots. I have roots of my own in Buffalo, and in certain ways it remains my home, but it would have stifled my personal and artistic development to have remained there.

Everyone, I suspect, has a spiritual home. Those of us who are fortunate get to find out where it is. Those of us who are supremely lucky get to live there.

New York is one of my spiritual homes. (Ireland is another, and I may discover more.) I draw a tremendous amount of energy from this city. I always have. I suspect I always will.

Forget the cultural advantages, the museums, the concerts, the galleries, the theater. My mother goes to more of that sort of thing in Buffalo than I do in New York; then she comes to New York once a year and samples more of the city's art and theater in four days than I do in twelve months. There's such an embarrassment of cultural riches here, with dozens of options every single day, that it's very easy to pass things up, secure in the knowledge that there'll be other equally attractive choices tomorrow. People in less abundant cities are less apt to do this; they latch on to everything that comes along.

However you experience this city, don't be afraid of it.

So it's not the shows, it's not the pro teams, it's not the night clubs. There are other things that probably matter more to me. That I can walk out the door and walk easily to any of a hundred restaurants. That I can get along perfectly well without a car. That I can buy virtually anything at virtually any hour of the day.

But those are just entries on some sort of urban balance sheet, and they could be offset. The relative cost of the restaurants, say, and of almost everything else. The extreme difficulty of owning a car. The noise, the pollution, the crime.

What really makes the difference, I think, is that New York is so unfailingly interesting to me. I love to explore it, to take the subway out to some unknown area of the outer boroughs and just walk around for a couple of hours. I like to wander through the different ethnic neighborhoods. I like to know how the city has changed, and where the street names came from, and all the stuff you find in old guidebooks. I like to take in all the crazy-quilt architecture, with a dozen different styles crammed into a single block.

I like the way all of this feeds my writing.

In the summer of '76 I was in Los Angeles, living there quite happily, reasonably certain I'd go on living there for the foreseeable future. The climate was wonderful, the rents were reasonable, and it was, like New York, a writer's town. I'd just spent most of a year knocking around the country, and it was comforting to be back again in a city where people found writing to be a perfectly natural occupation for a human being to have. I'd been in no end of places where people found it remarkable enough that I could actually type, let alone that I made up all the sentences myself. So it was nice to be back in a writer's town and I thought I might stay there forever.

Then it was time to write a book, and I got the idea for what turned out to be *Burglars Can't Be Choosers*, the first appearance of Bernie Rhodenbarr. I assumed I'd set it in L.A., since that was where I lived. And I sat down at the typewriter and my mind shifted gears and I started writing about a burglar who lived in New York. Because, while I didn't have the faintest idea how I'd go about operating as a burglar in Los Angeles, I found it astonishingly simple to slip into the fictional skin of an urbane sophisticated Manhattan second-story man.

And so I had Bernie sail past an East Side doorman, a Bloomingdale's shopping bag in his hand. On his way out of that same apartment building, running pell mell from the cops who caught him in the apartment with a murdered man, the same doorman holds the door for Bernie, who calls out a promise to take care of him at Christmas.

See, that's New York. That's my home.

Whether New York was home to me or not, whatever the nature of my feelings for the city, it would cost me money to live elsewhere.

Let it be said, as far as that goes, that it costs me money to live here. Almost everything is more expensive in New York than it is anywhere else in the country. Cabs aren't too bad, and municipal transportation is average, and breakfast in a coffee shop is actually a bargain, but almost everything else is crazy. Rents are outrageous, and, because commercial rents are at least as bad, store prices are correspondingly inflated. Welfare cases in the rest of the country typically have more commodious accommodations than do hardworking and reasonably successful New Yorkers.

When I start having fantasies about moving to Coos Bay, Oregon, say, I remind myself how my income would suffer if I did. And I have to remind myself, because it's easy to forget. Logic suggests that my writing income would be the same wherever I lived. Writers, after all, can work anywhere. All we require is a place to put the typewriter and another place to throw crumpled sheets of paper. Why should the rewards of this activity depend upon where it's done?

There are several answers, and all of them seem to derive from the fact that New York is the unquestioned center of the American publishing industry. This is where business is done, and this is where the people are, and my proximity to other people in my industry has a very tangible payoff.

A couple of weeks ago I wrote a long short story about Matthew Scudder, a boozy ex-cop who has figured in five novels of mine. I intended to send it to one of the mystery magazines, but my wife read it and liked it a whole lot, and it occurred to me that it might be worth a shot at a better market.

So I called Alice Turner, fiction editor at *Playboy*. It ran a little long for a magazine story, I said, but would she like a peek at it? She had a look and liked what she saw. We got together of an evening to work out a few changes, and I had my first sale to one of the country's top markets.

Couldn't I have called her from Coos Bay, or Brookings, South Dakota, or anywhere else in the country? And couldn't we have worked out revisions over the phone? For that matter, couldn't my agent have handled the entire matter?

Of course. But I wouldn't know Alice in the first place if I didn't live in New York, and I very likely wouldn't have made a long distance call anyway, and—believe me, if I didn't live in New York, that story would have wound up in one of the detective books for a nickel a word instead of in *Playboy* for twenty-five hundred bucks.

Being in New York gives me real access to my publishers. There is a difference between a local and a long-distance call beyond what shows up on the monthly statement. There is a difference between breezing into the city once or twice or four times a year and dropping into the Arbor House offices whenever the need arises, or simply because I happen to be in the neighborhood.

Largely as a result of living in New York, I have become friends with a lot of people in the business. This sort of friendship doesn't yield any unseemly favors for me or anyone else. No one I know buys stories out of friendship, or turns down material because it comes from strangers. But editors and writers and publishers are all human beings, and human beings in every industry I ever heard of prefer to do business with friends. All things being equal, we'd rather deal with the known and familiar.

Living in New York puts me frequently in the company of other writers. Actually, this is probably less true than it is in Los Angeles, where a screenwriter friend has complained that he seems *always* to be lunching with other screenwriters, to the point where his life has become rather narrow. Most of my friends are not writers, but quite a few of them are, and when I want shop talk with fellow professionals it's readily available. This is at least as valuable emotionally, in maintaining my self-image as a writer and warding off the isolation which the profession so often imposes, as it is in the practical area of shared information.

Does this mean you have to move to New York?

No, of course not. It's more a way to rationalize the expense and aggravation of living here if it's where you want to be in the first place. If you already have a spiritual home that nourishes and sustains you, you'd be crazy to leave it.

If that's the case, I would suggest that you do what you can to minimize the disadvantage of living away from the center of the action. Here are a few steps you can take:

1. *Run up a big phone bill.* Make calls to New York as if you lived around the corner from your agent and publisher. It may seem like a ridiculous expense to pick up the phone when you could convey the same message in a letter, but the phone does a lot to cut down the psychological distance.

2. *Make at least three trips a year to New York.* A couple of years ago, when I was indeed thinking of living in Oregon, I realized that I could fly in every other month for less than what I would be saving on rent. I would suggest that you make several regular trips a year to New York, and that you be fully prepared to come in any time at a moment's notice should circumstances require your presence. (And let your agent and publishers know that you feel this way; New Yorkers sometimes assume otherwise.)

    Get the most out of these trips. Give everyone you know in the business plenty of advance notice that you're coming. Visit everyone you know through correspondence whether you have business with them or not. Drop in to say hello, to get acquainted. Let the people you know through correspondence take you around the office and introduce you to the people whose names you haven't even heard before.

    This may go against the grain for you. Many of us were drawn to writing in the first place because we could do it all alone in a room with the door closed. Our shyness and fear of other people made a solitary profession safe and appealing. Remember, though, that our writing itself almost always represents a cry for recognition, for acknowledgment, for intimacy. Otherwise we wouldn't have to send the stuff out after we'd written it; we could just keep it in the locked room with us.

We want to be known, to be acknowledged, to be loved. Reaching out to business acquaintances on a personal level is not that different from reaching out to faceless strangers through our written work.

I'd suggest that you let those business trips to New York run a little longer than they have to. Do all the business you can, but treat yourself to a little tax-deductible pleasure while you're at it. And avoid the trap of always spending time in the same neighborhoods and eating at the same restaurants. Do some exploring. Experience the city.

3. *Reach out to other writers.* If there's a writer's club in your town, join it. If not, organize one.

But that's not enough. It's too insular—you want to be in contact with writers who live out of your area as well.

Write letters. If there's a writer whose work you admire, drop him a note and tell him so. I have several good relationships that originated in this fashion; one of us wrote the other a fan letter, we discovered we were each the other's fan, and in rather short order we became friends. But for heaven's sake, don't write to an author with the calculated intent of creating a friendship. Write simply to reach out, with no expectation even of a response. The simple act of writing a generous and honest letter of acknowledgment to another writer will expand your parameters and reduce your isolation even if you never hear a word in reply.

Join professional organizations. Attend their annual meetings. Go to writer's conferences, at least one a year. And don't go to the same one every time.

At the conferences, interact with other writers. The actual program of a writer's conference is probably the least important thing about it. (Unless I'm giving my "Write For Your Life" seminar there.) Seriously, the data, the criticism, the inspiration you'll get at a conference is all subordinate to the great benefit of associating with other people who are there for the same reason you are. Get to know them. Make friends of the ones with whom you feel a common bond. And keep in touch afterward through correspondence.

If you're not too firmly tied where you are, if you've always had a sneaking suspicion that, while New York's a great place to visit, it must be an even greater place to live, and if you'd like to make a terrific investment in your writing career, you might consider moving to New York for a year.

But don't do it the way a friend of mine did. His agent had been urging him for some time to move to New York as a way of getting hooked into the publishing world. My friend lived in a suburb of a southern city. He moved, reasonably enough, to a suburb of New York, where he leased another writer's house for a year. He and his wife moved in and recreated their other life fifteen hundred miles further north of the Equator, and without friends and family around. It was pointless. My friend was so situated that he could come into New York at a moment's notice, but he wasn't *in* New York and he wasn't a part of the city. In my experience, all cities are different and all suburbs are the same; all his relocation did was shrink the geographical distance between his suburban house and New York City.

If you're going to come, do it right. Move to Manhattan. You can live better for less money in Brooklyn or Queens, but I think it would be a false economy for you. Later on, if you become a New Yorker and decide to stick around, you might want to move to Brooklyn or Queens, or even to a suburb. For now, though, spend the extra buck and take a little less in the way of space and creature comfort. You'll be more plugged into the center of things staying at the Y or a rooming house in Chelsea than you will be in a more comfortable and commodious apartment a subway ride away from Manhattan. This investment in New York is easier to make for two sorts of writers—those who are just starting out and those who have already reached the point where they are making a living at the typewriter. The former don't have a good job to give up and the latter have no job but writing.

If you're somewhere in the middle, working at a good job and writing as a sideline, you may prefer to postpone the move, perhaps indefinitely. But if it feels right to you, I suggest that you might want to do it no matter how clearly impractical it may appear to be. Good jobs and comfortable living situations keep a lot of writers from starving to death, but they also can keep you a part-time writer all your life. No one can tell you when it's time to take a chance, but you can tell yourself, and you can take the action.

This needn't involve going to New York; perhaps you'd be more inclined and better advised to take your savings to some part of the country where the living is cheap. But if you do decide on New York, you can find subsistence work here readily enough, waiting table or clerking in a store or shlepping other people's possessions for a moving company. Menial flexible-schedule stuff like this is best for a writer in New York, just as it's a must for actors and musicians. It allows you to give your real work—your writing and your experience of the city—top priority.

However you experience this city, as an occasional visitor or as an immigrant from elsewhere, don't be afraid of it. Helene Hanff has written about a honeymoon couple from England who flew to New York, cabbed to the Plaza Hotel, never left the confines of the hotel for the duration of their visit, cabbed back to the airport and flew back to London. They did so, we are given to understand, not out of pardonable unbridled passion but out of fear. They had picked up so much nonsense from television about crime in New York that they were terrified to venture outside.

Why, I wonder, did they come in the first place? They missed the entire city. The Plaza's a great hotel, but they could have had the identical experience at any of several London hotels and saved airfare and travel time.

This is, after all, a great city for strangers. While people in the outer boroughs tend to live where they were born and raised, almost everyone in Manhattan seems to have moved here from somewhere else. Thus the new arrival doesn't feel nearly so shut out here. A week after you move in, you'll find yourself giving directions to some greenhorn who just got off the bus the day before yesterday.

I'll tell you, this is some town. Even if you wind up hating it, even if you decide quite reasonably that you'd rather live almost anywhere else, you'll be a better writer and a richer person for having experienced New York and absorbed a sense of the city into your consciousness.

And you may wind up agreeing with John Steinbeck. There's something he wrote that I wish I could find to quote. I used to read it in the window of a saloon near Carnegie Hall. Steinbeck spent a few sentences detailing what was wrong with the city. And then he went on to say that, once you've come here, once you've let this city become a part of you and once you've become a part of it, no matter where you go for the rest of your life you'll know one thing—that no place else is ever quite good enough.

And if you don't agree, then as they'd tell you in my old neighborhood in Greenpoint, well, the hell with youse, and who asked youse anyways?

37. This Pen for Hire

Write your own book. Tell your own story. To thine own self be true. Hunt the buffalo, and let the chips fall where they may.

That's a message I've imparted intermittently in this column over the past decade, and one I'll probably urge upon you again in the fullness of time. In the long run, every writer best achieves his goals by following his own star.

In the short run, however, it sometimes profits us to take a detour. A great many of us, at one or another point in our careers, find it worthwhile to write someone else's book, to do some sort of ghostwriting or work-for-hire.

In the world of nonfiction, the spectral presence of ghostwriters is assumed, if not always visible. The public more or less takes it for granted that the autobiographies of prominent persons are collaborative enterprises, with the celebrity supplying the memories and the writer putting them into words and arranging the words in some sort of order upon the page. Sometimes the ghostwriter gets a joint byline, sometimes a credit on the copyright page, sometimes an earnest note in the acknowledgments. Sometimes the ghost gets no credit at all, and the purported author goes on the talk shows and assures Johnny and David that he/she wrote every word of it, and gosh, writing is sure hard work. Some viewers believe the celebrity wrote all the words, just as some people believe that the planet Jupiter is actually a hollow sphere, and that all the survivors of the lost continent of Atlantis live on the inside of it. (And, let it be said, every once in a while some celebrity *does* write a book himself. It happens.)

The general public is rather less aware that ghostwriters function in the world of fiction, too. In the past few years, several novels have appeared by people prominent in other fields. In many if not all cases, the celebrity has had virtually nothing to do with the production of the book. A writer, generally unsung, has written the book. The celebrity has furnished a name for the cover, a photograph for the back, and has gone on the tube to flog the thing. Sometimes the purported author acknowledges the writer for "creative assistance" or "editorial help." More often the celebrity takes all the credit; the writer has to content himself with half the cash.

The celebrity novel is becoming increasingly common, and it's not hard to see why. The books sell rather well. They're easy to promote for a couple of reasons. First of all, the celebrity author has name value. The name's fun to drop in-house, at editorial meetings and sales conferences. Sales reps recognize the name right away, and so do the people they sell to. Just as important, it's a cinch to get the book plenty of ink and air. Gossip columnists take note of a novel by a celebrity while they would overlook the same book by a nonentity, or even by an established novelist. Celebrities are naturals for the talk-show circuit because, unlike professional novelists, they don't have to sit up there and talk about the book. They can talk instead about life in the fast lane, or about their career in Washington or Hollywood. Or they can just look beautiful.

Finally, readers figure the celebrity author brings some real expertise to the novel. He or she really knows where the bodies are buried. And the reader already has a relationship with the celebrity, already feels as though they know each other, so it's not like buying a book by a faceless stranger.

In the past two months, my agent called me twice to relay feelers from publishers. First he mentioned a rather prominent actor best known for his work in suspense films. "They think he should write a novel," he said.

"Perhaps he should," I agreed.

"But of course they don't want him to write it," he went on. "They think you would be the perfect person to write it. They thought it might have a Hollywood setting, and he'd help out with that, and possibly furnish some ideas. I told them I didn't think you were interested."

"How well you know me," I said.

A few weeks later he reported that a forensic medicine expert, already the published author of two works of nonfiction, was ready to turn his talents to the novel. He didn't actually want to *write* a novel, but he could supply a few ideas, and of course he'd furnish the medical expertise. The proposition was not entirely unattractive—I had met the gentleman in question, found him pleasant company, knew him as a tireless and enthusiastic promoter of his earlier books, and could believe that he would indeed contribute useful background material for the novel, and that the venture would be financially profitable for all concerned. Nevertheless, I said I wasn't interested.

Before I explain why, let's look at some other opportunities for fictional ghosts. The series provides frequent employment for spectral novelists. The paperback racks overflow with endless series of category fiction featuring the same lead character or characters over and over again, all ostensibly by the same writer. (All the books in a given series are supposedly by the same writer, that is. Not all the books in *all* the series.)

Sometimes one writer does indeed write all the books in a lengthy series. But sometimes a particular writer will do the first three or six or twelve books about a gunfighter in the old west, or an ex-mercenary going up against the mob, or five marines winning World War II a battle at a time, and will understandably tire of the sport. Because the series in profitable for all concerned, ghostwriters will be brought in to keep it alive. The original writer may furnish outlines, may vet manuscripts before they go to the publisher, or may do nothing but collect a piece of the action.

*V*arious forms of hackwork provide a paid apprenticeship.

Sometimes there is no original writer. On such occasions a packager dreams up the idea for a series, gets a proposal written, cuts a deal with a publisher, and finds writers to produce the various volumes. The packager may supply his writers with fully developed outlines or he may leave them largely on their own.

Occasionally an established writer simply leases out his byline. Twenty-five years ago, a series of paperback originals appeared carrying one of the most respected names in American mystery fiction. Some people probably wondered why the author, who had previously always published in hardcover, was now writing paperback originals. As it happened, his sole connection with the books was monetary; he was in ill health and bad financial straits, and his agent managed to set up a deal wherein lesser writers supplied the books and the Big Name took a cut. And all the royalties and sub rights.

Film novelizations and tie-in novels are not necessarily ghostwriting—one more often than not uses one's own name, or one's own pen name—but I'll mention them because, once again, the writer winds up writing someone else's book rather than his own. The novelization is what the name implies; one takes an original screenplay and turns it into a novel, which in turn is published at approximately the same time that the film is released. A tie-in is a little different; it's a novel based on the characters in a TV show, with the plot devised by the book writer. There haven't been many tie-ins lately, but some years ago they were common, and tie-ins based on *The Man From U.N.C.L.E.* and *The Partridge Family* were quite successful.

Novelizations and tie-ins are successful because the publicity generated by the film or TV show creates a ready-made audience for the book. Movie and TV people like them because their presence on the newsstand helps to promote the show or movie, and because they get a licensing fee and royalty on copies sold. As far as the writer is concerned, both are generally considered a rather low form of hackwork, which is curious when one considers that the process of turning a screenplay into a novel is not philosophically different from that of turning a novel into a screenplay.

I did a couple of tie-ins twenty-five years ago; one of them, curiously, is coming out later this year from Foul Play Press, retitled *You Could Call It Murder*. My publisher thinks it's good enough to merit reissuing, although I have my doubts. I had never done a novelization, and was counting on that distinction to get me into heaven at a later date, but this past summer I did indeed do one—of which more later.

Is this sort of writing a good deal for the writer?

Well, it depends. It depends on the deal, of course, and it depends on the stage one is in in one's career. And, to be sure, it depends how badly you need the money.

Most of the writers I know have done some sort of ghosting or writing-for-hire early in their careers. Most of us, when we're starting out, are not capable of writing our own books out of our own inner selves and supporting ourselves in the process. Sometimes we have to learn how to write before we can manage more ambitious books, and various forms of hackwork (if you want to call it that) provide a paid apprenticeship. Anyone capable of learning in the first place will unquestionably learn a great deal by writing a book from someone else's outline, or with characters supplied by another. Similarly, sooner or later one will no longer be learning much by writing these books, and persisting in their production will hinder one's growth rather than contribute to it. The trick is knowing when to stop; as with most forms of self-destructive behavior, one generally stops a little later than one should have, and some people never stop at all.

Suppose one is past one's apprenticeship. Can one then justify writing books for a packager, or ghosting novels for an actor or politician?

It depends what sort of justification works for you. There is a series of mystery novels set in Washington which has consistently hit the bestseller list and has made their actual author a considerable amount of money, more than he ever made on books for which he received full credit. Has he made a mistake?

Only he could tell you. Only he could guess what he might have written, under his own name and out of his own self, if he hadn't been writing these books instead.

I know a writer who eked out a living for years in several areas of category fiction before he began writing an extended series of paperback historical novels for a book packager. The packager developed plotlines and set up a deal with a publisher and took, as I understand it, half the income from the books; the writer undertook laborious research and wrote the books for the other 50 percent. And made a fortune, and broke through to bestsellerdom, and turned out to find himself as a writer in these books as he never had previously.

And why did I turn down the two ghosting jobs I was recently offered?

Not because I don't think they might have been lucrative. I'm sure either of them would have paid me as much in front as I normally receive for a novel, and either of them could have done very well, possibly achieving best-seller status. From a dollars-and-cents standpoint, it would seem that both books offered me great potential and no real risk.

On the other hand, this kind of writing doesn't do much for one's career. It is anonymous. There is no glory in it, and the people who read and like the book won't rush out to buy your other books because they won't know who you are. It would take me at least as much time and energy to write a book under the actor's name, or under the doctor's name, as it would to write a book of my own. And it would add nothing to my body of work.

And, because I have a limited amount of time and energy and creative ideas available, to write either of these books would mean to forgo writing a book of my own. I'm not sure just what books of my own I'll wind up writing, or just how I'll employ that time and energy, but at this stage I'm unwilling to spend it on someone else's book.

Why, then, did I do the novelization?

Good question. It was a sort of special case, in that the pub-lisher thought I was just the person to turn this particular screen-play into a novel, and was willing to back up this conviction with a much higher advance than one generally gets for a novelization, and a generous royalty on top of it. (The writers of novelizations do not routinely get royalty contracts.) Furthermore, I read the screenplay and liked the story and characters. Finally, the publisher wanted a real novel, with my own creativity brought to bear and the whole book to be something of substance, on which I would put my own name.

It looked to me like a lucrative project which would be artisti-cally engaging and, because I had the whole thing outlined, a rather straightforward piece of work. I wound up writing it very rapidly and turned out a book that pleased both me and the publisher. (As it turned out, the author of the original screenplay had the legal right to bar the publication of the book, and he exercised it; thus, al-though I was paid in full, the book will never be published.)

Before I knew of the book's fate, however, I had decided two things—that I was glad to have written it, and that I would never want to undertake another novelization. Explaining this to my agent, I cited the story of Voltaire, who once accompanied a friend to a specialized Parisian bordello and enjoyed himself. A week or so later, the friend invited him to go again, and Voltaire declined em-phatically.

"I am surprised," the friend said. "You seemed to have such a good time."

"I did," said Voltaire, "but I should not care to repeat it. Once, a philosopher. Twice, a pervert."

38. Getting By on a Writer's Income

A writer, James Michener has said, can make a fortune in America. But he can't make a living.

I think the point is a good one. It's hardly a secret that a few people get rich every year at their typewriters. The same media attention which fifty years ago lionized a handful of writers as important cultural leaders now trumpets the incomes of a comparable handful. The tabloid reader knows nowadays about paperback auctions and movie tie-ins and multi-volume book contracts with sky-high advances and elevator clauses.

Balanced against this image of the writer as fortune's darling is a similarly glamorous picture of the unsuccessful writer starving in an airless garret, eating baked beans out of the can and pawning his overcoat to buy carbon paper. The poor blighter's starving for his art, and he'll either go on starving in pursuit of his pure artistic vision until they lay his bones in Potter's Field, or else he'll suddenly break through to literary superstardom, and the next we'll see of him he'll be at poolside sipping champers and snorting lines with the Beautiful People.

The validity of both of these images notwithstanding, most of the writers I know have never gotten rich and have always gotten by. This has certainly been the case with me. I have, to be sure, had good years and bad years. I had a couple of years when I made more money than I knew what to do with—although I always thought of something—and I had other years, and rather more of them, when I might have switched to another line of work had there been anything else for which I was qualified.

I did live in a garret once, in a rather pleasant area under a sloping roof atop a barbershop in Hyannis, Massachusetts. For a couple of weeks I subsisted solely on peanut butter sandwiches and Maine sardines, and I wrote a short story every day, one of which ultimately became my first sale. (The room was eight dollars a week, the sardines were fifteen cents a can, and I got a hundred bucks for the story.)

"I've been rich and I've been poor," Sophie Tucker said, "and believe me, rich is better." I suppose I believe her, but I also believed showman Mike Todd when he said he'd been broke innumerable times, but he'd never been poor.

I think the distinction's a useful one. The writing life has had me broke any number of times, and I suspect it will continue to do so as long as I pursue it. I won't be poor, though, not so long as I'm able to recognize that being broke is a temporary thing, that it's part of the business, and that it doesn't have to interfere with either my writing or my living.

There are several reasons why being broke is inevitable now and then. Sometimes the fault is my own. My ability to produce marketable material varies with the ups and downs of my own emotional life. Writers are not machines, and even machines do break down from time to time. Like most writers I've known and known of, I have occasional periods when I can't get anything written and other stretches when what I write just doesn't work.

Other times my writing goes along just fine but I can't seem to get money to come into my house. Sometimes changes in the market leave me in the position of a dress manufacturer with a warehouse full of midi skirts. Other times the entire publishing industry seems to have gone on hold, and manuscripts sit on editors' desks for months without being either accepted or rejected. Sometimes I get slow-paid by publishers intent on solving their entire cash flow problems at my personal expense. Sometimes a publisher decides his inventory is too large and elects not to publish dozens of books he's already bought and paid for; I get to keep the advance but I can forget about royalties, foreign sales, and all of the subsidiary income that make the difference between profit and loss.

Any number of things can happen to render a freelance writer insolvent, and if you stay in the game long enough all of them will happen to you sooner or later. But the point of this piece is not that dire events will occur but that you can survive them. You may decide it's not worth it—some of us are not temperamentally suited to the financial ups and downs of full-time freelancing. If you can't stand that kind of heat, then you should probably stay out of this particular kitchen.

If you can stand it, and would like to survive as gracefully as possible, here are some survival tips.

1. *Don't run scared.* While fear may not be the only thing we have to be afraid of, it's certainly up there at the top of the list. It can be an absolutely paralyzing emotion, utterly undercutting the self-confidence it takes in order to put words on paper

in the expectation that someone will be eager to read them.

Fear keeps a lot of writers from freelancing in the first place. Some people are never comfortable with the financial insecurity of freelance writing, and do better emotionally if they remain employed and write on the side. Those of us who do choose to write full-time have to balance fear with faith—in ourselves, in Providence, or in both.

Just about the time I was starting to write stories, Richard S. Prather published an article in *Writer's Digest* explaining how he'd become a full-time writer. He'd begun with the revelation that nobody starves in America; accordingly he'd decided to quit his job and invest a year in the process of establishing himself. It was, of course, the best investment he ever made, and before the year was out he had sold novels about private eye Shell Scott and had launched what was to be an extremely successful career.

There are several reasons why being broke is inevitable now and then.

Prather's piece must have made an impression on me; not only do I remember it after all these years, but my own first published story began with the line "Anybody who starves in this country deserves it," an observation of dubious socioeconomic validity, perhaps, but a not-bad opening shot for a suspense story.

In any event, it was easy enough for me to decide to freelance. My salary and expenses were so low at the time that I didn't have to sit down and write *Forever Amber* to make ends meet. Some years later, when I returned to freelancing after a year and a half's gainful employment, I had a wife and two children and a somewhat higher standard of living. But I also had the knowledge based on previous experience that writing was something I could make a living at, and I made the move without thinking to be afraid of the outcome.

2. *Watch out for sure money.* There are more ways than one to run scared. In my own case, fear has tended to manifest itself more in terms of an inability to take chances *at the typewriter*. For a few too many years I wrote pulp novels on regular assignment for sure money rather than risk failure by attempting something more ambitious.

This is even more of a hazard for writers who are rather better established than I was. Not long ago, for example, I was talking with a successful Hollywood screenwriter. He had had some success with a novel some years ago and was talking about wanting to write another novel—and did a pretty good job of talking himself out of it.

"It would take a minimum of six months and probably more like a year," he explained, "and then what could I expect to see out of it? A ten thousand dollar advance? A couple grand more in royalties if it gets lucky? Maybe a few thousand in foreign sales? You write one half-hour sitcom script and you make more than that by the time you're done with the residuals. And what does that take, a week's worth of real work? I'd love to write a novel but I don't see how I can afford it."

It's hard to fault his dollars-and-cents logic. But when I start thinking along those lines, I try to take a step back and remind myself that I never got into this business for the money in the first place. I became a writer so that I could do what I wanted, and if I reach a point where my "success" as a writer keeps me from doing what I want to do, then there would seem to be something seriously wrong with the turn my career has taken.

In my friend's case, it may be close to impossible for him to gamble the six months or a year required for that novel's production. If he's used to living on a six-figure income, how can he survive the drop in income which writing that novel will almost inevitably entail? Prather may be right, and perhaps nobody does starve around here, but mortgages get foreclosed on and cars get repossessed. Should a simple urge to write a novel leave a family living in Griffith Park on nuts and berries?

Which brings up another point.

3. *Keep the nut down.* However good we are at what we do, however much acclaim we win for our efforts, we are not working for the government or IBM. We do not have that kind of job security. We have security of another sort, the knowledge that we possess a marketable skill which no one can take away from us and which will ultimately carry us through adversity. But the operative word there is "ultimately." We can't count on a weekly check the way others can.

For this reason, and to keep from painting myself into a financial corner where I can't afford to take professional chances, I find it worthwhile to keep my fixed costs as low as possible. I don't buy things on time, and my rent is relatively low in proportion to my income. (I did buy a house on time, there being no other way for most of us to purchase real property, but when a Hollywood windfall came along I paid off the mortgage rather than spend the money upgrading the property, or enhancing my standard of living, or invest for future gain. Paying off the mortgage, several people assured me, was not a sound move economically. I knew what they meant and I knew they were right, but I knew the best thing I as a self-employed writer could do with that windfall was knock out that monthly payment, and I never regretted doing it.

I don't want to give the impression that I live like a church-mouse; I very likely spend as high a percentage of my income as the next wastrel. But I try to squander it on luxuries rather than saddle myself with a heavy burden of ongoing necessities. I'll spend money on travel, blow it on high living, or otherwise find a way to divest myself of it without increasing my day-to-day expenditures. Thus, when the money supply dries up and I have to cut back, I simply go without. I don't own a car; I take cabs when I'm flush and use the subway when I'm not. I treat myself to a lot of good dinners when there's money on hand, and I stay home and eat rice when it's gone.

4. *Don't take income for granted.* When pests asked J.P. Morgan what the stock market was going to do, he always gave the same answer. "It will fluctuate," he told them.

So will a writer's income. If anything, my income seems more subject to fluctuation now than it ever did, and seems concurrently to depend less on how hard I work than ever before. When I started out, I wrote a book a month for one publisher, working on regular assignment and knowing that I was going to get a certain check every month. I would write the book and I would get the check. Nowadays I'll work hard and produce a lot and make next to nothing, and then the next year I'll goof off and get little done and earn a lot.

Just recently, for example, a book of mine was published and sold to a paperback house. The publisher was as certain as he'd ever been that he was going to get a six-figure advance for this property, and his track record shows he doesn't make many mistakes along these lines. Well, there was no book club sale, and no paperback publisher submitted a floor bid, and they finally had the auction and he got the six-figure price, all right, but two of those figures came after the decimal point.

Well, these things happen, and I'm glad I've been in the business long enough to roll with the punches. The real heartache comes when you take the big money for granted and act accordingly.

Friend of mine writes mysteries. For quite a few years there he had a movie sale every year, regular as clockwork. Sometimes two books sold in a year, but there was always one that came through for him, and that was half his income.

Not surprisingly, he learned to count on it. If you make, say, sixty thousand dollars a year, year in and year out, and half of that comes from film sales, it's not too long before you're living on sixty thousand a year, and in the expectation of sixty thousand a year. It would be hard to do otherwise.

Then the well ran dry. Nobody bought movie rights to his books, and he sat around wondering what he was doing wrong. Well, he wasn't doing anything wrong, any more than he'd been doing anything especially right previously. You just can't take windfalls for granted, and when they come with regularity it's an easy mistake to make.

There are other ways to take income for granted. When I write a mystery, my income is realized from several sources. There's the advance my hardcover publisher pays me. There's the royalties the book earns over and above the advance—they don't amount to an awful lot—and there's the paperback money. There's another small chunk from a book club specializing in mysteries, and there are checks from the six or eight foreign countries where my books are regularly published.

Every now and then, these sources of subsidiary income dry up. There was a two-year stretch, for instance, when my French publisher didn't buy a single American mystery. There was another point when the Scandinavians suddenly ceased buying foreign books. It's important—but almost impossible—for me to remember that the only thing I can take for granted when I write a book is the initial advance. Other sources of income may be probable, but they're a long way from certain.

Fortunately, there are so many diverse sources of subsidiary income that I can survive when one or two of them dries up. Which leads us to our next point.

5. *Don't put all your eggs in one basket.* As I said, when I was first in the business I wrote a book a month for one publisher. Then I had a falling out with my agent and we parted company, and the publisher in question turned out to be a closed

shop, dealing only through that particular agent. Although I liked writing for him and he very much liked publishing my work, we both had to live without each other. This was manifestly easier for him than it was for me.

Well, I survived, and in the long run the experience was enormously beneficial for me. I was forced to grow as a writer. But I had made a mistake. I had grown far too dependent upon a single market, and when it was closed to me I found it extremely difficult to make a living.

This happens to lots of people. You can take a market for granted just as you can take certain income for granted, and an abrupt change in that market can be devastating. Sometimes there's not much you can do about it. In the fifties, the market for pulp westerns dropped absolutely dead. A whole slew of writers had done all their writing for these magazines for a couple of decades. They didn't know how to write anything else. Some of them managed to write western novels for the paperbacks, but that market couldn't absorb all of them nor could all of them produce novel-length stories successfully. Others switched and wrote mysteries, or got into television work, or somehow adapted.

But some of them stopped being writers.

Now you can say with some justification that these fellows should have seen the scribbling on the side of the building. The pulps didn't all die on the same afternoon. There was a point where some western writers realized they were going to have to develop new markets while others missed the boat—or stagecoach, if you prefer.

Any market can dry up. While it's hard to guard against the collapse of a whole genre, a writer can avoid being too dependent upon a single publisher. If too much of your income comes from a single source, you might as well be on that man's payroll. You're working for him and he can fire you at will. Or he can go out of business.

Or the editor who likes your work can move elsewhere. This is almost certain to happen repeatedly in the course of a writing career, and it has its good and bad aspects. While it can mean the end of a relationship with one publisher, it can also mean the beginning with another. And that's one way to:

6. *Make friends in the business.* I haven't heard of a business yet, with the possible exception of the undertaking trade, where people wouldn't prefer to deal with people they know. Some

writers use this fact of life to explain their own lack of success, muttering darkly that a conspiracy of old friends is keeping their work from getting published.

That's paranoia. Editors don't keep their jobs and publishers don't remain in business by buying inferior work from their buddies. (And yes, I have known an editor or two who bought garbage and took kickbacks, and another who published his old pals out of friendship even when their work was no good, and none of these people are working today.) What a good relationship with an editor or publisher will do is assure that they will use you if they can. They would rather work with you than with an unknown quantity. They know you're reliable. They know you can deliver. They know you won't make a pain in the ass of yourself over some minor point. And, all things being equal, they'll do business with you rather than take a chance on some yoyo they've never laid eyes on.

Publishing is an extremely small business in relation to its importance and influence. Editors commonly change jobs many times in the course of a career, even as writers commonly change publishers. One happy result of this—there are unhappy results, too—is that sooner or later you wind up knowing a whole lot of people at a whole lot of publishing houses.

It's worthwhile to cultivate these friendships. This doesn't mean sending out a ton of Christmas presents. It means becoming as genuinely friendly as your nature permits with the people you do business with. If you don't live near New York, it means budgeting for one or two trips a year just to allow yourself the chance to know personally some of the people with whom you've been corresponding.

It means, too, that you've got to get past thinking of the relationship between writer and editor or writer and publisher as on a par with that of tenant and landlord. It's hard not to regard it as essentially an adversary relationship, especially during the early years when the chief function of an editor seems to be that of spilling coffee on your story prefatory to returning it to you with a form rejection slip. But we are all of us in this silly business together, and working for the same ends, and it's useful to remember this.

7. *Be careful with advances.* William Faulkner once wrote a friend that the best way to get published was to secure an advance from a publisher. Then, he explained, the only way they

can get their money back is by publishing your book.

Faulkner's point is not altogether off the mark. There's a definite advantage in getting a publisher to make a commitment in advance. While he still may elect not to publish a book if it falls short of his expectations, he at least has a vested interest in publishing it and this can make him more receptive to the final product.

There are dangers, though, in living on advances. You find yourself trying to come up with an idea that will lead to two chapters and an outline and a fast contract, not something that will evolve into the best possible book. Some years ago, when I was more prolific than I am now and landed virtually all of my contracts on the basis of an outline or a brief proposal, I could hardly avoid the realization that I was writing a couple of hundred words for half the money and then had to write an entire book just to get the other half. It seemed economically sensible to stick to outlines—I could write dozens of them in the course of a year far more easily than I could produce half a dozen actual books. But sooner or later, I found, you have to deliver the book, or after a while they won't make more deals with you.

Years ago I knew a writer who was always living on advances. His agent operated as a sort of banker; whenever my acquaintance sold a story, the agent would advance him the sum due him, reimbursing himself when the check ultimately arrived from the publisher. At other times, when the writer needed money and had not sold anything, the agent would extend an advance against future sales, which is really nothing more than a polite term for a loan. On one such occasion, the writer turned up to collect a fifty dollar advance, and received a check for forty-five dollars; the agent was so accustomed to taking ten percent out of everything he'd even done so with the loan.

If you live on advances you're always behind, working to get even. You're like a coal miner in debt to the company store. I think it's sound business sense to contract for one's work in advance rather than write all the time on speculation, and it's undeniably true that the greater a publisher's cash commitment to a book, the more likely he is to promote it effectively. Still, living on advances has its dangers.

8. *Have a way to make the rent.* My grandfather started out as a plumber. He saved a few dollars and bought a couple of buildings, and he ultimately made his living in real estate. But he

never let his card in the plumbers' union expire. He paid his dues every year, just in case.

Writing's the only trade I know, so I can't go down to the union hall if the rent's due and the wolf is at the door. I've often wished I could. I think a writer should know how to do something, preferably the sort of thing that enables him to pick up day work when the going gets tough. I know writers who are experienced bartenders or waitresses. They can get work whenever they need it. Experience as a fry cook, for example, is probably more useful to a writer than experience writing ad copy or selling insurance, because it's the sort of thing you can walk into on the spur of the moment and keep as long as the financial shoe pinches.

While I don't have that sort of fall-back skill, I do have some things I can do to bring in small sums on a steady basis while my main business of bookwriting blows hot and cold. I write my *WD* column, for example; it provides a steady monthly check and gives me a regular monthly task to perform. I do occasional reviewing for a book club. I teach a course at a university.

Occasionally I've thought about getting a hack license, or doing office temp work, but I haven't had to yet. When the time comes that I do, I hope I won't let pride stand in the way. Having to do something else to make a few bucks doesn't mean that one has failed as a writer. It just means you've got a case of the shorts, and that, as we've seen, is part of the game.

9. *Remember the difference between poor and broke.* And act accordingly. Being broke is not a crime, nor is it proof of one's inadequacy as a writer or as a human being. If you go around with an attitude of implicit apology for being temporarily without funds, it's going to do you more harm than good.

Conversely, an air of confidence can get you through some tight spots. Some years ago I bought a house in New Jersey. I made the deal and set the closing date with the intention of making the down payment with a chunk of movie dough that was coming my way.

Now this didn't seem unrealistic at the time. The deal with the movie company was already made when I arranged to buy the house. It was just a question of drawing up the contract and getting the cash.

Terrific. Various lawyers dragged their feet on the contract, and then when it was finally signed the producer found a way to stall. He kept being out of town and unreachable by phone, and the closing date on the house kept approaching, and I didn't have any money. My then-wife asked if I didn't think I should tell the seller. "No," I said. "I can't see how it will help me to give him that information in advance." Well, then, didn't I think I ought to engage a lawyer? "No," I said, "because if I have a lawyer and he has a lawyer, the two lawyers'll fight." Then what did I intend to do? "I'll just play it by ear," I said. "Maybe the money will come in by then." And if it didn't? "Maybe I'll think of something."

Well, I went to the closing and explained the situation. I offered to pay the down payment with a post-dated check, which would enable the sellers to sue me if I couldn't cover it but which wouldn't really get them their property back, since title would have passed to me by then. Still, they were anxious to sell, and they knew I wasn't going to put the house on wheels and truck it across the state line, and I knew the money was going to come in from Hollywood sooner or later, and because I didn't have a lawyer their lawyer didn't have anybody to fight with, and I bought the house. I think the fact that I was really quite confident about the whole thing had a lot to do with its outcome.

10. *Let financial need be a spur, not a sledgehammer.* Mickey Spillane has told of the time when he was living on an offshore island, spending a lot of time on the beach and generally taking life easy. "I decided it would be fun to write a story," he recalls, "but I couldn't get an idea. I took long walks, I sat at the typewriter, but I couldn't seem to come up with an idea. Then one day I got a call from my accountant. He said the money was starting to run short. And you know what? All of a sudden I started getting one idea after the other."

I love that story, and I can believe it. Financial need can very well be necessary to goad the unconscious to come up with story ideas. But when the need is too great, when it weighs too heavily upon the mind, it can have the opposite effect, serving not as a spur in the horse's flank but a sledgehammer blow between his eyes that stops him dead in his tracks.

I try to avoid this by divorcing myself from financial matters as far as I possibly can. I have an accountant, and for a couple of years now all my income has gone directly from my agent to him. Similarly, all my bills go straight to him as well. Sometimes there's a lot of money in my account and sometimes there's not, but unless matters are very urgent I don't know how high the stack of bills is, and that's fine with me. I can forget all that and concentrate on writing.

Not everyone would be comfortable turning over financial management to another party. Sometimes I wonder if I shouldn't be handling this aspect of my life myself. But all in all I like things as they are.

11. *Remember it's only money.* According to Dr. Johnson, no man but a blockhead ever wrote except for money. Now you can read that line in more than one way, and I prefer to believe that Johnson meant that one is not justified in writing in the *expectation* of anything but financial gain, that he who writes hoping to be rewarded by fame, or to change the world, is unrealistic in his expectations.

I write for money, and if I struck oil in my backyard I can't be certain I'd ever write another line. All the same, I try to remember that it's only money and that money is just not all that important. I didn't get into this business for money and I don't stay in it for money. If I write something I don't want to write, I'm giving up some personal freedom. Perhaps more important, if financial considerations induce me to forgo writing something I would really like to write, I'm giving up a large measure of freedom and defeating my own purpose in having become a writer in the first place.

I have come to believe that freedom is ultimately the chief attraction of the writing life. I believe, too, that we are about as free as we recognize ourselves to be. The more I realize that material possessions have little to do with my happiness and that money is accordingly of rather little importance, the freer I am to enjoy this life and to fulfill whatever potential I have.

And that's as much as I have to say on the subject of living on a writer's income. Now that I've said it, they better pay me for it. And fast.

39. *Summary Judgment*

Good morning, class. Today I'd like to give you a quick rundown on the plot of a novel. The lead character is an elderly widow in a small town in North Carolina, and when the book opens there's this stray dog hanging around the house where she lives alone. She keeps telling people that she can't take on the responsibility of caring for a dog at her age, but at the same time she keeps on fixing food for it, and the dog keeps hanging around.

She wants to have her chairs redone, so she takes the seats off, and when the fellow who's going to fix them comes to pick them up she feeds him lunch. Then, before washing the dishes, she sits down to watch a soap opera, and she sits on one of the chairs with the seat removed, and wouldn't you know she gets stuck in it and can't move? And she can't call to anyone or reach anyone, and her big fear is that whoever rescues her will discover that she watches that soap opera, and that she let her lunch dishes just sit while the program was on instead of doing them up right away. I'll tell you, this really worries her.

Well, earlier she called the dogcatcher, and he comes by and gets her out of the chair, but first she makes him wash up her dishes so she won't be scandalized. He has to cut the chair frame to get her out of it, but he's a handyman when he's not a dogcatcher, and he offers to repair the chair for her, and he figures he'll bring it back on Saturday and come around lunchtime, because the food she has just given him is about the best he's ever had.

He drops his wallet while he's there, and in it there's a letter from his nephew who's just a few years younger than he is, and who's over at the local reformatory for auto theft. The old lady goes and visits the youngster and takes him some food, of course, and later he breaks out of the reformatory and comes by her house. She makes him take a bath and takes him to church, and the police get a tip about him and come to the church, and it winds up that he and one of the deputies are both wearing robes up in the choir loft and blending with the choir, one to catch the fugitive and the other to avoid getting caught. He gets out and steals another church member's car, but he winds up driving it to the old woman's house and gets caught, and they take him back to the reformatory, and he wants the old woman to adopt him, but . . .

Well, that's the gist of it. There are other things that happen, of course, like when the old woman's unmarried son climbs up to get some leaves out of the roof gutters and the ladder buckles with him on it and he's hanging from the roof and the next-door neighbor sees him there and thinks he's a prowler and is going to shoot him but then doesn't. There's lots of amusing incidents of that sort.

Well, what do you think, boys and girls? Think it'll play in Peoria? If it ran up the flagpole, would you salute? If it shouted "Frog," how far would you jump? More to the point, if it came in over your transom, would you offer it a chair or show it the door?

It sounds slight, sir.

Slight, Arnold?

Yes, sir. The problems seem like minor problems, don't they, sir? I mean, so what if the old lady can't get out of the chair? So what if her friends find out she's been watching soap operas?

They find out ultimately anyway, as it happens.

And is it the end of the world, sir?

No, she just makes a joke about it, and has to tell the story to everybody at church.

I'd call that a big yawn, sir.

I see. What do you think, Rachel?

Well, sir, I think it sounds suspiciously like a mid-list book, sir.

Oh, dear, Not a mid-list book!

I'm afraid so, sir. You know, the sort of novel publishers used to publish five years ago, but that they're all cutting back on these days. You want to know something funny, sir? Five years ago they were saying the same thing, and five years before that, too.

I know.

I wonder why that is?

I think it's the middle aspect of it, Rachel. As you all know, middle age is what starts five years older than you are now, no matter how old you happen to be. And a mid-list book is one every publisher will assure you could have been published five years ago, no matter what year it is now. For at least twenty years publishers have said that they're cutting back on mid-list books, and for all those years they have indeed been cutting back on mid-list books, and one may understandably wonder at this stage how they have any mid-list books left to cut back on.

But never mind. The book I've described is unmistakably of that endangered species, and any publisher might be expected to start cutting back on it the minute he set eyes on it.

How, then, did this particular book happen to get published? *It's been published, sir?*

Did you think I was just making up that plot on the spur of the moment? The book in question is *Walking Across Egypt*, by Clyde Edgerton, and it was published this year by Algonquin Books of Chapel Hill, North Carolina, in association with Taylor Publishing Company of Dallas. It is, I should add, thoroughly delightful from first page to last, warm and amusing and satisfying, with not a false word or a clumsy turn of phrase to be found within its pages.

And why am I telling you all this?

Because several points occurred to me while I was reading *Walking Across Egypt*, and I wanted to share them with you. The book made me think about What Publishers Want, and made me wonder how much it matters what publishers do or don't want. And the book made me think, too, about the value of outlines and summaries and synopses.

*I*t is almost always a mistake to submit anything other than a complete manuscript.

First off, let's agree that *Walking Across Egypt* is no-question slight, that its concerns are the small problems of small people, and that any agent or publisher who read it would despair at the likelihood of being able to publish it profitably. The author's skill and the book's considerable quality don't change all this. I don't know if Algonquin Books of Chapel Hill will make a profit on this title, but I'm pretty sure they won't get rich off it. According to the book's flap copy, Mr. Edgerton teaches education and creative writing at St. Andrews Presbyterian College in Laurinburg, North Carolina, and he and his wife sing and play folk music professionally. I doubt that he'll be able to quit his day job on the strength of his royalties. Or his night job either.

But *Walking Across Egypt* got published, didn't it? I don't know how many copies it has sold, but one of them wound up in the Fort Myers Beach public library. It is the author's second book; his first, *Raney*, seems also to have been a mid-list book, and received excellent notices in the *Washington Post*, *Sewanee Review*, the *New York Times*, and the *Kansas City Star*.

What exactly is my point here? I suppose it's that, if a writer is good enough and if his book is good enough, it will get published and it will find the audience it deserves. When all is said and done, you're still better off writing your own book than trying to write someone else's. If your book, like Mr. Edgerton's, is not categorically what the publishing industry is clamoring for, the odds against you are longer and the rewards smaller—but when did I ever tell you this was going to be easy, or that you were likely to get rich at it?

Having said that, now let's talk about synopses.

Any agent or publisher who made Mr. Edgerton's acquaintance by reading a synopsis of *Walking Across Egypt* would turn it down.

This is not because the book is poorly plotted. On the contrary, the structure of the book's plot is one of the factors in the novel's success. But the book could not possibly succeed without the author's enormous skill in narration and characterization, and a synopsis cannot convey these abilities. All I could find in a plot synopsis would be a dozen reasons to send the book back to its author.

I think that's usually the case with synopses. The more I consider the question, the more I am drawn to the conclusion that it is almost always a mistake to submit anything other than a complete manuscript to an agent or publisher.

I'm going to repeat that, just because it's such a radical departure from the prevailing wisdom: *It is almost always a mistake to submit anything other than a complete manuscript to an agent or publisher.*

What do you accomplish by submitting a synopsis? Well, it expedites things for all concerned. You don't have to write an entire two-hundred- or three-hundred- or five-hundred-page novel and have it get rejected. Instead, you can write a five- or ten- or twenty-page synopsis—and have it rejected. It's less work for you, and it's substantially less work for whoever reads it, the agent or publisher who only has to wade through five or ten or twenty pages before returning it with a nice note saying that it is regretfully not for us.

And this, I think, explains the popularity of the synopsis for writer and reader alike. It's important, I think, to bear in mind that agents and editors are in the rejection business. We don't like to think of it that way, and they certainly don't like to think of it that way, but isn't that the way it is? For every manuscript they take on, they reject dozens or hundreds or thousands. They occasionally create problems for themselves by accepting something that doesn't work, while they never make problems when they reject something that ultimately proves successful for someone else.

Well, put yourself for a moment in their Guccis. If you had to read a hundred items a day, and you knew full well you would be rejecting a minimum of ninety-nine of them, would you rather they were long or short? Would you like them five pages long, or would you prefer they ran five hundred pages?

Right.

While agents and editors might indeed prefer to read outlines, because they can be rejected so much more rapidly in that form, they would rather buy (if they're publishers) or take on (if they're agents) complete manuscripts. Because that way they know what they're getting. A synopsis is at best a pig in a poke, and the only way to buy one of those is to minimize one's risk. Typically, one does this by telling the writer that the outline looks promising, and inviting him to submit the manuscript when it's written. The agent or publisher risks nothing and makes no commitment, while the writer does all the work with no guarantee of getting anything for it.

Naturally, this is the way a publisher would prefer to do business. Failing that, he'll offer a contract that calls for a pittance on signature, with the real money held back until delivery of an acceptable manuscript. If for any reason the manuscript you ultimately turn in isn't acceptable, he doesn't accept it. He may let you hang on to the initial pittance, at least until you place the book elsewhere, but he won't pay you for the work you've done and he won't publish the book if he doesn't like it. And he may dislike it even though you've done exactly what you said you'd do in the outline; indeed, he may dislike it simply because the editor who signed up the book has left to try homesteading in Nova Scotia, and his replacement hates that kind of book, or the way you write, or just categorically doesn't like anything his predecessor took on.

Do you see what I'm getting at? The only advantage of placing a book before you've written it is that you're getting an advance commitment from a publisher, and you're not. It's an illusion. He's not really committed to anything, he still won't publish your book unless he likes it—and in the meantime you've accepted less desirable terms than you could have gotten with the complete manuscript, because the publisher has the excuse that he's taking a risk, buying something that hasn't been written yet.

What's the answer?

To my mind the answer is to write the book first. There's no way out of writing the damn book, you know. Sooner or later you're going to have to write it, so you might as well write it now. Then show it around until you find someone who wants to publish the very book you happen to have written.

And what about the publishers who insist they only want to look at summaries?

Remember, what they say and what they mean are not necessarily the same thing. It's true that they'd rather *read* synopses, but they'd rather *buy* whole books, and just as you're going to have to write the whole book somewhere along the line before it can be published, so are they going to have to read the whole thing somewhere along the line before they can publish it. Their policy notwithstanding, if you send along a manuscript with an inviting cover letter, it will probably get looked at, and if the opening pages are gripping it will probably get read. And, when the right publisher does read it and wants to publish it, you'll get better terms than you could have gotten for an incomplete novel.

On the other hand, if you want to get rejected, stick to synopses. You can write ten or twenty of them in less time than it would take you to write a whole book, and you can get them rejected left and right, and spend a lot less money on postage in the process.

If that's what you want.

40. *Writing for the Ages*

"A writer's ambition," wrote Arthur Koestler, "should be to trade a hundred contemporary readers for ten readers in ten years' time and one reader in a hundred years' time."

I wonder. Is that ratio a good one—a hundred now, ten in a decade, one in a century? More to the point, is the whole principle a valid one? Ought we to be concentrating less on the reader today than on the reader as yet unborn?

I suppose a desire for immortality of a sort is one of the reasons why we write, and why we publish our writings. We put our writings into print in order to broadcast our own visions of the universe; by publishing, our renown can extend further than the range of our own voice. By writing works that both endure and prevail, we triumph as well over time as space.

There is, to be sure, a point of diminishing returns. However good you are, eventually they forget you. There comes a point when you're read only by scholars. The language changes, and you're read only in a modern version, or with the aid of dictionaries. Sooner or later whatever footprints you've contrived to leave on the sands of time fade and are forgotten with the rest.

Still, one's work can outlast oneself, sometimes by decades, sometimes by centuries. Looking backward, we unquestioningly equate merit with endurance. Shakespeare, we know, was greater than his contemporaries; he is performed today and they are not. We look at the Victorian novelists—Dickens, Reade, Thackeray, Trollope, Hardy, et al.—and rank them by the state of their present reputations. We note that many books, great critical and popular successes in their time, are no longer read at all; on the other hand, we point to Melville, forgotten in his own lifetime and elevated to fame and wide readership half a century after his death.

Are many of us fixated on the question of how long our work will be read? I don't think so. Painters and composers are more likely to be obsessed with the judgment of future generations, perhaps because they are less likely to be appreciated in their own time. Typically, the same person who prefers Rembrandt to today's painters and Beethoven to today's composers will nevertheless prefer to-day's novelists to last century's. We seem to want our reading to reflect contemporary concerns, a demand we are less likely to make on less literal artistic media.

Still, one wants to be read, if not forever, at least as long as possible. One wants one's books to stay in print. One wants to leave *something* behind.

Should this desire affect the way we write now? And how?

Let me tell you how the question came up. I recently read a copy of *Pardon My Ghoulish Laughter*, the seventh volume of Fredric Brown's pulp detective stories to be collected and published by Dennis McMillan in limited printings for collectors. Various mystery writers have supplied introductions for the books (I had the pleasure of providing one of them myself) and this particular volume's intro was the work of Donald E. Westlake.

In it, Mr. Westlake recounts how the manuscript sent to him was missing the last page of one of the stories. While he waited for the missing page to arrive, he read all the stories, including the one with its ending absent. The story hinged upon a puzzle, with its solution to be found on the missing page, and circumstances had so arranged matters that Mr. Westlake had two weeks to work out the solution.

"When I'd read the final page of the story," he reported, "my sense of failure changed to irritation and a vague feeling I'd been cheated; it turns out there was *no way* I could have solved the puzzle."

Why? Not because Fredric Brown had cheated, but because Westlake and any others of us reading the story some forty-four years after its initial publication, have been cheated by Time. The puzzle's solution hinged upon a radio program of the Forties. The story had outlived the plot element, and the puzzle had thus been rendered unsolvable.

Mr. Westlake went on to make the point that Brown's story was a pulp story, that pulp writers were writing not for the ages but for the rent, and that it would never have occurred to Brown or another in his position to worry that the shifting sands of time would obscure the solution to his story. What is remarkable, he points out, is not that the stories are dated but that they are as readable as they are. The talent and genius of their author has enabled them to remain readable and diverting, the effects of time notwithstanding.

What can we learn from this? Should we avoid details which will fix our stories in their time?

I don't know that we can. The example cited above is a special case, and Mr. Westlake points out that he would not have been struck by the time-imposed unfairness of the puzzle if he had been able to read the story all at once. But it seems to me that all our stories are very much creatures of their time.

This was brought home to me years ago when I read an anthology of detective stories presumably edited by Alfred Hitchcock. (Let it be said that Mr. Hitchcock had about as much to do with the anthologies published under his name as Grover Cleveland has to do with the Cleveland Indians.) This particular anthology consisted of some stories a year or two old and some others twenty or thirty years old, and the editor evidently felt a need to do something about this. Accordingly, he tried to edit the older stories. In one story, obviously written in the late thirties, he had the narrator drop a dime in a pay phone rather than the nickel the author must have had him spend. In another, written in the forties, the lead character drops into a movie theater and watches a film with Paul Newman and Tuesday Weld. Fearing that a nickel phone call and a pair of forties actors would date the story, he had resolutely updated it, patching in contemporary references whenever the mood struck him.

B y writing works that both endure and prevail, we triumph as well over time as space.

What a lamentable idea. All he managed to do was ruin the stories, because they remained rooted in the time of their writing irrespective of his patchwork job. His changes were jarring; after one had comfortably settled into the period of the story, one was forever being yanked out of the story's time by references which belonged to a more recent world. He should have left the stories alone entirely; the only way to make them contemporary would have been to rewrite them entirely from the first word to the last, keeping only the plot, and even that might not have worked, because the plot itself might have been, too, a creation of its time.

Consider any piece of writing. Even if the writer doesn't mention newspaper headlines or baseball scores, even if there are no references to celebrities of the day or media events, everything about the work reflects the moment in which it was written. I am using the language a certain way in this column because I am writing it in the late spring of 1986. Had I written it five years earlier, or were I to write it five years hence, I would write it differently. Not by design, but because time is one of the dimensions of a piece of work.

I've been especially aware of books as creatures of their time lately because I've had the extremely gratifying experience of seeing all my earlier works coming back into print. Some of the titles seem to me to be immature work, or at least youthful work, and I don't know how well they stand up in comparison with my more recent efforts. But that consideration is a different matter from our topic this month. I find myself questioning the merits of some of the things I wrote twenty-five years ago, not because time has eroded them, but because I'm not convinced they were all that wonderful in the first place.

With some of them, however, I was concerned specifically about the effects of time. I wrote seven books in the late sixties about one Evan Tanner, an adventurous and eccentric globetrotting insomniac. The books were rooted in the political realities (or unrealities) of the day, and I wondered if time would treat Tanner kindly. I worried that the books might be too much part and parcel of the sixties to entertain and amuse readers in the eighties.

Happily, that doesn't seem to have been the case. Berkley brought the books out over a two-year period, and sales increased along the way, suggesting that readers who bought the first books stayed with the series. I read one of them myself a month or two ago, the first time I'd read that particular book since its publication, and I have to admit that I found myself laughing aloud. I could not possibly write that book today, nor do I suppose it would be salable today as an original, but as a book of the sixties reprinted in the eighties it seemed to me to be still readable, and even entertaining.

Then again, it's possible that I'm easily amused.

How then do we write for the ages? How do we avoid including elements that will date our work adversely?

I don't know that we can. "The man who writes about himself and his own time," observed George Bernard Shaw, "is the only man who writes about all people and about all time." If we portray our own time with sufficient honesty and insight, our work will reveal all that is universal about our time. If we treat the true concerns of our years, we touch the true concerns of all time.

"Ah, take the cash and let the credit go," Omar Khayyam advised us, "Nor heed the rumble of a distant drum."

Still sounds good, doesn't it? After all these years . . .

41. On Growing Older

Growing old, Maurice Chevalier used to say, wasn't all that bad. Not when you considered the alternative.

With another birthday just around the corner and the odd gray hair turning up in the comb, I find I'm thinking rather more often about the aging process than is my wont. Specifically, I've been thinking of the ways in which growing older affects one as a writer. It seems to me that—yes, Arnold?

You're not getting older, sir. You're getting better.

You're very kind, Arnold. You're also only half right. I *am* getting better, but I'm also getting older. One of the nice things about writing is that the two are not mutually exclusive.

It must be hell for athletes. However durable their God-given physiques, however diligently they nourish themselves with wheat germ oil, sooner or later Time nails 'em. The legs, I'm told, are generally the first to go. One way or another, the body won't do what it did in the past. The jab loses its sting. The fastball, a few miles per hour below its standard, falls prey to .230 hitters. Hungry younger players move in and take over—on the football field, on the tennis court, or wherever.

The age when all this happens, of course, varies with the sport. Swimmers and gymnasts peak early on. Baseball and football players are on borrowed time not long after thirty. Golfers, though they'll lose distance on their drives and dull the cutting edge of their competitive nature with the passage of time, can keep going almost forever.

And writers? What, if anything, do we lose to the years? And what do we gain?

There are losses. Some writers are successful early on because of the freshness of their vision. There is something new and exciting about the way they see the world, and it is this novelty which wins them readership. If there's no considerable underlying talent, or if they fail to develop such a talent as they go along, they may have nothing left to sustain them when the novelty of their work wears off.

Similarly, some of us make an initial impact upon the reading public because of what we are able to write about. There are innumerable cases in American letters of writers who won a wide audience with a first novel that drew directly or indirectly upon their background and experience and who never recapture that initial success after they've used up that resource. Sometimes the failure is a commercial matter. Sometimes it is artistic as well, with the writer incapable of seeing or feeling deeply in his fiction once he's exorcised the demon that compelled the writing of that first book.

Less dramatically, it is extremely common for writers to write more and more about less and less as the years go by. The profligate youth turns stingy with age. In a first novel, the writer will often throw in everything but the cat and the kitchen sink. Every character he's met, every scrap of background he's lived with, every bit of plot business he can invent, lends richness and flavor to his stew. The passing years teach parsimony, and the writer learns to mete out his ideas and experiences, until sometimes he writes far too much about far too little.

This said, perhaps we can have a look at the bright side. And there is indeed a bright side, because it is very much in the natural order of things for writers to improve with age. We *should* get better as we add years. If we don't, it probably means we're doing something wrong.

For one thing, the passing years ought to bring an increase in technical proficiency. Even for those of us to whom writing comes naturally, the process of creating fiction involves a considerable amount of learned technique. We learn both from our own processes of trial and error and from observing the trials and errors of other writers. Technical ability is not all there is to writing, certainly, and no end of clumsy craftspersons produce artistically and commercially successful fiction, but no book was ever the better for being poorly written.

In my own case, I'm frequently astonished when I reread work of twenty years ago. I can almost always see better ways of doing certain things. I am aware of options now that would never have occurred to me in my youth.

This, incidentally, may in part explain why I'm not as fast a writer as I used to be. When I could only see one way to put a scene together, one direction for a plot to move, all I had to do was plunge straight ahead. Now I have more choices to make, and they take consideration.

At least as important as the growth of one's technical proficiency, I suspect, is the deepening and maturing of one's vision. When I was twenty years old I had the insights and perceptions of a twenty year old, and a rather callow one at that. While I'm hardly the Wise Old Man on the Mountaintop at the moment, I like to think I've learned a little bit about the world in the intervening years. Inevitably, my work reflects this ripening. Many of the characters who peopled my early fiction seem now to lack dimension. They are less complicated than I have since discovered people to be. If I am at the same time rather less certain of things than I used to be, that too will reflect itself in what I write.

Another gain that comes with time is one of confidence. If I have lost some of the brashness of youth, perhaps I have acquired a greater measure of confidence growing out of an improved sense of who I am and what I can and cannot do. This knowledge helps me avoid writing books that are wrong for me. It enables me to hold my own in wrestling matches with editors and publishers. And it takes some

The passing years teach parsimony.

(but certainly not all) of the fear out of that most frightening article, the blank page in the typewriter.

As far as one's audience is concerned, gray hair doesn't hurt a bit. The public, so often denounced as fickle, strikes me as extraordinarily loyal to writers. The more one writes and publishes, the more one establishes oneself as a recognizable brand name in the marketplace. While writers without number fade away after an early burst of success, those of us who steadfastly produce book after book year after year generally record a steady increase in sales as the volumes pile up.

This is even true with writers who don't deserve such loyalty. Some of us, I'm afraid, deteriorate with age, for one reason or another, but if we've achieved a certain measure of popularity over the years, it generally takes our public a while to catch up with us. I could offhand name half a dozen writers who have been significantly off their form for several books each, with no consequent slump in their sales.

One advantage of age, as far as the public is concerned, is that the older one gets, the more one is presumed to know something. Many of us are leery of placing much credence in persons significantly younger than ourselves. When a writer is older than we are, we're more willing to believe that he knows what he's talking about.

And the older a writer gets, the more people out there are younger than he is. Some writers, as I mentioned above, do fade with the years, and it might be interesting to examine some of the ways this comes about.

Some writers decline because they fail to grow. If a writer is not open to new experience, if he is not willing and able to enlarge his field of vision, then he is going to run out of things to write about. Some writers isolate themselves. Writing itself is a solitary pastime, and some of us compound its isolation by associating only with other writers or with a small and homogeneous group of acquaintances. University campuses and writer's colonies are cozy places, but they can become sterile soil for the writer.

Some writers are spoiled by success. Approval, so essential to most of us, can be toxic in overdoses. We can very easily become careless and self-indulgent when everything we do draws applause. Editors are reluctant to tell us when our work is off the mark, and we find it hard to listen if they do. I just last night finished a book by a writer who's been a favorite of mine for over two decades. It's the latest volume in a series, and it's a bad book in just about every respect, and I'll bet nobody told him.

Some writers dry up. Many of us produce fiction as oysters produce pearls, to assuage pain and irritation. As we grow, the need to do this may disappear. Sometimes, having written out what's been bothering us, we don't have to keep on writing. There's nothing wrong with that. After all, we none of us signed any lifetime contracts. When it stops being rewarding, we're allowed to quit.

Some writers waste themselves. Alcoholism, drug addiction, depression, madness—these are virtually occupational illnesses for writers. Even when they don't kill us outright, they can grind our talent in the dust.

Some writers outlive their talent. For those of us who live a long time, a certain falling off toward the very end may be inevitable. I can think of a few novelists whose last books were embarrassing. Perhaps they were already being weakened artistically by whatever was destroying them physically. The list of pitfalls is a long one, and one could easily extend it. The wonder is not that there are so many ways in which one's writing ability can decline, but that for so many of us it does *not* decline, that such a high percentage of us maintain and improve our level of performance right up to the end. We may write fewer books and put in fewer hours as we get older, but it's exceptional for us to retire altogether.

How lucky we are. How very lucky we are.

42. Welcome to Hard Times

"In these hard economic times," writes Pamela R. Landis of Gilbertsville, Pennsylvania, "the morale of a struggling writer can sometimes drop low. Everyone has to tighten their belts, including the publishers. I think I can say this without a doubt; fifteen years ago, maybe even ten years ago, some of the writers in our local writer's club would have been published. They are good. But they are up against some stiff competition from established writers as well as writers who have agents to sell their work. I'm not saying that all the new writers being published today have done it through the assistance of an agent, but many have.

"Our members are up against tired editors suffering from bad cases of eyestrain and boredom. Frustration has been our biggest enemy and it is difficult to keep up our morale. Anything you can offer will be appreciated."

Now my own morale was not at its best on the day this letter arrived, nor was I any stranger to eyestrain and boredom. But I could hardly forbear to answer Ms. Landis's plaint. After all, she had said some very nice things about my own writing, had enclosed a check in payment for one of my books, and had sent along a self-addressed stamped envelope. How could I do other than reply?

I don't have a copy of my letter, but I seem to recall something bracing and stiff-upper-lippish. In any case, Ms. Landis's letter was still resonating in the little echo chamber I call a mind when I fell into a conversation with a friend of mine, a freelance writer-editor. She too has fallen on hard times and was thinking of supplementing her income reading slush for A Major Magazine.

"So I made some inquiries," she said, "and I found out what they pay. Do you know what they pay?"

No, I said. I did not.

"They pay forty cents a manuscript," she said.

I volunteered that this was not exactly a king's ransom.

"Or a queen's either," she said. "Forty cents a manuscript! Who could possibly read for that figure? If you read a script in five minutes you'd still barely make minimum wage."

I pointed out that one could average rather less than five minutes a manuscript. In the vast majority of cases, a quick scanning of the first page or two would be enough to determine that the manuscript did not merit a second reading and could be returned to its author forthwith. "You could probably do twenty an hour without killing yourself," I suggested. "It strikes me as a hard way to make eight bucks an hour, but you could probably do it."

"I'm not sure I could," she said. "And as a writer I'm appalled by the idea. People sweat and strain and mail off their manuscripts, and somebody who gets forty cents a shot for piecework glances at them and sends them back. It doesn't seem fair."

Who ever said it would be fair? In point of fact, I suspect a slush pile manuscript gets a better shot from a piecework reader, whose sole task is to sift the slush, than from an editor who attends to that chore in his spare time. Reading unsolicited manuscripts is a low-priority task as well as being a time-consuming and generally thankless one, and several editors have admitted to me that they do not always do an honest job of it.

"Sometimes the stuff comes in faster than you can deal with it," an editor told me just the other day, "and I'll fall behind in dealing with it, and it becomes a matter of shoveling, uh, stuff against the tide, and then the day comes when I just reject everything. I take every single manuscript in the pile and pin a rejection slip to it and stuff it back in its envelope and send it to its writer. Nobody likes doing that, but you don't always have a choice."

There's another side to the forty-cents-a-manuscript routine, and it's not particularly comforting, either. And that's the realization of just how much it costs publishers to deal with the manuscripts that come in over the transom. Every year, a magazine has to spend thousands of dollars just to return manuscripts it didn't solicit in the first place, and that's only the cost of getting the stuff read and processed. Some writers don't enclose a postpaid return envelope, and some editors are softhearted enough to address an envelope and stamp it and send the script back.

I wouldn't. I swear I'd throw the thing out. I had a letter a couple months back from someone who honestly couldn't figure out why editors expected one to send SASEs with submissions. Wasn't it enough on his part that he was submitting his stuff? The fellow didn't have much grounding in reality.

If a publisher pays forty cents a script to a freelancer, that's because it's cheaper than having his own fulltime staffers sift the chaff. Standard publishing practice has called for editorial trainees to serve as first readers. It's a way for them to learn the business while they screen the slush, and it is perhaps a sign of the times that some publishers find it a worthwhile economy to cut their staff and use freelancers.

Other publishers, of course, have dealt with the problem by getting rid of the slush pile altogether. A simple refusal to consider unsolicited manuscripts saves them thousands of dollars annually. In return, it costs them the opportunity to discover a pearl beyond price in their slush, and they acknowledge this, but figure the odds are better on turning up a needle in a haystack.

Some magazines which do read unsolicited manuscripts would prefer not to, but don't want to alienate readers who are also would-be writers. But for this consideration, they'd be closed markets for over-the-transom submissions.

> *E*very year, magazines spend thousands just to return manuscripts.

What does all of this mean to those of us who are trying to get started writing fiction?

Well, it's hard to pretend it's good news. It's no simple task to build up a lot of enthusiasm for the idea of sending off a manuscript when you know somebody's going to get forty cents for reading it, somebody who's got every incentive to dispose of it as rapidly as possible. And how easy is it to do one's best work at the typewriter with this state of affairs hovering in the background?

But is it that much worse than it used to be?

Maybe it is, but I'm not sure the difference is substantial. Breaking into print as a writer of fiction has always been impossible. It is true, to be sure, that the pulp magazines in the thirties and forties constituted a receptive market for magazine fiction, albeit a low-paying one. But it is at least as true that certain fiction categories constitute a receptive market now. Publishers in these categories seem to be eager for submissions. Some of them actively seek new writers. Imagine that, will you? Publishers actively seeking new writers!

They'd still rather deal with established professionals whose work they know. And they'll still turn down dozens or hundreds or even thousands of manuscripts for every one they publish. And that, I submit, is as it should be. If everyone who sat down and wrote something wound up getting it published, it would be impossible to find anything decent to read. It has always been true, and it will always be true, that only a small percentage of those of us who want to write will wind up getting published. What's wrong with that? Only a handful of the kids who play Little League baseball ever become professional ballplayers, and I don't think that means there's something wrong with the structure of the sport, or that they ought to lower the pitcher's mound.

Maybe there's more to the analogy than meets the eye. Ted Williams used to say that there was nothing harder than hitting a ball thrown by a major league pitcher. I might say in reply that the man never tried to publish a piece of fiction. It's difficult, and it always has been, and I suspect it always will be.

And yet we keep trying. And some of us manage it.

I was about a thousand words into this column when I broke off to do a radio interview over the telephone with John Otto, at WGR in Buffalo, New York. It was a call-in show, and one of the callers had some very generous things to say about my column and my book, *Telling Lies for Fun and Profit.* Very helpful, she said.

Mr. Otto asked if she'd ever written fiction herself. Indeed she had, she replied, and that very day she'd sold her first story. "I took your advice," she said, "and wrote a confession story, and it sold."

I told her I thought that was terrific. And it is. But I don't think I had to tell her. I think she knew.

Because there's really no feeling quite like it.

I recall one of Lord Chesterfield's letters, in which the good gentleman commented upon the illogic of pursuing another pastime entirely, one rather more universally enjoyed than the writing of fiction. "The pleasure is momentary," he observed, "the price exorbitant, and the posture ridiculous."

I quote from memory and may have a word wrong, but you get the idea. The point remains that Lord Chesterfield's remarks are unquestionably correct, yet I know of no one who ever avoided the activity in question for those reasons. And is it any different for those of us who were born to write fiction? God knows it's given me some fleeting joys and cold comforts, that it has cost me much and forced me into some ridiculous postures, but how could I have done otherwise? How could I have lived these years without it?

What advice do I have for you? The very best advice of all. Stop writing. Quit wasting your time. Instead of postage and envelopes and typewriter ribbons, put your money into something sound, like lottery tickets and czarist bonds. Come to your senses!

What advice could be better? And I know it's perfectly safe to offer it to you. Because, if you were meant to be a writer, you won't listen to me. Will you?

That's what I thought.

43. Truth to Tell

Good morning, boys and girls.

Good morning, sir.

Today I'd like to talk a bit about honesty, about telling the truth. What do we know about the truth? Yes, Arnold?

It's stranger than fiction, sir.

Stranger than some fiction, Arnold. It's also, I would submit, an essential ingredient of fiction. There might seem to be a contradiction here. As the title of a superior text on the subject would have it, successful fiction writing is largely a matter of telling lies for fun and profit. And yet it is the inner truth in fiction that makes it work, and the fictioneer's willingness to hew to the truth that lends strength to his or her work.

By way of illustration, I'd like to depart from the usual format of this class and read something aloud to you. This material is—yes, Rachel?

You've said you don't believe in reading work aloud in class, sir.

I have indeed.

You've called it a waste of class time, and you've said that we can best criticize one another's work if we read it in silence on our own time.

Quite true, Rachel. But I'm reading this to you not so that you can criticize it but because I think the content will be meaningful to you. This isn't a piece of fiction. It's an essay, and it came to me the other day in the mail. Its author is a young woman now in her senior year at Clark University in Worcester, Massachusetts. She has assisted a couple of times at my "Write For Your Life" seminar. She's a pre-law student and, as you'll see, she's a writer.

Listen up, Rachel.

It is time to set myself free. For four years I've been holding back in my writing, afraid to let go. I have been hiding under a shadow, a shadow formed by The Story. The Story holds me back, it blocks my writing, it follows me like a ball and chain. It is time to let go, to break the blood-line.

I am sending Daddy a copy of The Story.

I used to love to write—fiction, especially. I would make up stories on my way home from school, just so I would be able to make my mother laugh over dinner. I created characters, and sometimes began to believe they were real. My characters would converse in my head, I would write their dialogue in my mind. There were continuing sagas that I would return to each night as I lay in bed waiting for sleep.

I rarely wrote those stories down. They were more flexible existing only in my imagination. Besides, Daddy wrote books, not me. But I did write a lot. Even at seven and eight I kept a journal. It wasn't a diary, I certainly didn't write every day. But in my childhood, writing was a place to be free. I could swear on paper and no one would know. I could write, "I hate you, everyone!" and would never have to apologize.

As I got older, my writing took on a more definite purpose. I became a great writer of letters. In my early teens I found that I preferred the written to the spoken word, especially if the matter at hand was an emotional one. It's easier, I discovered, to state your position or argue your point when no one is there to argue back. And, I learned, it is far too difficult to be honest face to face. Tell the truth on paper, and don't be there when it's read.

The first time I wrote with a real audience in mind was my senior year in high school. I took an English class called The Modern Short Story. For our final assignment we were given a choice: write either a research paper on the life and work of a particular author or an original short story. An original short story? Easy. All I would have to do was write down the ideas and conversations that went on in my head.

That is when I wrote The Story. And it was easy. I wrote in a composition notebook and worked on it on subways and between classes. It wrote itself when I was in the shower or lying in bed at night. The words just poured out of my head onto the paper. Two days before it was due I lost the first seven pages. I have trouble believing it now, but I didn't cry, I didn't swear, I didn't even ask for an extension; I bought a new composition book and began again. It was a breeze. The hardest part was making my hand keep up with my head.

My teacher loved it. Not only did he give me an A, but he had me read it aloud to my class and to his two other senior classes. I showed it to my friends; they loved it too. My mother, my sisters—I showed everyone. Except my father.

It is a good story. It's funny and sad, honest and easy to read. It gets in deep, rings true, and touches close to the heart.

It is the best thing I've ever written, before or since. I was more proud of myself than I had ever been. And I felt guiltier than I've ever felt.

You see, the story is about a girl and her father. No, let's be honest. It's about me and my father. It's about our relationship since my parents' divorce. It was written with a great deal of anger and hostility that I hadn't even known existed. I never showed The Story to my father. There are two reasons for that: one, because he would think it was about him and would be hurt; two, because he is a writer and, while I can handle his criticism, I fear his praise.

*T**he basic negative idea embodied here is "It's not safe for me to tell the truth."***

I was really torn apart. On the one hand I wanted to show him. I mean, he's a novelist. And I knew he would think it was good. I wanted him to be proud, impressed. I wanted him to say, "Welcome aboard." But I couldn't show him. He would be hurt, crushed. He was better off not knowing my anger. I was terrified of the reactions I imagined.

For the past four years, The Story has followed me. It's been there, lingering in the background every time I've picked up a pen since the day I wrote it. Each time I sit down to write, it warns me of my capacity for hurting people. It reminds me of the simple "fact" that the better I write, the more I can hurt the people I care about.

My writing has changed since I wrote The Story. I can feel myself copping out. I have ideas that I don't bother with, and I pretend not to notice as I push them away. I decide that whatever I'm writing—a short story, a research paper, a journal entry—will get too involved, will take too long. I rush, I hedge, and I feel myself just skimming the surface, never bothering to dig deep.

Writing isn't fun anymore. I spend hours at my desk, writing until my hand is cramped, my back aching. I try until my head hurts. I stay up until I see the sky turning light. And as the minutes and hours tick by, I know that I am trying harder than I have to, taking longer than I need to. And I know that I am just not writing as well as I used to, as well as I can.

I am a writer. I write because I can, because I like to and because I have to. But my belief in an untrue fact makes me work harder than I have to and prevents me from writing as well as I know I can. I've made it a chore and I've made it some sort of a test. I am using my writing to test my ability to love and my ability to hurt.

But today I am ready to let go. Today I will put a copy of The Story in the mail. My father will read it and he will understand. And then maybe I will understand. Good writing doesn't hurt people. And honesty isn't bad. It is worthwhile to take the time and expose the nerves, to get to the heart of the matter. I am sending Daddy The Story and setting myself free.

Now the reason I elected to read you this—Rachel, are you all right? Arnold, could you lend Rachel your handkerchief?

It's kind of grungy, sir.

Edna, if you could let Rachel have a Kleenex . . .

Thanks, Edna. I'm sorry, sir.

Quite all right, Rachel.

I was moved to tears, sir.

Well, that's nothing to apologize for. The reason I read you this, above and beyond my desire to move you all to tears, is that I think it illustrates vividly the way a fear springing from an unfounded negative belief can handcuff a writer.

The basic negative idea embodied here is "It's not safe for me to tell the truth." A lot of writers subscribe to this notion in one form or another. Here are a few versions of it, some of which might strike a particular chord with you:

The truth will hurt the ones I love.

People won't like me if I tell the truth.
People will hate me if they know the truth about me.
The way I perceive the truth proves that I am a bad person.

I've written before about our false negative beliefs and how they can stand in the way of our success as writers. An interesting thing about such beliefs is that we often spend our lives trying to disprove them, even as we constantly allow them to sabotage our efforts.

An interesting illustration of this phenomenon in respect to truth-telling in writing came up at a "Write For Your Life" seminar this past spring. One of the participants was my friend Bob Mandel, author of *Open-Heart Therapy* and national director of the Loving Relationships Training. During the section where we focus on our most negative thoughts about our own writing, Bob determined that his was *The truth hurts.* Now a motto of the Loving Relationships Training is "Tell the whole truth faster," and I don't think it's entirely coincidental that Bob chose to combat his negative belief about the truth by heading an organization with such a byword, and by being rigorously honest in all his own relationships. But imagine how believing that telling the truth will hurt others has stood in the way of his own writing!

In the essay quoted above, the writer tells us how easy writing was for her, and how it has since become a struggle. It seems quite clear to me that the struggle consists of the war between her desire to tell the truth and her fear of its effects. Writing is best when it's struggle-free, and the writer who struggles at the typewriter is like a driver who's got the gas pedal pressed to the floor—and his other foot exerting similar pressure on the brake.

Part of this fear of the truth flows out of negative self-esteem. "I'm bad," the writer reasons, "and if I show myself in my work, everyone'll know." Another side of it, more in evidence in the quoted essay, flows out of the ego-based conviction that other people can't be trusted to respond as intelligently as we would. They won't understand, they won't get the point, they'll take things the wrong way. In this particular instance, for example, the girl's father couldn't be trusted to distinguish between honest fiction and objective reality, to understand that The Story revealed one particular aspect of their relationship, examined her feelings from one particular perspective.

"Beauty is truth, truth beauty," wrote John Keats. "That is all ye know on earth, and all ye need to know." I'm not sure it's *all* I need to know; my tenth-grade biology teacher would be distraught if I failed to remember that ontogeny recapitulates philogeny, and I feel a similar commitment to knowing that Pierre is the capital of South Dakota.

Beauty is truth, truth beauty. And here are a couple of other affirmations to work with in internalizing the idea that it's safe to let your truth shine in your fiction:

"It's always safe to tell the truth."

"The truth is always beautiful."

"I can always afford to be honest."

"The more I tell the truth, the safer I am."

"The truth is good for me and everyone else."

In the case of the essay's author—what is it, Rachel?

Could you tell us her name, sir?

Her name?

The young woman who wrote the essay, sir. You didn't tell us her name.

Oh, didn't I mention it? Her name is Jyl Block.

Jyl Block. And her father is a novelist?

That's right. Oh, dear. Edna, you'd better give Rachel another Kleenex.

I'm all right, sir. Sir? You must be very proud of Jyl, sir.

Indeed I am, Rachel. Very very proud.